sick of nature

sick of nature

David Gessner

To Molly,
My fellow non-nature writer.
I love the quiet moments and look
forward to reading you in print!
In your work!
In Friendship,

[signature]

August 2004

Dartmouth College Press

Hanover, New Hampshire

PUBLISHED BY

UNIVERSITY PRESS OF NEW ENGLAND

HANOVER AND LONDON

DARTMOUTH COLLEGE PRESS
Published by University Press of New England,
One Court Street, Lebanon, NH 03766
www.upne.com
© 2004 by David Gessner
Printed in the United States of America

5 4 3 2 1

Library of Congress Cataloging-in-Publication Data

Gessner, David, 1961–
Sick of nature / David Gessner.
   p.   cm.
Includes bibliographical references.
ISBN 1–58465–358–2 (cloth : alk. paper)
1. Natural history—Authorship.   2. Gessner, David, 1961–   I. Title.
QH14.G47 2004
508—dc22   2004003028

The author gratefully acknowledges permission to reprint the following material:
Excerpt from "East Coker" in FOUR QUARTETS, Copyright 1940 by T. S. Eliot and renewed in 1968 by Earne Valarie Eliot, reprinted by permission of Harcourt, Inc.
Excerpt from "To My Twenties" in *New Addresses*, by Kenneth Koch, reprinted by permission of Karen Koch.
"Sick of Nature," a Roy Y. Ames Memorial essay contest winner, was published in the September 1998 issue of *Literal Latte*.
"A Letter to A Neighbor" was published in the winter 1999 issue of *Orion*.
"To the Fatherland" will appear in the Spring 2004 issue of *American Scholar*.
"A Polygamist of Place" first appeared in the September 14, 1998, issue of *High Country News*.
Parts of "Soliloquy in Spartina" appeared in the Autumn issue of *Sanctuary*. Other parts, in different form, appeared in the Los Angleles *Times* Sunday Book Section.
"Trickster in the City" appeared in the Fall 2003 issue of the *Harvard Review*.
"Benediction" (finally) appeared in the Spring 2004 issue of the *Georgia Review*.

To Hadley Mariette Gessner

I resist anything better than my own diversity. —WHITMAN

Contents

I.

Sick

My moods hate each other.
—EMERSON

Sick of Nature

I am sick of nature. Sick of trees, sick of birds, sick of the ocean. It has been almost four years now, four years of sitting quietly in my study and sipping tea and contemplating the migratory patterns of the semipalmated plover. Four years of writing essays praised as "quiet" by quiet magazines. Four years of having neighborhood children ask their fathers why the man down the street comes to the post office dressed in his pajamas ("Doesn't he work, Daddy?") or having those same fathers wonder why, when the man actually does dress, he dons the eccentric costume of an English bird watcher, complete with binoculars. Four years of being constrained by the gentle straitjacket of genre; that is, four years of writing about the world without being able to say the word "shit." (While talking a lot of scat.) And let's not forget four years of being the official "nature guy" among my circle of friends. Of going on walks and having them pick up every leaf and newt and turd and asking "what's this?" and, when I (defenseless unless armed with my field guides and even then a bumbler) admit I don't know, having to shrug and watch the sinking disappointment in their eyes.

Worse still, it's been four years of living within a genre that, for all its wonder and beauty, can be a little like going to Sunday School. A strange Sunday School where I alternate between sitting in the pews (reading nature) and standing at the pulpit (writing nature.) And not only do I preach from my pulpit, I preach to the converted. After all, who reads nature books? Fellow nature lovers who already believe that the land shouldn't be destroyed. Meanwhile my more hardnosed and sensible neighbors on Cape Cod are concerned with more hardnosed and sensible reading material (*People, Time, Playboy*—not a quiet magazine in the house), when occasionally resting from the happy exertion of gobbling up what's left of our neighborhood, selling and subdividing. Being honest (one of the nature writer's supposed virtues), I have to admit that an essay is a much less effective way of protecting the land than a cudgel. In other words, I have to admit to impotence.

Which isn't much fun. Today, the morning after yet another legislative defeat for conservation on Cape Cod, I find myself feeling particularly pessimistic about the possibility of affecting change. The original land bank bill, which marked my first minor foray into volunteer politics, was a modest and sensible proposal for putting aside some money to spare the remaining undeveloped land on the Cape, a still beautiful place that's quickly going the way of the Jersey Shore. But because that money would come from the profits of the sellers of real estate (one percent on sales over $100,000), conservatives (is there a more tediously ironic word in the language?) decided that the time was ripe for another Boston Tea Party. The real issue was that developers and realtors and builders wanted to keep on developing and realting and building, but of course they couldn't come right out and say that. So they pooled a big pile of money and called in a big telemarketting firm from Washington that proceeded to reframe the debate entirely in terms of that highly original catchphrase "no new taxes" (while also, just for the fun of it, scaring the bejesus out of the Cape's substantial elderly population).

The standard response to this unfairness of things is to curse and wave our little fists at the wicked telemarketers, but today I have a different reaction. I marvel at their effectiveness. Had the pro–land bank forces called in a team of essayists, what would we have done to help? Assembled, we'd have looked like a reunion of Unabombers: solitary, hollow-eyed, scraggly-bearded characters ranting against progress. Likely our strategy would have been to abandon the phone lines and take to the beaches to wander, alone and aimless, in search of terns and profundities. Not only that, but had we somehow—despite ourselves—won, the victory party wouldn't exactly have been a barrel of laughs. You can bet you wouldn't find a single lampshade-wearing party guy in the group.

Which is part of the problem, or, at least, part of my current problem. Throw an imaginary kegger and fill the room with nature writers throughout history and you'll get the idea. Henry Beston, looking dapper if overdressed, alternates tentative taco dabs at the cheese dip with Aldo Leopold; Barry Lopez sits in the corner whispering to Thoreau about the sacredness of beaver dams; Joseph Wood Krutch stands by the punch bowl and tells Rachel Carson the story of how he first came to the desert as Carson listens earnestly. In fact, everything is done earnestly; the air reeks with earnestness. As usual with this crowd, there's a whole lot of *listening* and *observing* going on, not a lot of merriment. Writers from earlier times drift off alone to scribble notes, modern ones talk into microcassette recorders. You might think Ed Abbey could spark the party to life, but until the booze to blood ratio rises he remains painfully shy. Everyone else merely sips their drinks; buffoonery is in short supply; no one tells bawdy anecdotes. In short, the party is a dud.

Perhaps in real life these writers wouldn't restrict their discussions to the mating habits of the spoonbill roseate (*Ajaia ajaja*). In my present state of mind, I'd like to imagine them talking about anything other than nature. Sex maybe. Certainly sex must have played at least a minor role in all their lives, even Thoreau's. Perhaps one reason for the retreat to Walden, unexplored by most critics of American Romanticism, was to have more time and freedom for masturbatory binges. We'll never know. We do know that Thoreau exalted in that most underrated aspect of nature appreciation: pissing outside. "I have watered the red huckleberry, the sand cherry and the nettle tree," he wrote. Hell, maybe Thoreau himself would be just the man to break the ice at my party. "Water is the only drink for the wise man," he said piously, but since I'm imagining I'll imagine having someone, Abbey maybe, spike his water. Perhaps for one night, throwing off his teetotaling ways, he could sing and dance, putting folks at ease by showing that even the great stuffy father figure could tie one on. And with Thoreau—Thoreau of all people, the one they respect the most, their God!—acting the buffoon, the rest of them could let their hair down and start to drink and talk about normal party things like lust or the score of the Celtics game.

I, a relative neophyte, wouldn't have merited an invitation to the big shindig, but, along with the rest of the Corps of Junior Nature Writers, I'd watch Thoreau's wild-man antics through the window. And maybe, just maybe, Henry would stumble out and bullshit with me late at night, and together, just two drunk guys, we could water the sand cherry.

~

The preceding scenario may suggest that I am losing my grip (on this essay as well as my mind). Maybe so. Not long ago I moved from Colorado to Cape Cod to live in Thoreauvian isolation, and for a while I was convinced solitude was driving me insane. (I'll admit that, unlike Thoreau, I had a wife with me, but we still felt isolated together.) Since coming back, I have been a literary Euel Gibbons, subsisting on a diet of pure nature reading as well as writing. Assuming the mantle of genre, I began my adventure determined to deepen my connection to the natural world, inscribing the front of my journal with Henry Beston's words: "A year in outer nature is the accomplishment of a tremendous ritual." But at some point I cracked. I started writing pieces like this one, tossing aside the stage craft of birds and bugs and beaches, and focusing on what I really cared about—*me*. Usually I rate about an 7.3 on the narcissism scale, but suddenly, finding myself with long hours to contemplate an empty beach and my own deep thoughts, my rating shot off the charts. Working at a job in the city, it's easy to dream of the rustic life, but actually living it entails dangers. It's not just nature that abhors a vacuum. Deprived of its usual gripes, the imagination creates elaborate dissatisfactions and paints masterpieces of hypochondria. There's a reason Cape Cod, our seaside paradise, has such high suicide and alcoholism rates. Though it isn't fashionable to admit, I wouldn't have made it through the fall without television. ("Our only friend," my wife called it.) As the sages have long reminded us, when we get away from it all we still bring our minds along.

As I turned inward, I forgot about the beautiful world outside. Nature became, if not a malevolent presence, at least an irritating one. Gulls shat on my back deck, raccoons rummaged through the trash cans, and the powder post beetles (close cousin to the termite) drilled into the beams day and night with a sharp *tcckkk tcckk tcckk* noise that made me feel as if they were burrowing into the meat of my temples. And then, suddenly, I realized that I hated nature, or at least hated writing about it in a quiet and reasonable way. Why? Because the whole enterprise struck me as humorless, which in turn struck me as odd, given that comedy often draws on a strain of wildness. Gary Synder wrote that those who are comfortable in wilderness are often comfortable in their own subconscious. And it seemed to me that those who are comfortable with the uncertainty of nature should also be comfortable on the same shaky ground of humor. Why was it, then, that so often love of nature seemed to breed earnestness?

And then there was this: With only a couple of obvious exceptions, the modern nature writer is most often praised for his or her "restrained" voice. Restrained as in shackles, it seemed to me. "Quietly subversive," is the phrase usually tossed out by critics when referring to nature writing. Well, while I sit here carving out my quietly subversive prose, the bulldozers down the street at Stone's bluff are loudly subverting the soil. Hollowing out the Cape just as the beetles hollow out our beams.

But I'm not telling the full story (which in this case is a crime since what this essay is really about is the frustration of not telling the full story). When we choose to do a thing, we in effect choose not to do many other things. The same with genre. As I complain about my previous genre's restrictions, I find myself bristling at my present constraints (those of the curmudgeonly personal essayist). Yes, Cape Cod can sometimes seem as desolate as Siberia, and yes, the sound of hammers banging is never far off, and yes, there have been plenty of times when, sitting in my cold room listening to the beetles *tcckk, tcckk, tcckk*-ing I longed for an escape from this drear peninsula. But something else has also happened. After my crack-up in early fall, I actually began to settle in. As the year sprawled on, moving slowly, ambling like no year I'd known before, I, despite myself, began to remember some not-unpleasant things about Cape Cod. Like October. A month when the tourists finally packed up and cleared out for good. A month when the full moon rose over the pink-blue pastel of the harbor sunset and the blue-grey juniper berries shone with chalky iridescence at dusk, and when masses of speckle-bellied starlings filled the trees (and the air with their squeaky-wheeled sounds). A month when the ocean vacillated between the foreboding slate grey of November and a summery, almost tropical blue (while occasionally hinting at its darker winter shades). Most of all, a month of color, a month when the entire neck caught fire in a hundred shades of red.

And though this is not what I intended to write about, these memories lead to other memories of the fall (a time that's becoming more romantic with each retrospective second). Like the first husky wisps of woodsmoke rising from my neighbor's chimneys, or the time I saw the seals playing tag between the offshore rocks or the haze of wood dust in the sunlight as I stacked the logs against the side of the house, fortifying us for winter, or the time I kayaked into the marsh and, sliding in through the channels, low and quiet, caught the great blue heron off guard and watched it walk across the spartina with its funky seventies TV pimp strut, head bobbing forward and back . . .

But there, you see. I'm going off again. Like heroin or nicotine, the nature habit's hard to break. I could, without much prodding, turn this essay into a paean to the beauty of the past year on Cape Cod, on how the year has been a deepening, a wedging into the physical world, a slowing down. If that was my story, then I would, of necessity, edit out certain details (like any mention of those sustained periods when I was sure that the beetles were sending messages to me through the phone lines). It wouldn't be so much lying to exclude these, as much as it would be a genre choice. The sort of choice we make semiconsciously almost any time we open our mouths.

And maybe what I'm sick of isn't the birds and trees and beach or even writing about the birds and trees and beach. Maybe what I'm really sick of is making the same choice over and over again. Of being one thing. Of constraint. Maybe I'm rebelling against my too-safe self. Rebelling against the formulaic in me, the way we squirm uneasily at a too-pat Hollywood movie.

But I'm the one calling the shots, after all, so why keep calling the same shot? Much has been written about the modern tendency toward specialization, and I won't add another long-winded celebration of the amateur. But it *is* true that from a young age Americans are taught that there's nothing like success, and that the way to *really* succeed is to do one thing well. Having spent a half dozen years out West, I can say this is particularly true of New Englanders. We proudly celebrate our uptightness. Our heroes as a rule are monomaniacally devoted—Larry Bird, John Irving, Ahab—and whether these heroes focus on basketball, novels, or whales, they are praised for directing their energy toward one thing without wasting time on diversions. But as the good Captain illustrates, this isn't always the surest road to mental health. In my case, focusing on one thing (even a thing as seemingly benign as nature-writing) was an invitation to those beetles to crawl into my skull.

It is now the middle of February on Cape Cod, a time that I dreaded during the melancholy of late November. The odd thing is that I really *am* settling in, really starting to enjoy it here. Winter insists on its own pace, dispensing with ambition, and when I do write I turn to whatever takes my fancy. Specialists may bring home more bacon in our society, but the impulse to variety is healthy, even thrilling. The pursuit of only one thing eventually grinds down to a grumbling feeling of work and obligation.

In that spirit, I have been undergoing a sects change operation, switching genres rather than gender. To support myself, I work for half the week as a substitute teacher and when I go into school, the real teachers always greet me with the same question. Wondering which of their peers I'm subbing for, they ask, "Who are you today?" I like the question and have written it down and taped it over my computer. Each day I strive to be a different who. If I feel like writing a haiku about the chickadees at the feeder, that's okay, but if I feel like creating a story about lying naked in a lawn chair, drunk, and blasting the chickadees with a scatter-gun, that's okay, too. These days I write as I please. To use a simile that would be scorned by my fellow nature writers, it's like watching TV with your thumb on the remote, a hundred channels at your disposal (and, honestly, how long do you ever really rest on the nature shows?—one good chase and kill by the lion and, click, it's off to *Baywatch*). Or to turn to a simile the nature-writing gestapo might like better, the health of the individual, as well as the ecosystem, is in diversity.

"A change is as good as a rest," said Churchill, and I do feel rested these days, jumping from genre to genre. Letting different voices fight it out inside me, I'm ignited by the spark of variety. Tabernash, our adopted stray cat, is never more cuddly than right after he's killed something. The thing that the confirmed specialist neglects is the incredible stores of energy that remain in other parts of us once one part is depleted. Though heretical, it could be suggested that variety isn't only more fun, it's more efficient.

I have already mentioned Ed Abbey (note to New Yorkers: not Edward *Albee*), and it is thanks in part to his consistent irreverence that I've always been a big fan. One thing a nature essay isn't supposed to be is funny. Or sexual. In this regard, I remain an admirer of Abbey's, who insisted on constantly broadening the nature corral. Abbey fought against the nature label long before I did, lamenting, "I am not a naturalist" and complaining that what others called nature books were really volumes of personal history. He has been a kind of patron saint for my own efforts to break free. In his introduction to *Abbey's Road*, he complained that critics are always calling some nature writer or other the "Thoreau" of this or that place. He wrote of nature writing that it "should be a broader and happier field" and that, "Like vacuum cleaner salesmen, we scramble for exclusive territory on this oversold, swarming, shrivelling planet." It's only gotten worse in the years since Abbey's death: As the world grows more crowded, our fiefdoms shrink. Ten years ago, Cape Cod had only two living Thoreaus: Robert Finch and John Hay. Now there are a dozen more of us, scrambling and clawing for the remaining turf, happy to be called the Thoreau of East Harwich or the Thoreau of Dennisport. No less than the developers we revile, we try to make a living off the land

and scenery, and so it's necessary to subdivide and develop new areas. And it's not only our plots of land that are smaller. Step right up and observe that freakish character—The Incredible Shrinking Nature Writer. If you drew us to scale and made Thoreau a giant, and placed Leopold and Carson at about his shoulder, you could keep drawing us smaller and smaller until you sketched in me and my crop of peers at insect size. It may be, as some suggest, that our time marks a renaissance of nature writing. But it's a renaissance of ants.

Fear has always led to the taming of diversity and wildness, and, in writing, as in so many other professions in this increasingly crowded and competitive world, fear breeds specialization. With more and more of us competing for the same food source, it's wise to stick to one genre and to the specific rules of that genre. It makes you identifiable. Marketable. Commodifiable. After all, we don't want to buy *Lemon Pledge* once and find out it works—"Boy, this stuff can really clean!"—only to buy it again and discover it has transformed itself into an underarm deodorant. That wouldn't be convenient. Or neat. And neatness counts, now more than ever.

So maybe it's neatness I'm really sick of. A born slob, I admire writers who jump from genre to genre, break-out artists not content to stay in one pasture for long. But I better watch myself: The genre border guards never rest. When I first moved back East, the Cape Cod Museum of Natural History refused to keep my book in stock or let me speak there, apparently fearing both fart jokes and activism. "We really only carry *nature* books," the manager of the bookstore told me, to which I replied, for once, that mine *was* a nature book, it even said so on the back cover. "It's really more of a personal narrative, isn't it?" the manager asked in a scolding voice. Particularly damning, it seems, is the fact that some reviewers used the word "funny" to describe the book. You don't want to do anything as drastic or volatile as mixing humor with nature; that wouldn't be proper, wouldn't be safe. When I speak to someone else about giving a talk, she tells me that, "We only deal with nature here and we don't want anything political," as if, in this day and age, the two could possibly be peeled apart.

For my part, I'll take writing that spills sloppily over genre walls, always expanding its borders. We all pay lip service to Whitman and his famous "contradictions," but it's not all that common to see writers contradicting themselves on the page. "My moods hate each other," wrote Emerson. Amen. I love to see Thoreau overcome by an urge to strangle a woodchuck or Abbey take a break from celebrating the stark beauty of the desert to throw a rock at a rabbit or Annie Dillard admitting she wrote of the beauties of nature while locked in her windowless, cinder-block study. I admire Rick Bass, for instance, when he interrupts an essay to practically grab readers by the collar and insist that they write their congressman to save his beloved Yaak Valley, and I also admire him for the way his "nature writing" has permeated his fiction. Another writer I admire, Reg Saner, has warned me not to make the natural world a stage for merely personal drama, and these are wise words. He points out that Emerson's little book got this whole mess started. "The trouble with *Nature*," Reg said. "Is that there's very little actual *nature* in it. No rocks or trees or birds." But I *like* Emerson's self-contradictory title. And I want nature to occasionally act as a stage, as long as it's not only and always that. For instance, I want novels—where personal drama is imperative—set deeply in nature. After all, to write about humans is naturally to write about the things that matter in their world: weather, wind, plants, trees, animals, and water.

But today I want to make a plea not for wilderness, but for wildness. For freedom. For sloppiness. For the exhilaration of breaking down the Berlin Wall of genre. A plea for amateurism, variety, danger, spontaneity, and honesty in a world growing increasingly professional, specialized, safe, pre-packaged, partitioned, and phony. As novels are set more and more often in lands walled by style and concrete, it has been up to today's nonfiction writers to usurp the themes that have concerned us since the great romantics, reminding us that writing isn't some impotent, inert thing unrelated to actual life, and that stories don't all have to end with some subtle New Yorker flicker of hair that subtly signals something few of us get. On the other hand, there's no reason these larger concerns can't be re-invested in fiction, no reason other than prevailing fashion. We have all seen the damage done by the contemporary mania for partitioning. If nature writing is to prove worthy of a new, more noble name, it must become less genteel and it must expand considerably. It's time to take down the NO TRESPASSING signs. Time for a radical cross-pollination of genres. Why not let farce occasionally bully its way into the nature essay? Or tragedy? Or sex? How about painting and words combined to simulate immersion in the natural world? How about some retrograde essayist who suddenly breaks into verse like the old timers? How about some African American nature writers? (There are currently more black players in the NHL than in the Nature Writing League.) How about somebody other than Abbey who will admit to drinking in nature? (As if most of us don't tote booze as well as binoculars into the backcountry.) And how about a nature writer who actually seems to have a job? (Almost all seem to be men of leisure, often white guys from Harvard.)

Of course, genres help critics box things (and not incidentally allow us to write), but breaking through genres can be as exhilarating and dangerous as waves crashing over a sea wall. And that's where the action is today, when writing spills and splashes over genre barriers. Not just the fictional techniques in today's creative nonfiction—which is exciting in itself—but letting the material go where it will, even if it's "bad" and misbehaves and trespasses in Old Man McGinty's fictional backyard (and makes our fictional parents mad). Thorny, uncategorizable writing. Of course, this is nothing new. Revealing myself as an Emersonian recidivist, I say let the pages fit the man.

After all, though it gives critics and marketers fits, it's where things get most fuzzy that they're most interesting. There are always those ready to wield the word "autobiographical" like a club, to claim the current interest in memoir signals the end of civilization, but the overlapping of fiction and nonfiction is ultimately freeing. "Consider Philip Roth's *The Facts*—which isn't the facts at all . . ." wrote Wallace Stegner. "*The Facts* is as surely a novel posing as an autobiography as *Zuckerman Unbound* is an autobiography masquerading as a novel." Or as the writer Luis Urrea said: "I tell the truth in my novels and make things up in my non-fiction." Genre confusion, like gender confusion, is disconcerting, but it's overall a happy development, a sign of play and freedom. As Stegner says, it doesn't matter if it's autobiography. It matters if it's art.

But it's time to reel myself in.

I'm willing to write manifestos, but I'd prefer having others act them out. For all my declarations of freedom, I, too, am constrained. If genre were an invisible dog fence, I would already have been jolted by several zaps, and would have retreated meekly. So here comes the traditional twist and summary that marks the end of a personal essay. Of course I'm not sick of nature at all. Just sick of being boxed in, and of the genre itself being boxed too narrowly. In fact, having declared myself done with nature, I suddenly feel the itch of the contrary. Hell, after three days of sitting in the attic typing this too-personal essay while listening to an endless loop of the Butthole Surfer's second-to-last album (*Independent Worm Saloon*), I'm ready to get down to the beach and commune with some semipalmated plovers. Maybe even to write about them.

"Bigger than Shakespeare,"
Or How I Weathered the Perfect Storm

My boat was well-caulked, tightly built of pine planking hung over an oak frame. Having failed for ten years to build a grandiose schooner of a novel, I settled finally on a small, quiet fiction-less vessel. Nothing spectacular, maybe some laminated mahogany for the stern and transom, but solid, a work of craft if not art. She was a good Cape Cod boat, a dory let's say, and when I launched her with little fanfare from Sesuit Harbor in April of 1997, I had great confidence that she was, if nothing else, seaworthy. But I didn't know there was weather coming in. Not just the usual nor'easter, mind you, but waves of the once-in-a-hundred-years variety. My little boat could have handled almost anything out there on the Bay. But it couldn't handle the perfect storm.

~

From the first time I saw his picture I knew he was trouble. Our books had come out at the same time and we were asked to do a reading together down in Falmouth. The sponsors of the reading sent out a flier with both of our jacket photos on it. In mine I looked like a homelier, mildly constipated version of Jackson Brown, staring glumly at the camera, wearing a white T-shirt with arms crossed sternly. My wife took the photo and liked it, so I used it. But *his*! It was and remains to this day the undisputed king, the mother of all jacket photos. He stares out like some impossible mix of Jean Claude Van Damme, a Calvin Klein underwear model, and Dolph Lundgren. And the name matched the photo. *Sebastian Junger*! It was as if a computer had created The Perfect Author,

The Perfect Face, and The Perfect Name. Was there any question that he was about to embark on that modern-day sleigh ride of FAME? The second I saw the picture I began to consider having a stand-in for my next jacket. And a name change. I mulled over various dashing nom de plumes. Cornelius Kaiser, maybe, or Estaban Ernst.

I approached our reading with excitement and trepidation. It's not very literary to admit to going into a reading hoping to "win," but I'm competitive by nature (maybe, in part, because I had a father who staged among other things, "lobster races," each child assigned a crustacean to root for as they crawled backward across our patio before boiling them alive). Whatever the complex roots of my troubles, I had the sudden desire to *train*. I can't say that I was training specifically for the reading— that would have made no sense—but I was training nonetheless. As an inspirational aid I turned to my video collection, and selected that masterpiece of cinematic understatement, *Rocky IV*. You may laugh at my mention of this movie, but watch it through and you'll admit that the Siberian training montages are unrivalled in film. It was those montages I focused on. I cast Junger as the superhuman Russian fighter, Drago (played by the above mentioned Lundgren) and myself, of course, as everybody's favorite underdog and big-hearted lug—Rocky Balboa. In the film, Stallone's character flies off to "Russia" (which looks a whole lot like Colorado) to train for his big fight with the Ruskie. He is frightened of Drago at first, justifiably so as the Russian has just punched to death his old rival and buddy, Apollo Creed. Arriving at a rustic cabin out on the tundra, Rocky pins Drago's picture up on his bedroom mirror and then sets to training. While Drago works out on futuristic machines and gets stabbed with daily steroid needles, Rocky trains as no boxer ever has before or since: running around in the snow in his leather jacket with an enormous ox yolk over the back of his neck, tossing mini-boulders into some kind of rock hauler's chute, and chopping down pines in the Siberian Forest. At the end of his weeks of training, he crumples the picture of Drago in his hand.

And so with two weeks to go before my reading, I taped Junger's picture above my computer. My training regime wasn't quite as manly as Stallone's: I wrote in the morning, jogged the beach, and practiced reading in front of a video camera in the afternoon. At cocktail hour one night, my wife Nina and I tried to guess the height of this mythical Junger-creature. Six foot five and not an inch shorter, I maintained. Nina, always in closer contact with reality, suggested he might be a normal-sized person, perhaps even shorter than me, and we shook and bet a dollar on it. As the day got closer, I considered strategies for our first encounter. Maybe I should walk up with a smile and sucker punch him when he reached out to shake my hand.

Sadly, Sebastian spoiled all of my dramatic (pugilistic) plans. Like a lot of Hollywood stars (particularly action heroes) he was of average height (I slipped my wife a dollar) and, worse still, turned out to be one of the nicest, calmest people I'd ever met. Even more unsettling, he was obviously shy during his reading, blushing when he mispronounced a word, hardly an überman. All this made it difficult to hate him, but not, for one trained in the bitter arts, impossible. Particularly over the next few weeks when the inevitable started happening. The Perfect Jacket Photo got things stirred up, but then the book itself turned out to be not half-bad. As he suddenly began appearing everywhere, pangs of jealousy stung more frequently, growing more personal when my wife brought his book to bed and, staying up late, muttered "I can't put it down." My own book had featured a testicle, not a hurricane, and I grumbled something about true art not being appreciated and pulled the blankets over my head to block the light. Over the following weeks, Junger was everywhere: there were Perfect Storm articles, Perfect Storm TV spots, Perfect Storm lunch boxes. The marketers had found their dream boy, not just looks and dash, but good reviews. And then he reached literary nirvana: a glowing cover piece in the *New York Times Book Review*.

By the next time we signed books together, over the July 4th weekend, it was Beatlemania. I prepared for the book-signing by drinking beers on the beach, then showed up unshowered, sand staining my elbows, wearing a loud Hawaiian shirt. Already slightly drunk, I proceeded to gulp down the glasses of wine the generous store owners offered. At one point I asked someone to look on the computer and compare sales of all of Shakespeare's plays over the last year to sales of *The Perfect Storm* since April, and sure enough the Bard was badly beaten. "He's bigger than Shakespeare," gushed one of the young women in line. I suggested it probably was due to Shakespeare's jacket photo, what with that pointy Bozo hair and funny collar.

Sebastian, meanwhile, was as friendly and polite as ever, actually recommending my book to people, and, due probably to the tidal pull of The Storm, I sold a lot of copies that day. But, always the ingrate, I responded by needling Sebastian.

"Next thing you know you're going to be in *People*," I teased.

He laughed modestly.

"I hate to admit it but I'm in this week's issue," he said.

I went over to the racks and picked up the magazine. Sure enough, there he was with his arms crossed, standing on a dock in front of a half-sunken boat. This was the real deal: true American celebrity. Not just a paragraph in *Picks and Pans* either, but a full-blown article (called "The Muse of the Fishermen") with a full-blown picture.

"Jesus Christ," I muttered.

"I know, it's weird," he said. "It's like it's all happening to someone else."

I thought about this for a minute.

"That's exactly how I feel," I finally said.

I exaggerate my own competitiveness. And my bitterness. But the question I ask myself today is how much truth is there in my hyperbole? Literary pettiness is something I'd always read about but never understood. After all, as another writer-friend said, it's not horseshoes or wrestling, where one person wins and the other loses. Back in Poetry School in Colorado, my peers and I would celebrate if one of us got a piece accepted in some magazine that nobody but us had ever heard of (and that nobody read unless they had a story in). The idea of actually having a book published seemed like heaven. That was the pending miracle, the dreamed-of event that would transform years of pain and failure and rationalizing, that would change the answer to the question "What do you *do*?" from a kind of embarrassed "I try to write" to a confident "I'm a writer," that would, quite simply, change *everything*.

I should have guessed it wouldn't be quite that miraculous a metamorphosis, but after almost two decades of struggle, I couldn't help but imagine. After all, we live "in idea," as Samuel Johnson told us over two hundred years ago, driven on by "the hunger of the imagination." It's a perfect image: the imagination as a big gaping mouth, swallowing whatever comes near it, always needing to feed. And always in movement, like a shark, no sooner swallowing down one meal than looking for the next. But that picture is a shade too dark. Without our imaginations we wouldn't write books in the first place, and we certainly wouldn't be able to write book after book without publication. The imagination is a shark, yes, but it's also a surging green thing, a wave that we can surf on, if not control. And though it isn't fashionable to suggest, we *can* to some extent control it. As Johnson reminds us, not only is the imagination always feeding, it is colored by what it digests. In short, we are what we eat.

So we'd better watch our diets. Fame makes idiots of us all, and so does the lust for fame. While writing my book, I'd subsisted on a steady diet of Henry David Thoreau, and, under his fatherly guidance, I'd honestly begun to believe that my time as a failure—that is, an apprentice—had helped make me strong, that it was healthy to work hard without superficial rewards. "The life that men praise and call successful is but one kind," Thoreau preached, and I believed. I called it the "luxury of failure" and felt I drew my strength from years of rejection and self-reliance. But once my book came out, my imagination snuck around back and started smelling through the garbage, sniffing for *People* magazine and *Entertainment Tonight*. Sure, the Thoreauvian vegetarian diet had been fine, but now my shining hour had arrived and it was time for the raw American gluttony of glory—time to eat Henry the Eighth legs-of-mutton and pour booze down my throat and fly to New York to be the toast of the town. Time for people to gasp and quote my witticisms to each other and for society pages to report another "Gessner sighting." Fuck Thoreau. Let's party!

Even the most moral among us must momentarily harbor these fantasies of transformation. We all need to believe that, for Sebastian, the world's ills have been banished and life is a dance from one witty jig to the next. After a champagne breakfast in bed, he pulls on his smoking jacket and ascot, and marches confidently out into the day. He never gets in bad moods or is paralyzed by anxiety or worries about growing older or going bald. "Thank God that year's over," he said when I called him a year after we first met. "I feel like I have my life back." I couldn't quite bring myself to believe he actually felt that way. Part of me didn't want to hear it, the way my unpublished friends back in Colorado don't want to hear me gripe about the difficulties of being published. The truth is we all have a need to believe that some imaginary future event—a winning lottery ticket, a wedding, the publication of a book, a promotion—will transform us, will suddenly make our life blessed. And if we don't get that, we reserve the right to feel bitter.

Of course, it isn't unusual to crave fame and attention. Everything in our fast-forward TV culture teaches us to lust for magazine covers and glory, for what Wallace Stegner called "the big rock candy mountain," that one gold strike that will change us forever. But there's a small problem with allowing the mind to wander in this direction, that being it's childish. We've become like a pack of oversexed high school kids, horny for celebrity. But calling us teenagers is perhaps overestimating our level of maturity. The books tell us to embrace our inner child and so we do, forgetting that our inner children are, more often than not, whiny, attention-seeking little brats. Maybe we should try getting in touch with our inner adults instead. My mother recently told me a story about myself as an infant when she left me unattended in my crib despite my cries for her presence. How dare she ignore me, I must have thought—*me!*—the center of the universe. I responded by stripping off my diaper and shitting, and then smearing the excrement over my crib, every object in it, and every inch of my body. There's your inner child at work.

But enough moralizing. Back to envy. I found that, as the summer wore on, I started mentioning Sebastian's name more often, getting that slight name-dropper's buzz by making myself important by association. I also took some perverse delight in undermining my own achievement by comparing it with Sebastian's. Since then, I've noticed that many writers, living so much in their imaginations, like to focus on the success of a particular other: the fellow graduate student who got a big advance, the famous hotshot who scooped their idea. We use these others as sticks to beat ourselves with. Before my book was published, my jocky Boston friends and I had always gotten along by ridiculing each other, and they didn't know what to make of my suddenly being a respected author. I helped them out a little by making a public joke out of my secret competition with Junger, so that rather than being befuddled by my success, they could mock my comparative failure. And mock they did. Especially the night my buddy Mark called and told me about the sale of Junger's paperback rights. *One point two million!* I laughed and joked along with Mark, but when I got off the phone and walked outside into the summer night, I felt the first surge of true bile rising. This was no joke; this hit me where it hurt. My book had brought me a lot, but one thing it hadn't brought was cash, and come fall I would be looking to go back to what I'd been doing on and off for the past fifteen years: some sort of menial labor.

But, after a brief spasm of real bitterness, I soon was back to lighter grumbling. I watched as Sebastian's sleigh ride continued, complete with the obligatory fame-backlash when a magazine or two questioned his sources. I thought he handled it all pretty well and I actually found myself defending him during that time. I even managed to laugh when an old friend of my father's, a red-faced fishing captain who'd bought my father's boat after he died, greeted me thusly at Hill's Wharf, our local bar: "Hey, David, why don't you write a book like that *Perfect Storm*?" Of course, Sebastian's crowning achievement was yet to come. Maybe the Nobel Prize used to be the highest acclaim a writer could receive. No longer. Topping off his year of triumph, Sebastian took home the prize that all of us secretly covet. In late fall, *People* magazine proclaimed him their "Sexiest Author." Ripped off again, I retreated, grumbling, to my garret and the solace of Thoreau. It wasn't much consolation, but I assured myself that Henry David wouldn't have won any plaudits for being sexy either.

And so, to return finally to my original water-logged metaphor, my boat, planks battered, half-swamped, limped back to Sesuit Harbor. I now store the boat in dry dock down at the marina, and when I walk by it, I feel a growing fondness of the sort you would feel for a dear old friend. I don't have much time to think about Sebastian these days because I'm too busy working on my new boat. This one's a Mackenzie with overlapping planks on the bottom. Yesterday, I screwed in the planks and felt a surge of satisfaction when I sunk the last screw. A bigger boat than the last, she's capable of taking me farther. Capable, too, I say to myself, of weathering almost any storm.

Benediction

On Being Boswell's Boswell

I sat in the front row like a rock groupie, straining forward so that I could catch every word. He sometimes spoke in a plaintive whisper and, never having quite mastered the use of the clip-on microphone, presented no more than a dramatic mime show to those seated in the back of the class. He was frail, with wispy tufts of white hair floating out above his large ears and thin bones canopied in oversized clothes, a mismatched plaid jacket and striped pants. Occasionally his lectures, like his appearance, were haphazard, dissolving into wistful monologue.

"Let's skip some of this stuff," he'd say, waving it off.

Once, I remember, he looked down at his watch and, startled by the amount of time left in the class, exhaled a loud "woof." His comments could be dream-like: "I may have mentioned that to you earlier—or was that years ago?" Or halfway through the lecture, he'd apologize: "I'm sorry that this wasn't better."

The transition of English literature from neoclassicism to romanticism was our stated theme, but a leitmotif of old age and melancholy ran through the classes. Aging and Loneliness 104. "Don't let anyone tell you about how wonderful it is to grow old," he sighed. "The only value of getting older is that you care less about what other people think of you." He looked down from the podium with his elastic face, twisting and pulling at it as if it were made of putty. It was a great comic face, a gentle clown's face that had led a studious and difficult life. Introducing Keats' *Endymion*, he took off his glasses and stared out with his blue eyes. He referred to the biography of Keats he'd written "in my greener, happier days."

Those were the moments that made me love the man, but there were other moments, too. Moments when an idea would catch his fancy, and he would spark alive. Then his hands slid from their resting place below his chin. First, the right hand would pulse to life, slowly rising up from the podium in a circling flight. It opened and closed steadily, then began fluttering and darting, dipping and rising as if barely within his control. When his point was made, the hand would fall gently, a leaf dropping in slow, unpredictable swoops, back and forth, never twice along the same path, finally landing on the podium, or nestling back into the folds of his face and resting for its next flight. Then, just as the room was calming, the other hand would take off, dipping and flying out toward the class.

"We must look to the past's great examples," he exhorted, and it took all my will not to shout "Amen!" He spoke of Samuel Johnson, and as he did, his left arm flew up so violently that it looked as if it might pull him off the ground. He stood there strict, masterful, and commanding. His white fingers balled up into a fist, but then, abruptly, a second later, broke into a undulating dance. With this same light pulse, he removed his thick black glasses, and, with that, underwent another miraculous change. The glasses off, the hand and voice in unison again, all was sweetness and light. He rubbed the creases arcing below his eyes, and looked out with an expression watery and kind. The transformation was complete. There again stood the most gentle man in the world.

~

I was drunk, in one way or another, the better part of my time at Harvard. Like a lot of people, I felt I had no right being there in the first place—this was a place for geniuses and Thurston Howells, after all— and so I threw myself into a bacchanalian frenzy: drinking, skipping classes, smoking pot from the hookah I bought at the Leavit and Pierce tobacco shop, sleeping late, playing Ultimate Frisbee by the stadium in the afternoons. I didn't take Harvard too seriously, or maybe I took it *too* seriously and so, as a defense, acted in very silly ways. During my freshman year, I tore a sink off the wall of our communal bathroom in a fit of drunken fury, and the next year, hoping to impress a girl, I leapt out of the second-floor window of her dorm after bidding her good-bye. I thought I would catch a branch and swing to the ground, Erroll Flynn– like, in a dazzling exit. Instead, the branch snapped and I fell fifteen feet down backward and fractured my skull on the concrete. It was a pattern that would repeat itself throughout my twenties: grandiose visions, impulsive decisions, disastrous results.

For me, the campus was less an ivory tower than it was a territory that I prowled at night like an animal, full of beer and lust. I remember a particular oak tree in the quadrangle in front of Eliot House where I liked to mark my territory. Often I roamed through the night, staying up until the garbage trucks came rumbling and roaring like dinosaurs down the Cambridge streets. I grew my hair long and did countless push-ups, the latter my only concession to discipline. Feigning a deep lack of ambition, I was secretly, intensely ambitious. Though I had no definite idea what it was yet, I knew deep down that I would do something great. This secret vision, coupled with my profligate behavior, caused no small amount of self-loathing.

My one saving grace in college was that I loved to read. It was the dark secret I hid under my brutish exterior: I was bookish. I discovered Rabelais and then Montaigne, whose earthiness and constant self-examination struck a chord; and Dostoyevsky, taught by a brilliant gnome-like Russian professor, and, of course, Thomas Wolfe, who stoked my delusions. It was after reading Wolfe that my previously vague and inchoate ambitions began to coalesce into clarity. I became more interested in Wolfe's biography than in his actual writing, which bored me after a while. What I loved was the myth, the idea of being a famous writer, and also of being, not incidentally, a giant (he was 6'7"), bigger than other men (though I, not quite six feet, could only imagine). And I found that I loved reading about his life: the fame of it, the intensity of it, the anguish of it, the oh-so-exciting-wrought-upness of it.

I learned that Wolfe had gone to Harvard for graduate school and had reacted to his new surroundings with characteristic volatility. He was, as always, overwhelmed by the "pity, terror, strangeness, and magnificence of it all." But he was also lonely. "He felt more lost at Harvard than ever before," wrote an early biographer, Elizabeth Nowell. I understood: After the leaves fell that first autumn in Cambridge, the cold winds whipped down the brick streets between the buildings and I felt lost too. Partly in response to his loneliness, Wolfe spent hours prowling the deep stacks of Widener library. My first encounter with those book-lined catacombs was not quite so literary: I was playing a stoned game of tag with my five roommates, running through the underground corridors and catacombs. But later I went back on my own. I descended three floors below the ground into the darkness (you had to flick on the lights in each row) of acres and acres of books. I loved the smell of the place and the sense of possibility. There was an added layer of self-consciousness to my explorations, of course, since I had just recently read about Wolfe's own monumental assault on the Widener stacks. Unlike me, he gorged systematically, timing his reading with a stopwatch. He records his rapacity in *Of Time and the River*:

> To prowl the stacks of an enormous library at night, to tear the books out of the shelves. . . . The thought of these vast stacks of books drove him mad . . . He pictured himself tearing the entrails from a book as from a fowl . . .

And I, prowling the same stacks sixty years later, pictured Wolfe and then pictured myself picturing him while ripping through books of my own.

But if reading Thomas Wolfe was like the lighting of a fuse for what would become my incipient megalomania, then by far the most important event of my college life was my discovery of Walter Jackson Bate. Bate, who had recently won the second of his two Pulitzers, was one of Harvard's fabled great men, a lineage that extended back to Alfred North Whitehead (whom he'd heard lecture in the thirties) and beyond. I blew off many of my classes, but I never missed "The Age of Johnson."

The thrill of Bate's lectures came first—his malleable face, trembling voice, and hand floating above the podium—but soon his ideas began to infect me. I took long walks by the Charles River, muttering to myself, mulling over the notion that literature must retreat from modern games and return to essentialism, whatever that was. I did poorly in the rest of my classes; this was the only class that mattered. Back in my room, I hunched over his biographies of Johnson and Keats, and his little book, *The Burden of the Past*, ripping deep furrows beneath the sentences with my ball point, feverishly scrawling down notes and quotations.

By my sophomore year, Walter Jackson Bate—the great man himself—lived only a few doors down from me and I often saw him eating in the dining hall, not ten feet away. There he was, taking his breakfast or lunch, wearing mismatched plaids or what looked like pajamas, often eating alone, absorbed in his Salisbury steak and profound thoughts. At least a hundred times, I would pick up my tray and start across the room to sit with him, but would always chicken out. Though I was taking another of his lecture courses, I had never encountered him in person outside of class. I could have gone to see him during office hours, but by then he meant—he *symbolized*—too much to me, and I didn't have the courage to approach him.

That was left to Jon, my bolder and less self-conscious roommate. Jon and I had become good friends and it was in Jon that I confided my growing hope that I might someday become a writer. I also confided how much Bate meant to me. "Why don't you just go over and talk?" Jon asked, logically enough. Finally, one day, fed up with my equivocations, Jon, with my halting blessing, marched over to Bate.

Jon introduced himself and soon the two were friends. Three months later, when Bate invited him up to his New Hampshire farmhouse, it seemed like a crushing blow. I hated hearing the stories from that weekend, but, of course, I asked Jon to tell them again and again, until I knew them by heart. I heard about Bate and Jon spending the day pitching horseshoes and walking through the woods, then spending the evening drinking hot cider and rum in front of the fire with Bate reading out loud the poetry of his "old friend Archie Macleish."

I was devastated.

But if Jon knew the actual man, I still believed that I alone understood his ideas. I'd entered college flirting with the notion of going to law school, but Bate's lectures permanently derailed that course. "The boldness desired involves directly facing up to what we admire and then trying to be like it," I read. "It is like the habit of Keats of beginning each new effort by rereading Lear and keeping close at hand the engraving of Shakespeare . . ." And so I tacked pictures of Keats and Johnson, and yes, of Bate, too, above my desk. In his biographies, his *stories* as I saw them, great writers always struggled and, eventually, persevered.

"The hunger of youth is for greatness," was a line from Longinus that Bate often quoted. By my senior year, my own hunger was a gnawing one. Near the end of that year, I finally got up the nerve to visit Walter Jackson Bate during office hours. There he was in person, white hair disheveled, sitting behind a large desk and slamming his empty pipe on a glass ashtray. I stared into his watery blue eyes and wondered what to say. I knew I needed to make an impression, needed to become his friend the way that Jon had. We had just begun to talk when he managed to shatter the glass of the ashtray with a particularly sharp whack from his pipe. He called in his secretary and the three of us got down on our knees, sweeping up ash and picking up broken shards.

When we resumed talking, I tried to explain how much his courses and books had meant to me. I admitted that I wasn't a very good student overall but that I'd spent the better part of the last four years prowling Widener and reading, as Samuel Johnson had put it, "by inclination."

He studied me closely, brushing ash off his pants.

"It sounds like you've given yourself quite a self-education," he said.

That was as close as I would come to a blessing that day. We had a nice chat, but there were no invites up to the old New Hampshire farmhouse, no special advice conferred. I left his office happy to have finally spoken to him, but disappointed that I hadn't performed better or garnered more pearls of wisdom. "There are a series of answers available in man's long and groping quest," he had said in class. "Answers that can shed some light on our problems now, can teach us what might work, and what not to do." That was what I really wanted, some of those answers.

It didn't matter, though, not really. Bate, unbeknownst to him, had already given me his blessing almost a year before. It had been during a survey class called "From Classic to Romantic" in the spring of my junior year. In a lecture during that course, I heard him speak about the possibility of a "new romanticism," a return to the essential tenets of romanticism that might rise out of the compost heap of post-modernism. He described how the romantic movement itself grew out of neo-classicism, in part born of a rebellion against neo-classicism's "worst excesses": the eighteenth century's increasingly rigid emphasis on unity of form, order, decorum—that is, "the rules." Then he suggested the parallels to our current situation, comparing the worst excesses of post-modernism and deconstructionism to those of neo-classicism: a dry emphasis on reason, on mind; a focus on games, a literature that had moved away from essentialism, from a direct connection to life. "What is literature if it isn't relevant to how we live?" he asked the class. Though a scholar, not a prophet, Bate speculated that the next logical movement in the arts would be toward a kind of "new romanticism."

It was just a theory, of course, maybe even an off-hand remark, but in my fervid young brain it quickly became much more than that. In my mind's eye, I saw Walter Jackson Bate floating above the stage, clad in a tunic, reaching over with a blazing sword that he placed on my shoulders. In my head, his new romanticism became THE NEW ROMANTICISM. Was there any doubt who the first great New Romantic writer would be?

I graduated from college in 1983. For the next seven years I tried to write my NEW ROMANTIC novel. I wrote it in every conceivable fashion from every conceivable point of view. I had many titles, but I might have aptly called the book *Quagmire*. I never found an angle into my material or, more to the point, I found too many angles. Too much freedom, I was beginning to learn, could be just as deadly as too much restraint.

My classmates grew rich as I labored at my intangible, and possibly insane, project. On the years I actually filed my taxes, the profession I wrote insistently down on the forms was "writer." What that meant, for practical purposes, was that I worked in bookstores, substituted at high schools, framed houses, and even once did a stint as a security guard at a phone store. At the time, I thought these jobs the gravest injustice on the planet. With a wild sense of entitlement, I once actually asked my girlfriend what Shakespeare's fate would have been had he been forced to labor as I did. I said this in anger and without irony. I thought I, and my situation, were unique, not understanding that I was just a type. The type I was was an apprentice writer, and the side effects of that vocation— the bitterness, the occasional megalomania, the sense of injustice and impotence, the envy and frustration and rage—were as much a part of the job as carpal tunnel or tennis elbow were part of my work as a framing carpenter.

I felt a growing sense of panic and failure, but deep inside I was sure that if I finally completed my book, it would change everything. Then I'd be hailed as the great artist I secretly dreamed I was. I saw myself creating a Wolfian tome that I would someday bring to Bate and drop on his doorstep, just as Thomas Wolfe had brought his manuscript to Max Perkins. Samuel Johnson spoke of the "epidemical conspiracy for the destruction of paper," and during those years I did my part. I created new drafts, destroyed them, created dozens more. The trouble was that while I had a romantic vision of a great writer writing a great book, I had little else.

But it wasn't only delusion that Bate spurred. Looking back, it seems that the important thing was to continue writing, to get the bad out and get to the good, and Bate's books helped keep me going. There's a profound impotence to apprenticeship. Beginning is terrifying business, and chaos is inherent in beginning. Most of us are unable to see that beginnings will ever end. "I spit on the grave of my twenties," wrote Mencken. I can't quite build up that much anger for the character I was. He was silly and immature, but I don't hate him. If anything, I feel a little sorry for him, and, at times, even feel gently admiring. I like the fact that when the whole world was saying "Pick door A and you'll be a success," he picked door B. And I like the fact that, when everyone was saying that the most important thing in the world was to make money, he tried, however clumsily, to make art.

It isn't just how to write that a writer learns during his or her apprenticeship, and, looking back, I can't help but feel that there's something healthy about spending years banging one's head against a wall. We gain, among other things, the luxury of failure, a necessary luxury for an artist. It builds the muscles of nonconformity to work long and hard at things that others consider ridiculous. And perhaps delusion is a necessary tool. "Without hope there is no endeavor," was a line of Samuel Johnson's that Bate was fond of quoting. I wonder if any young writers would ever finish a book if they knew just how long and hard the effort would be, and how little the end result would impact the world. Without the drunkenness of excitement, would we ever even start anything? Some delusion, some exaggeration of rewards, is essential, and without the pot of gold we'd get nowhere. Of course we don't usually win the pot. Looking back, I admire the grit of that character I was, but I also know that much of his energy sprang from his delusions. He would never receive the fame and glory he so craved but in its stead he would establish regular habits and pleasure and the sanity of work. Not such a bad trade-off in the end. Looking back, I'm glad it wasn't easy for him. Our failures are our strengths; our calluses define us.

My extended adolescence showed no signs of abating as I approached my thirtieth birthday, and it was only through the good fortune of a life-threatening illness that I finally stopped my obsessive scribbling. Had I not gotten sick, I'm sure I would be sinking in my *Quagmire* to this day.

I learned I had testicular cancer. For a month or two, the prognosis was uncertain and I wasn't sure if I would live or die. When it became clear that I would survive, I felt like a snake that had shed its old skin. I secretly hoped the surgeon had cut the old book away with the tumor. I began to make a story out of what was happening to me as soon as I got sick; I understood I now finally had something to say. But during the enervation of the radiation treatments, I couldn't yet muster the energy to begin to say it.

In April, in the midst of radiation, I received some good news. I had been accepted into a graduate writing program in Colorado and would move West in September. But before I left the East, I had some unfinished business. Perhaps freed by the desperation of sickness, I finally had the courage to contact Walter Jackson Bate. I wrote him a long, honest letter, telling him how much he and his books had meant to me over the years, how I had struggled to begin to write, and how I would like to visit him. He responded by inviting me to his home in Cambridge. A few weeks later he was greeting me at his door, wearing a light blue flannel shirt with blue suspenders and blue pin-striped pants. His hair was whiter now, and I noticed, as we shook hello, that his fingers were smaller than I recalled, not the elongated flesh spiders they had grown into in my imagination.

We retired to the living room where he reclined in a brown La-Z-Boy. I sat on the edge of the couch across the room, leaning forward again like the old days, eager to catch every word. Tobacco spilled out over his side table and he pinched up a fingerful and jammed it into his pipe.

I sat silent and waited, with no thought of starting the conversation. Older, a little wiser maybe, I was still deeply intimidated by the sleepy-looking septuagenarian with blue smoke swirling up and around his face. What could I possibly say that would be significant to such a man?

Around his waist Bate wore a white cummerbund, or girdle, that I now realized was a brace. He leaned back further in his La-Z-Boy.

"I can't sit up for long," he sighed.

"Your back's bad?" I asked quickly.

He studied me. His eyes were a soft blue, weighed down at their ends by the slight droop of age.

"Oh, it's not good, I'm afraid," he said.

I had mentioned my own health problems in my letter, and now I saw an opening, a way to at once change the subject and sound literary.

"I'm thinking of moving out to Colorado," I said. "Like Hans Castrop going to the mountains to recover."

"Oh, yes, *The Magic Mountain*," he smiled. "I'm afraid I could never bring myself to re-read it. Every time I started it would bring out my hypochondriacal tendencies."

His pipe had gone out and he began to distractedly bang it on the ash tray, dislodging old tobacco, but then he blinked once, and looked up at me, his blue eyes shining alert.

"But *your* health," he said. "You *are* feeling well again?"

Up until that moment he had sounded weary, but now he was wide awake. I like to think that it was empathy, the quality that so distinguished and enlivened his work, that woke him up that day. In his books he had always *become* those he wrote about. The legend in college was that he had grown sick and developed a nearly tubercular cough as he neared the end of his life of Keats, and in the same way my sickness seemed to draw him out of himself. Worried about *my* health, he leaped to his feet to cook us a lunch of broccoli soup and grilled cheese. During lunch, of course I was on my best behavior, as if my literary future were being judged by my table manners, but I couldn't help but smile when he put down his spoon and his right hand began to flutter above our sandwiches.

I listened as he railed against former Harvard presidents and decon-structionists and the excesses of modern art.

"Perhaps I'm lost in the past," he said. "But I have a preference for the nineteenth-century straight narrative novel. Since Joyce, it seems that fiction has become a puzzle built for academics to figure out."

I reminded him of a comment he'd made in class once.

"You were talking about that Henry Moore statue in front of Lamont. You said it looked like a giant pretzel left out in the rain."

He laughed. "That might have been a little harsh."

For the rest of the afternoon his mind reached like tendrils into dif-ferent subjects, crawling out into them, exploring one idea, moving on to explore the next. I drove him to the Mt. Auburn cemetery, where we walked for over an hour. Anything seemed capable of sparking new thoughts.

He pricked his finger on a rosebush and swore. Immediately the sub-ject turned to the derivation of common curses. He began a discourse on the word "shit."

"It comes from the Latin, you see. It means to *shoot*—to expel."

He shot his arm out quickly as he said the last word.

"And what about 'fuck'?" I heard myself asking.

He laughed.

"Quite a *direct* word, isn't it?"

Directness led to indirectness which led to Samuel Johnson's disdain for periphrasis. He pointed at me.

"He wouldn't have liked the way you called the toilet a 'washroom' after lunch," he laughed. "He had no patience for roundabout talk. Like calling fish 'the scaly breed.' "

I asked him if he still lectured.

"Oh, no, no. They've put me out to pasture, you see. This retirement age is a relatively new thing, but they're quite steadfast about it. Even Galbraith couldn't fight it. When I was an undergraduate it was different. I remember listening to Alfred North Whitehead lecture in a course called 'Cosmology.' His voice was thin and frail by then, and you had to lean forward to catch his words, but what he said was fascinating."

He sighed.

"Yes, they let people carry on a good deal longer back then."

It was a good day. We wrote each other and spoke on the phone a few times afterward, and, later that summer, right before I left for Colorado,

Walter Jackson Bate called and invited me up to the mythic farmhouse in New Hampshire. It had taken over ten years, but I had finally achieved the same status as my roommate Jon.

In early August, I made the trip to New Hampshire. On the first afternoon we toured the property in his old Jeep, just like Jon had. I had to bite my tongue to keep from crying out as we bombed down dirt paths, through briars, and across farmland. Here was my old professor wearing a pair of flip-up sunglasses and smiling with delight at the speed and rushing wind. I'd heard stories about him charging round campus on a motorcycle as a young man, but I'd never before been able to imagine Walter Jackson Bate as daredevil. This was a new twist.

After dinner that night, he poured us drinks. We drank several "Italian kisses," a mixture of red and white vermouth, then small glasses of Madeira, or "old Maumsby" as he called it. "The liquor that Richard the Third had his brother drowned in," he muttered.

I nodded as if I knew the allusion. That night, as usual, his talk was varied, ranging from cows to religion. The first subject came up because it turned out he had owned a small dairy farm "after the war." The second came up when I, emboldened by liquor, asked him if he believed in God.

"Oh, yes, I suppose . . ." he said. He pointed out through the plate-glass window. Rain poured down hard on the flower beds and mist rose above the rolling hills. "I have to believe that there is something behind such a miraculous world."

I was surprised by his statement, even more surprised by the adamancy of my response.

"I can't believe in Heaven," I said. "Heaven seems the worst case of wishful thinking. Like believing in Santa Claus."

He studied me.

"I said I believed in a God who created the universe," he said. "I never said I believed in an afterlife."

He stood up and excused himself, and I wondered if I had committed a grave faux pas. But he returned a moment later with a book in his hands.

He sat down and, without introduction, began to read from T. S. Eliot's "East Coker." At first he read in a near monotone, but then his voice began to quaver, becoming more dramatic, and his hand—the wonderful right hand—fluttered and rose off his lap. Throughout the poem, he held his hand up by the side of his head. It trembled slightly like a dry leaf as he read:

Home is where one starts from. As we grow older
The world becomes stranger, the pattern more complicated
Of dead and living. Not the intense moment
Isolated, with no before and after
But a lifetime burning in every moment
And not the lifetime of one man only
But of old stones that cannot be deciphered
There is a time for the evening under starlight,
A time for the evening under lamplight
(The evening with the photograph album).
Love is most nearly itself
When here and now cease to matter.
Old men ought to be explorers
Here and there does not matter
We must be still and still moving
Into another intensity
For a further union, a deeper communion
Through the dark cold and empty desolation
The wave cry, the wind cry, the vast waters
Of the petrel and the porpoise. In my end is my beginning.

He sighed as he finished, cupped wrinkles drooping below his eyes. At that point in my life his reading was the most dramatic thing I'd ever heard. I had no idea what to say.

"Thank you," I managed.

"Thank *you*," he said. "It's been years since I read poetry out loud. The last time I read this piece was at Eliot's memorial service."

If I had not already been transported to some other mythical literary stratosphere, this last bit of casual name-dropping sent me there. The poetry, the liquor—"Old Maumsby," *here even the booze was poetic!*— and Bate's presence intoxicated me. Of course I should have let the moment settle, should have savoured it, but that wasn't my style. Before I could stop myself, my lips began to flap and words spilled out of my mouth.

"I don't really know how to tell you this, or even if I should," I blurted. "But I feel I *have* to tell you. Since I first heard your lectures I've tried to write the book I mentioned in my letter. For seven years now I've been writing it and re-writing it, but I can't stop. No matter how I try I can't get it right. You see, I want it to be a great book, but . . ."

I carried on in this vein for a good ten minutes, my words becoming more and more tangled. I tried to explain how I had begun a new story, about my cancer, but I didn't feel it would be right to start the new book until the old was finished. Wasn't it logical to kill off the old and put it to rest before starting the new?

When I finally finished my confession, I stared down at the floor. I had no idea what to expect, but wouldn't have been too surprised if he'd walked across the room and slapped me.

"A tar baby."

I heard the words and looked up. His chin rested in one hand while the other rubbed his eyes.

"What?" I asked.

"A tar baby. That's what we used to call it before the word became unfashionable. A tar baby. You put your hands on it, get stuck to it, caught on it, never get away from it. I've seen the same thing happen to friends and colleagues. Seen it ruin careers."

He paused to sip his drink.

"They say that knowing too much about a historical period makes it impossible to write historical novels. Maybe you know too much about your book. Maybe it's time to stop for a while, to put it aside and work on other things."

"But I feel like I have to finish it. I feel like if I don't the last decade will be a failure."

"Of course you feel that way," he said sharply. "If you didn't it wouldn't be a tar baby. But despite how you feel, you *must* put it aside. Keats had the right idea when he refused to further revise *Endymion*. He wrote: '*Let this youngster die away.*'"

The next two days passed quietly. We read, walked, talked, and toured the property in his jeep. I took notes in my journal, a Boswell to his Boswell. During those days, Bate spoke of many things but never mentioned my outburst over my writing or his response, and I thought perhaps he'd forgotten about it, since we'd both been a little drunk. Our conversations grew less literary, often revolving around domestic affairs.

"The one rule is we don't let the cat out at night. If we do a fox might get her. You've got to be careful. She waits by the door and then—*zip!*" With the last word he shot his finger and whole arm forward with amazing speed.

Another day passed and I imagined that I was perhaps overstaying my welcome. I decided to leave a day early. The night before my departure, Bate left me in his study as he headed up to do his nightly reading.

"The TV is set on channel three for the VCR," he said as he left. "You just call me if you want to turn it on. It's easier to do than to explain, like so many things in life."

I had no interest in watching TV. Instead I sat quietly at the plain oak desk without drawers where he'd composed the Johnson and Keats biographies. He had written them, he'd told me, while teaching full time.

"The teaching is the pleasure," he said. "The writing the work."

I began to examine his bookcase, the classics and the Agatha Christies and *The History of Hand Cut Nails in America.* I came across an old, particularly tattered book, an "Avon Classic" that had cost thirty-five cents. The book was *The Aims of Education* by Alfred North Whitehead. The pages were working their way free of the spine, and I picked each page up delicately and turned them over one by one. It wouldn't be going too far to say that there was an air of religious discovery about my enterprise. I couldn't tell what was more exciting—Whitehead's own words or Bate's notes scribbled excitedly in the margins. "Knowledge does not keep any better than fish" had a checkmark next to it, and "Above all the art of reading aloud should be cultivated" was underscored twice. "Interest is the *sine qua non* for attention and apprehension," Whitehead had written. Next to that, scrawled in the margin, was Bate's response; "So literature, when it is taught, must be tied up with a student's concerns. It must be shown as projecting or dramatizing the problems of life with which he is familiar." At times Bate argued with his old professor. "The second-handedness of the learned world is the secret of its mediocrity," Whitehead wrote. Bate took exception: "But the second-handedness can be supplemental. Also, it depends on how the feeling is felt. If felt directly, it is not second-hand."

I was lost in his books when Bate himself called down goodnight. Jamming Whitehead back into the case, I returned to my bedroom. But I was far too excited to sleep and soon was back in the study. I took a volume of Johnson's *Ramblers* off the shelf, copying down in my notebook the sections Bate had underlined. Among the sections was one from *Rambler* #60, on biography, a section I'd heard Bate quote often before and one that would become a guide for me in my future work. "There are many who think it an act of piety to hide the faults or failings of their friends," I read, but "If we owe regard to the memory of the dead, there is yet more respect to be paid to knowledge, to virtue, and to truth."

Next I took Bate's own biography of Johnson down and, on a whim, skimmed forward to the front pages. According to the title page, Bate had been born in 1918. I checked that date against the date of publication of his various books. Despite being obsessed with Johnson, Bate had not written his first book about him until 1955, at the age of thirty-six. He'd written the Keats biography eight years later at forty-four, and hadn't written his great life of Johnson until 1975, at the age of fifty-six.

There was something comforting about those numbers. I hadn't yet experienced the exhilarating feeling of rebirth and regeneration that I would feel the next year while living and writing my new book in a cabin in the Rockies, but perhaps it was then, in Bate's study, that I got my first hint of it. I remembered Johnson's phrase: "Without hope there is no endeavor." I put the books aside and turned off the light, and that night, for the first time in many nights, fell asleep comforted by a feeling of hope.

Before I left New Hampshire I already knew that I would follow my Boswellian impulse and write an essay about the experience. Of course I would. That weekend had been about the most thrilling event of my life and I would do what almost any writer would do: I would record it.

What I didn't know was that Bate would react with indignation to that essay, which I thought a tribute, ending its chances at publication and, effectively, ending our friendship. As any sophisticated reader knows, these mentor/disciple stories rarely have happy endings—following a fairly standard arc of infatuation to worship to disillusionment—and my story is no exception. I wrote my essay a couple of years after my visit, having by then abandoned my "tar baby." I wrote about Bate well, I think, and sent it out to a prestigious review where it was accepted, my very first acceptance as a writer. To be polite, I also sent the piece to Bate, sure that he would appreciate the admiring, even loving, spirit in which it had been conceived. What he saw instead was a caricature of an enfeebled, senile old man. He called the editor of the review and raged, and the editor promised not to run the piece.

Due to the miracle of modern technology, I got the news of my first acceptance and subsequent rejection within seconds of each other, both singing out to me from my answering machine. I had been away for a weekend of cross-country skiing and had come back home, my face flush from the outdoors and from the beer I'd drunk while driving back down the mountain roads. My fine mood got better as I listened to the first message on the machine, accepting my essay. I was in the middle of a celebratory dance when I heard—and was crushed by—the second message. Walter Jackson Bate had called the editor and would not allow the essay's publication. The effect of this double message was like that of a pro wrestler's body slam: I was lifted high above the mat before being thrown down.

Bate wrote me a scathing letter, along with a marked-up version of the essay. He particularly objected to my description of his overactive hands, saying they made him look crazy, like something from "Hogarth's pictures of Bedlam." The essay's pages were filled with his scrawled notes: "Too much fluttering of hands!" "*Hands* again!" "Do you have a *mania* for hands?"

Reading the old piece today, I agree with him, to a point. The essay verges on caricature, but my admiration for my subject—why call him anything other than my *hero*?—comes through. At the time I was crushed. Wasn't this the man who embodied magnanimity and empathy? I sent a letter of apology, but Bate refused to respond to it or my phone calls. I wrote again, promising never to publish the piece, a promise I'm now breaking. I do so with Bate dead five years and the Johnson quotation about the salutary effect of honesty in biography in mind. Though I blamed myself for the incident, I later heard stories of Bate's occasional irrational rages, how he once threw his ashtray against an English Department wall, for instance. It didn't sit well with my image of the kindly, wise professor, but by then I was a little more inclined to believe it.

Of course it isn't big news that heroes have feet of clay. For all that we pained each other, Jack Bate remains my greatest teacher, an inspiring guide whose voice I still hear and who helped me define who I am. What I choose to remember about Bate is that he was heroic in the Johnsonian sense, struggling to manage his own imagination, disciplining it toward empathy and the creation of art. That that imagination might have been a bit more unruly and irrational than I first believed is no longer cause for despair or bitterness, but hope and reassurance.

~

But all this was some years in the future. At the farmhouse, I knew nothing of the feud to come and still regarded the idea that I might one day publish an actual book the way a dying skeptic regards the possibility of a miracle cure, hoping but unbelieving. And, of course, my infatuation with Bate was still in full bloom: I saw him as my Merlin, my Obi-Wan Kenobi. If this sounds mythic and overdone, it was. But also somewhat fitting. Recovering from cancer, coming back from the dead as it were, I was about to move to the West into a new life. And, now, how could I fail? I had the benediction of a wizard and wise man.

We took one final jeep ride around the property on that last day, the last day I would ever see Jack Bate, as it turned out. I had spent the better part of the morning thanking him, but before stepping into my car, I reached out my hand for one final "thank you." To my surprise he clasped my hand tightly and then laid his other hand on top of mine. His voice was gentle.

"I've been thinking about your book," he said. "The more I think of it, the more I think you must be done with it."

He let go of my hand.

"You understand?" he asked as I climbed into the car.

I nodded.

"There are plenty of other things to write. You can always go back to it. But for now be done with it. Let it die away."

I nodded again, and he turned and began to walk the cobbled path back to the house, the cat running in front of him. He didn't turn around as I pulled out of the driveway, but threw his right hand straight up above his head in a final backward wave.

A Letter to a Neighbor

You will be moving into your new home soon and, as ours is a small community, the neighborly thing for me to do would be to bring by a tin of cookies or fudge. Instead I send this letter. Cowardly by nature, I'll probably slip it under your door. It's not the sort of thing likely to elicit the smile brought on by a note from an old friend, or even the irritated glance aimed at junk mail, and you'll surely toss it aside at some point. If I had the courage to stick around while you read my words, you would no doubt turn to me and counter my own flimsy, idealistic arguments with more solid and practical ones. "What right do you have to tell me what to do with my land?" you'd ask. "I bought it with my own hard-earned money. Furthermore, if I hadn't built my house here, the place would be checkered with subdivisions."

You would be right of course. And I should be grateful the land wasn't further developed. But I'm an ingrate, and ingrates, by nature, complain.

"It's a goddamn desecration of place," another of your new neighbors said recently. That's the word—desecration—that keeps coming up when I think of what you've done to your land. I don't use the word lightly; in fact, I use it just as it was meant to be used.

I have walked the path to the bluff, *your* bluff, since I was a small child, first holding my mother's hand, then exploring on my own. From a young age, I understood that this land was different from the rest of Sesuit Neck. The sound of building is never far off on Cape Cod, but neither is the sound of the ocean, and the ocean insists on wildness. Your property, due to a coincidence of wealth and geography, remained the wild heart of Sesuit. Stone's Bluff heaved out from the shore like a great whale-backed beast, a jutting heath transported directly from a nineteenth-century romantic novel. Approaching it by beach from the harbor, one travels from tame to wild, first walking past the over-developed private beachfronts, then past the public beach and Bagley's, and finally leaving all houses behind. As an adolescent, I had a distinct sensation of relief when, moving past the last of the homes, no longer feeling windows or eyes staring down at me, I began to walk faster, excited, out to greet the bluff alone.

Part of what ensured this solitude was the rocky terrain. Except at dead low tide, the land below the bluff could only be walked by jumping from rock to rock, and most beachgoers, fearing bloody shins, didn't take the risk. But the brave were rewarded. Once past the sandy stretch, and headed toward the point, anything could happen. Seals basked on Tautog Rock, rafts of eiders bobbed off-shore, and, if I got there before dawn, I might see deer licking salt off the rocks. It was as if, by walking less than a mile from the harbor, I had passed through a door into another world.

Not a quiet world. Weather reached Stone's bluff first, and, often, summer turned to fall when I arrived at the jutting spit. The sky above would pile up with clouds, enormous cloud continents with dark violet interiors and flashes of gold escaping from the coasts. Long shadows shafted down the sand, my own goofy, dark doppelganger stretching out in front of me as I walked. Sometimes the open beach barely let me approach—warning me off with sand stinging my face. Gulls drifted by sideways. Trees and grasses bent and ran from water and wind. Light, dry sand flew spectral over the darker sandbar sand like a curtain revealing the blue-grey ocean and purpled clouds. Even on the rare days when the waves rested, the rocks seethed with life. Barnacles hissed and crabs scuttled and swallows darted and swooped down from their cave homes in the brown cliff wall.

As with any good relationship, mine with the bluff deepened over time. After college I came to Cape Cod to write, and that fall, standing on the point like the bow of a ship, I watched as the wind swept out summer's clinging heat and ushered in the clarifying Cape light. It was below the bluff that I learned that nature can provoke two profound and opposite reactions: stunning me into a near doltish silence when faced with the ineffable and causing me to run for my pen. The latter reaction was more common; lists gushed over the pages of my journal and punctuation fell away like something withered and dead. I recorded random sights and sensations: a red-tailed hawk treading air in the stiff wind . . . the smell of cut grass and grapes . . . the bloody mucous inside a periwinkle . . . the smell of celebratory cigars wafting to the beach the day the cranberries were harvested . . .

Then, just as it was as good as it could get, it got better. The real weather blew in and the leafy world reddened, poison ivy and sumac bloodying the edges of the cranberry bog. Not wanting to squander any opportunity for joy, I often reached the beach before dawn to watch the show. When the birds called up morning that was my sign to wake and head to the bluff. Later, at sunset, I'd return to catch the dying rays of light, sipping a beer and watching a pumpkin-orange moon rise.

This overindulgence, this binge of color, led to a long hangover, and I had to leave Cape Cod for a while. But over the years, I've kept coming back. Gradually, I've learned that for the bluff each time of year is both itself and a moving toward—the spare clutching of the pitch pines in mid-winter becoming the island bloom of late spring. For a while, in my twenties, I tried to write a novel, a kind of grandiose *Wuthering Heights*, which I set on the bluff. Years later, older and calmer, I wrote a book of essays about Cape Cod, and it wouldn't be much of an exaggeration to say that the bluff was the book's main character. The book ended with the spreading of my father's ashes on the bay beyond Stone's point, after which I walked out alone toward the bluff at sunset, seeking refuge.

Perhaps by now you've put this letter aside. But if I've gone overboard with my descriptions, it's only to try to impress upon you how much your land means to me. To convince you that, to the degree that places can be sacred to human beings, I hold this place sacred. Assuming that I have at least partly convinced you of this, I can begin to address what you have chosen to do to my sacred place.

In these times, half of truly loving a place is a healthy hate. Hate is a strong word, of course, and one that is often fenced out of the reasonable pastures of the nature essay. But *hate* is what I feel and hate, as well as love, is what compels me to write today. I apologize in advance if some of the things I'm about to say sound rude and unneighborly. But I would contend that you have acted quite discourteously yourself, that you came to Sesuit Neck, not like a neighbor or friend, but like a conqueror from another land, first unleashing a fleet of trucks like tanks rumbling through our streets, then securing a beachhead, and finally razing our beloved capitol. This is not generally considered polite behavior.

Furthermore, you seem not to have bothered to take the time (and it can take some time) to learn about the place you've moved to, but rather, acting with an intruder's mentality, have imposed your ideas from the outside. You'll be happy to know that there are many in the neighborhood who insist you are a "good guy," and I'm sure that in person you can be charming. I can be fairly charming myself, and perhaps if we'd met under different circumstances, we might have drunk a beer or two and become friends. But while I've no doubt that you're a "good guy," I also have no doubt that it's good guys like you, with your blissfully thoughtless adhesion to old-time progress and just plain BIGNESS, who are destroying sacred places like this one all over the world.

But before I work myself into full froth, let me climb down from my soap box and get specific. Your house. Since humans first settled here they built their homes low and strong, a logical and organic reaction to the daily assault of wind and water. This is how things grow on Cape Cod, and how they have long been built, a response that evolved directly from place, and an intimate knowledge of that place. For inspiration, you need have looked no farther than the pitch pines and scrub oaks that crawl mangily across the humpback of your new backyard, a yard you will find to be one of the windiest places on earth. If you had been in a listening mood, the trees would have spoken directly to you, whispering "stay low," and, heeding that advice, you could have still built a large and beautiful structure. "But," you may have reasoned, "with modern building materials and techniques making the old restraints irrelevant, why not spread as far and high as I can go? Why merely become part of the bluff when I can rise above it?" Why indeed. Well, stifling the moralist's urge to tell you to go back and read the story of Icarus, I'll suggest there were simpler reasons.

You might have paused and considered your neighbors. Not just the deer whose paths have forever weaved through the brambles you tore down or the swallows who for countless generations have made their homes in the undercusp of the bluff where tractors now rumble, but the three hundred or so *Homo sapiens* who dwell here in different seasons. You might have, dare I mention it in this day and age, minded your manners, and said, well, since I'm tearing down this mansion, this neighborhood landmark, I'll consider the others who live here and, while of course building a large place, will try to fit gracefully into my new home. This was not the option you chose. The house you chose to build would dwarf a shopping mall. Proof of that is the way it seems to dwarf what had previously been the Neck's most prominent feature, the bluff itself. For the first time since I was born, the silhouette from the beach is not of humped land descending like the back of a sleeping giant, but of a castle sprouting into the air, proclaiming dominion over its once wild surroundings.

Instead of wisely sitting back from the ocean, your building peers over at those of us who still try to walk this spit. In a way, I admire your nerve, daring the ocean. But of course you believe you can control large forces. This winter, I felt the ground shake as earth-moving machines dumped more of the $300,000 worth of fill. Most of the old mansion, which looked like a dollhouse beside your plywood palace, has been torn down, and most of the fields and brambles ripped up. Meanwhile, your grandson patrols the grounds in a golf cart, scaring off deer and neighbors, yelling at one long-time resident to "stay off my property." Below the bluff, the sounds of the ocean are now punctuated by the backward beeping, the mating call of trucks that invades every moment of our waking lives. Most of us were sure the frame was complete a few weeks ago, since your house already rose several stories above any structure we'd ever seen in these parts, besides Scargo and the water towers. But then you added a final room on top of it all, an observatory or walled-in widow's walk, as if to say, "Why not go just a little bit higher?"

Despite my state of high dudgeon, I, walking below on the beach, have looked up and fantasized about being the carpenter sinking those final nails, staring out at the neck from that wooden aerie. I'm not above the urge for a dream house myself, and I'd have been happy for you if you'd built a grand house, even an enormous house. That this would have been fairly easy should be evinced by the simple fact of the previous home. The bluff is of such magnificent scale that a mansion—a mansion!—was able to fit snugly into place. But the sad and frustrating thing, the thing that causes me daily depressions and stabbing pains—and this is especially sad if your are indeed a "good guy"—is that a dream house or mansion wasn't good enough for you. You could not tolerate merely becoming part of this beautiful, beautiful bluff, but had to dominate it. Yes, dominate. Sometimes the sexual metaphor is unavoidable. You haven't exactly sidled up and wooed this land, have you?

As I write, I try to hold myself back, to temper my impulse to use words like "rape." After all, it's only a piece of land. This sort of thing is going on every day, and we'd better inure ourselves to it. "Sesuit Neck was ruined already," said a neighbor, and maybe so. But in this neighborhood, two things have mercifully slowed the rush. One is the marsh, which winds through Sesuit Neck like a mucky subconscious, and the other is the land below your new home. Ticks and stink make walking the marsh on a daily basis impractical, so most often I go to Stone's Bluff to have my few moments in a world without people. But not completely without people, and that is the paradox of that bit of land: It's a place for the community as well as the solitary. Below the bluff, I may run into J.C., who collects shells for his driveway and gathers wood for his fire, or dog walkers who want a minute free to think. That is what this point has really meant to the neighborhood: a place where you could go to get away, a place where seals and wild birds exist.

"Our neighborhood Holiday Inn," an old friend of my father's calls your new home. People grumble, now that the true scale of your attack is being revealed, but I've noticed that few express outrage. They are used to it, you see, the gradual decline and destruction brought on by "improvements." Used to having every brambled corner of the neck torn up, every copse of locust chopped down. They accept it as "progress," the way of things, which I, of course, should also do.

But can't.

Again, I apologize. My parents raised me to be courteous, and fanaticism doesn't come naturally.

It's been a long road to get to where I am today. Please understand that if I sound angry it's only because I'm being stripped of thirty six years of connection and memory. I understand that, according to the law, your deeds and title say more than my little essays about who has the right to this land. It's yours unequivocally to do with as you will, and, again according to law, my love for this land means nothing.

The truth is, if I keep calm, I really do think I understand what you've tried to do. You're obviously an ambitious man and in that we are alike. While your workers hammer away up on the hill, I hammer away at my keyboard. Like you, I dream of creating something big, something great, and, like you, I sometimes feel as if my passion for this controls me, not me it. But we are in control more than we admit, more than it's fashionable to say these days. I don't suggest the laughable premise that humans are rational creatures, or that reason controls our lives. What I do suggest is that our imaginations can be nudged, and work best if nudged earthward. For me, it has been a question of learning that, when my words rise too high, they become brittle; that they are better when connected to earth. That is, I want my books to be like a good Cape Cod house that seems to grow out of the surrounding ground. It's not that I've given up ambition. Hardly. It's just that my ambition now is to stay closer to the earth.

Perhaps you thought you could simply plow into and over our neck without any cries of protest from us humble villagers. Well, this is my cry and it won't be my last. I'm a relatively young man with a long writing life ahead of me and, as long as I have strength to type, I plan to make your home into the symbol of everything I despise. I admit to taking some vindictive pleasure in this. But that is my worst motive. I have better ones. I write today with a purpose. I'm tired of creating lyrical nature essays. This piece really is for an audience of one—that is, for you. And, keeping that in mind, I'd like to swallow my anger and change my tone. Impotent rage gets old fast. I'm ready to stop ranting and turn this letter into what it really is.

What it really is is a plea. An appeal to your better instincts—to the "good guy" in you that my neighbors speak of—to the amateur, not the professional; to the man whose wild impulse made him want to live on this wind-swept bluff, not the man who built to dominate it. An appeal to the quieter, deeper voices inside you, to your own marshy subconscious.

My plea is this. Leave the beach wild, and leave as much of the bluff wild as you can. This morning, I saw the orange florescent paint on the rocks that you plan to plow away, and the fleet of tractors close to the bluff's edge, close enough possibly to scare off the swallows. Smoke wound out of the briars as if the bluff were a chimney; the sand on the beach vibrated. It looked and felt to me, as it must to the birds, like the end of the world. Hyperbolic perhaps, but true. Everything I know about the world, everything I love and hate, comes down to this single place.

Please have the tractors back up. Let the rim by the cliff's edge remain the territory of the deer and birds and of the coyote I saw hunting there the other day. Let the beach remain a place where people need to risk bloody shins to walk. Don't turn what has been home, classroom, gymnasium, observatory, study, and wild place into mere beach.

Leave it inaccessible. Resist the urge to domesticate, to tame. Give this one gift to your neighborhood—a last patch of wildness—and I guarantee that you will be surprised how much your neighborhood gives back to you.

By now you are truly sick of me and my thundering.
Who can blame you?

But let me try to end on a courteous note. Maybe we will never share that beer, but, perhaps, in the end, we can be considerate neighbors. While this isn't exactly a tin of fudge, it isn't a letter bomb either. My fantasy is that you will reconsider, pause, and keep the bluff as wild as you can. Perhaps if you do this, your house, despite its grand ambitions, will begin to take root in the land, connecting to the earth so it can weather the blasts of wind that will blow up from the sea.

Finally, bear in mind that if my words sound occasionally venomous, it's because this is a difficult time for me. It used to be that I was pulled out to the bluff, that I almost couldn't help walking there, my feet leading me excitedly to that place beyond human eyes where the seals were. Now I have to decide, on a day-to-day basis, whether I'm up for the depression, anger, and fear that will surely well up if I head in that direction. For me, it's a time of loss. So please remember that, if there is hate in this letter, it was born of the opposite emotion. To put it as bluntly as possible, I love your land. In time I hope you will too.

Ultimate Glory

A Frisbee Memoir

What you gave me you gave whole
But as for telling
Me how to best use it
You weren't a genius at that.
Twenties, my soul
Is yours for the asking
You know that, if you ever come back
—KENNETH KOCH, "To My Twenties," from Kenneth Koch's memorial service

We labor over our big decisions and big dreams, but sometimes it's the small things that change our lives forever. What could be smaller than this: It is the first week of my freshman year of college and I, looking for a sport to play, am walking down to the boathouse for crew, resigning myself to four years of servitude as a galley slave, when I see a Frisbee flying across the street. The Frisbee, tossed from one long-haired boy to another, looks like freedom to me. Then I notice that there are several Frisbees flying back and forth among a band of young men, all wearing shorts, with cleats hanging over their shoulders. At the time I am quite shy but, uncharacteristically, I cross the street and ask them where they are going. To Ultimate Frisbee practice, it turns out, and I am going with them.

It is my first practice, and almost my last. The college I am attending is Harvard but if I thought there would be plenty of snobbery at the boathouse, I didn't expect it out on an open field tossing Frisbees around with a bunch of semi-athletic half-hippies. But it's here all right, mostly in the form of a tall, skinny preppie-nosed boy named Paul Edwards. I'm not yet aware of the caste-like layers of the sport, not aware that Edwards has spent the last season playing for the soon-to-be national finalist Boston Aerodisc and considers himself laughably above practicing with a bunch of beginners (some, like me, *who can't even throw forehands!*). But if I am shy during that first practice it isn't because I'm naturally passive or subdued. I might not say much to other people, but inside my head, plans already broil, slights are carefully noted, and words wait to pour out. By the third time Edwards criticizes the way I cut for the disc, I am ready to storm off. Who does this skinny prick think he is? I played high school football and tennis, and am a decent basketball player, and though I might not know how to make the fancy little throws he can, I know right off that I'm a better athlete. It's true he can do almost anything with a Frisbee—on the sideline he very seriously sprays silicone on the disc (with the air of a doctor starting an IV) so that he can spin it on his well-trimmed nails—but does that give him the right to criticize *me*? The next time he opens his mouth, I storm off. *Fuck this*, I think, and start walking back toward the boathouse. Full of righteous indignation, huffing and puffing, I make it about fifty yards until one of the team's captains catches up with me. He is a small energetic man named Stuart and he gives me a pat on the back, acknowledging that Edwards can sometimes be hard to play with. He talks me into staying. As it turns out, he knows the right way to win me over. "You're going to be great at this," he says. Music to my young ears.

~

That was the beginning of almost twenty years lost in the world of Ultimate. A friend of mine once said that our bodies are like credit cards; we get the bills later on. I am forty now and have been paying my bills lately in the form of varicose veins, arthritis, and a torn rotator cuff from almost two decades of playing that silly sport; I've become like an old sailor who can feel weather coming in across the Bay in my bones. Not long ago, on a particularly achy day, I said to my wife: "If I were young again, I wouldn't play that stupid sport." She looked at me the way she does sometimes. "If you were young again," she said. "I'd give you a beer, toss you a Frisbee, and you'd chase after it like a border collie."

Ultimate Frisbee, which when I started to play was barely ten years old, was invented in a high school parking lot in Maplewood, New Jersey, in 1968, and is played by seven men or women to a side, on fields 70 yards long with 25-yard end zones, the object being to advance a plastic disc across a goal line in the air. But instead of running with the disc, the player who catches the disc must stop, establish a pivot foot, and throw it within ten seconds. If the disc is dropped or knocked down, play instantly changes direction, offense becoming defense. There are no stoppages of play until a goal is scored. Then the Ultimate equivalent of a kick-off occurs; the scoring team throws or "pulls" the disc to the receiving team, which waits to receive on its own goal line.

The sport is filled with running, jumping, and diving, but has the unfortunate distinction of being played with an object universally considered a child's toy. In fact, cardiovascular studies have shown Ultimate, with its non-stop running, to be a match for soccer, but though teams often share the fields with—and often practice harder than—rugby squads, they can never quite escape the taint of the whimsical. For those who devote their lives to the sport, it's a little more serious. For instance, the throws used to advance the disc are hardly the casual from-behind-the-hip flips seen thrown by old guys at picnics. Long passes, called "hucks," occasionally carry the full distance from end zone to end zone. Players uncurl traditional backhands or flick forehands, but they also employ a varied arsenal of non-floating passes. These include the spear-like overhead, where the disc is hurled in football style and can travel fifty yards upside down before turning back over and dropping into a receiver's hands, and the "blade," a knifing pass that describes an absurd parabola, and that the very best players slice surgically round the field.

When watching Ultimate (the "Frisbee" was dropped from the name some years ago), the first thing that strikes the uninitiated is the way men and women throw their bodies around. Often they do this on fields only a little more forgiving than the parking lot where the sport was invented. And if Ultimate is a game of moments—of improbable dives and acrobatic catches—then these moments are heightened by two physical facts: 1) a disc is a hell of a lot easier to catch than a football or basketball, and 2) a disc *hovers*. There's a bumper sticker that reads: "When a ball dreams, it dreams it's a Frisbee." Players make wild stabs or catch the trailing plastic edge, the disc seeming to stick to their hands. Throws curve twenty yards out of bounds and then boomerang back in, and sometimes the disc actually seems to *wait* for players to catch it.

For many, myself included, all this action can prove addictive. The Ultimate world is full of people who, for reasons they can never quite explain, have given up the normal benefits of life to chase plastic, men and women brimming with the passion and impracticality of the clichéd artist, a band of jock Van Goghs, painting on and on without the faintest hope of a sale.

Whatever the mysterious motivation, each year more innocents are drawn into Ultimate underworld, often leaving behind mystified parents wondering exactly where they went wrong. After graduating from some of the country's best schools, their minds are subtly warped, and, instead of putting their energies into sensible pursuits such as law or medicine, they throw them into this ridiculous sport. It's kind of like a new LSD in this way: Turn on and drop out. Suddenly Ivy League graduates are working at warehouses so that they can have time to pile in a van to drive, stuffed in with ten rank-smelling teammates, down to a tournament in Texas. Meanwhile, they live in warrens filled with other players, and drink beer and talk incessantly of Ultimate. It's enough to make parents want to call in the de-programmers.

~

My own immersion began on that field freshman year. Soon I became friends with two of my classmates, Jon and Simon, and when the older guys put us on the field together they called us the "freshman death squad." Both of my new teammates had attended Brookline High School, a progressive public school in the Boston area that had its own tradition of Ultimate, and they came into the game as full-blown players, complete with forehands (or, in Simon's case, an ugly but effective throw called the "thumber" in which the disc was launched from closer into the body with the thumb, not the fingers). While I lacked their skills, I made up for it through a kind of brutal effort, playing defense for the whole season in about the same mood I'd been in when I stormed away from Paul Edwards, and running deep to catch the passes that Jon and Simon threw.

My hands were my strength as a player. As college wore on, I became obsessed with catching—"You are what you catch," read a note on my wall—and this obsession, like most of mine, ran like a parent stream back to my father. When I was nine or ten, I loved nothing more than playing football with him on our front lawn. He had been a scrappy high school jock himself and would line up at quarterback, taking the imaginary snap, while I'd run patterns: buttonhooks and down-and-outs and square-outs. I remember the square-outs best because they sent me directly into the front hedges. He threw tight, mean, lefty spirals and if the ball was out of my reach, I would dive for it, often ending up sprawled and cut in the bushes. If the ball tipped off my fingertips, he always said the same thing: "If you can touch it you can catch it." This was a phrase that stayed with me, sometimes resurfacing in my dreams. Now, playing Ultimate at eighteen, I felt I could catch anything, however poorly thrown.

I loved running hard and throwing my body around and skying after discs, and I worked on my throws much harder than I worked on my classes. After practice, I would often head back to Simon's room and drink beer and listen to Springsteen and talk for hours about Ultimate. Like a lot of people who go to Harvard, I was unimpressed with my classmates as a whole. I'd expected to be in the presence of "genius" and though they were a lively group, with varied talents and interest, I wasn't nearly as dazzled by their intelligence as I had imagined I would be. But Simon was smart. Perhaps a little too delighted by his own raconteur's wit, but smart. Simon's favorite form of speech was the loud monologue, which he could keep going for surprising stretches of time, brooking no interruptions. But if it was sometimes hard to get in a word edgewise, Simon was a good and generous friend. Already, he was playing the stock market and, one day, after a lucrative surge, he bought me a gift. At first I'd played Ultimate barefoot, then in a pair of narrow Adidas cleats barely held together with athletic tape, but I was soon eyeing a new pair of expensive cleats in a local store window. Simon told me that if the stock market did a certain thing he would buy them for me, and when the market obeyed, he did. I was ecstatic. They were big, black, Johnny Unitas-style hightops with long plastic spikes that were painted silver so that almost everyone I covered asked the same frightened question: "Are those *metal* cleats?" Not only were the cleats physically impressive, but they had a name that I liked. They were called "Barbarians."

~

"You're playing *what?*" my father asked when I first told him what I was doing. If he still held any illusions that his son would evolve into the reincarnation of Frank Meriwether, this did them in. Frisbee, of all things. Clearly a sport for long-hairs and druggies.

But as well as laughing at Frisbee, my father would feel its sting. During my senior year, he drove to Cambridge to tailgate at a football game. The Ultimate team was playing in a tournament on a nearby field and so he decided to drop by to take a look at his son's eccentric preoccupation. I can still see him chortling with the friends he dragged along, amused that such a foolish game existed (as he waited to get into a stadium where he could watch a sport played with an oblong ball made from a pig), while concerned that the wayward son sounded a wee bit too passionate about his strange new obsession. It was nice of my father to come watch, but he was standing too close to the field, sipping drinks with his friends, and not really paying attention.

He *should* have been paying attention, if for no other reason than Nathan Salwen was roaming the field. With Nathan around, there was always potential for danger. Nate was a physics genius who dropped in and out of Harvard, taking a half-dozen years to get his degree. But while Nate's mind could soar and play subtly among quasars and string theory, he played Ultimate like the classic wild man. He had thick veined plowman's legs, a squat, powerful torso, and wore his wild red hair long, with a frayed red beard and moustache. When he tore around the field, you could squint and imagine, without much of a stretch, that this was how Neanderthals looked chasing after deer. Nathan was an "impact player"; he played passionate defense and dove at the slightest provocation and could run all day, but he also could make an impact in a less positive way. His throws weren't quite as developed or accurate as he imagined they were. And his first instinct was to make the most difficult and, if possible, longest throw. This instinct to punt the disc deep, an instinct that apparently could not be controlled, would sometimes cause his team-mates to cringe and mutter when Nathan got the disc. "No, Nate, no . . ." they would plead. But the answer was always yes. Nathan saw things that were sometimes there, sometimes not, and then he wound up and let 'er rip. As Simon liked to say, Nathan "had a notion."

Nathan's forehand flew like a dying quail. Sometimes when he launched it, Simon would look at me and say "duck full of buckshot" and then, after mimicking the motion of pumping a shotgun, would pretend to point his imaginary gun and shoot the wavering disc out of the air. But Nate's backhand was raw power. He would curl around the disc and then uncoil, launching it with a fury, sometimes heaving it right out of the end zone.

When he caught the disc around half-field, on the sideline where my father stood, his defender left Nate's ferocious backhand open. Someone was streaking deep and Nate's eyes lit up and we all knew what would happen next. Nate had a notion and if my father had been paying closer attention, and had noted Nathan's tendencies, he would have had a notion, too. Something, some atavistic, primal instinct would have tingled and warned him that this was a dangerous man nearby, a hunter from another clan, a clan not like his own. But at that moment my father, inebriated, oblivious, imagining himself safe watching a mere "Frisbee" game, foolishly ignored whatever subtle signals his brain or body was sending. He stood there smiling, barely an arm's length away from this wild red-headed troglodyte, as Nathan wound up, virtually coiling around his backhand, and then, his eyes glinting with notions, unwound himself in a violent, powerful jerk.

The disc travelled barely two feet. It caught my father on the side of the head and knocked him to the ground. The game stopped. My father instantly went from one of the spectators to the main attraction. A crowd gathered round him. "Are you all right, man?" Nathan asked. There was a cut and some blood, but my father was just dazed. An old athlete himself, he tried to make light of what had happened and, after gathering himself for a minute, gamely climbed to his feet.

My father and I would joke about it later. As would my teammates. And it *was* funny, a comic moment. But there was something else there, too. Looking back, my symbol-making imagination can't help but mold the incident into personal myth. If I had more Robert Bly in me, I might be inclined to explore the idea of my father, authority figure and businessman, knocked to the ground by the team's wildman, Id flooring Superego. Which, as it would play out over the next decade, was pretty much what Ultimate would do to any traditional career plans or hopes of financial success. It would be easy to say, and not entirely untrue, that the wildman in me, in coming years, would beat the stuffings out of the businessman within.

As graduation approached, my Harvard roommates worried about which companies to go to work for. Meanwhile, I'd secretly begun to wonder which of the great Boston Ultimate teams, the Hostages or the Rude Boys, to try out with after college. By then, I'd become completely wrapped up in the lore and the lure of the game, and it wasn't so much a decision as an inevitability that I would continue to play after school. Why? It was simple really. I wanted that feeling I experienced when I dove through the air and a disc stuck to my hand or when I jumped high and snatched one out of the air over someone else. The simple fact was that nothing else made me feel so alive; nothing else gave me that sensation that Tom Wolfe, speaking of Chuck Yeager and the other young fliers at Edwards Air Force Base, called "rude animal health." Playing Ultimate was one of the few times in my young life when I felt potent, and I was quickly becoming an addict of that feeling. Trying to describe the feeling now, I keep coming up with words like "primal" or "tribal" and I'm afraid this might reek of the once-fashionable neo-primitivism of the men's movement, but there was nothing contrived or literary about the feeling I was after, and I knew it to be real. I had been inside of it, and if anything in my world was true and to be trusted, it was that feeling. I was ready to follow it anywhere.

While I loved playing, from the very beginning I relished the stories about the sport almost as much as the sport itself. In college, up in Simon's room after practice, we would ride the buzz of endorphins, beer, and pot, acting giddy as we talked about Ultimate, barely able to contain our excitement. Simon and I would analyze the Hostages and Rude Boys, blatantly hero-worshiping great players and their best plays. We would also try to decide such weighty issues as who was the game's greatest player—the 6'7" Steve "Moons" Mooney of the Rude Boys was in contention, along with David Barkan and Steve Gustafson of the Hostages—and who would win at regionals and nationals.

Actually, there was plenty to be excited about. Within the city limits of Boston in 1982, we had, arguably, the two best Ultimate Frisbee teams in the world. That season, the Rude Boys would roll through the rest of the field on their way to taking the National Championships, their only serious challenge coming in the semifinal game, when they beat the cross-town Hostages. The previous year had been even more exciting. You couldn't have invented more perfectly contrasting rivals than the Hostages and Rude Boys. With Moons at the fore, the Rude Boys were the game's überteam, capable of sporting a starting seven with an average height of 6'4" and overwhelming other squads with size, talent, speed, and depth. And, if the Rude Boys blasted teams into oblivion like some sort of Frisbee version of Vader's death star, then the Hostages were a scraggly band of rebels, fighting against all odds. They had taken their name during the Iran crisis and, since Khomeni had taken fifty-two hostages, everyone painted that number on their shirts. While the Rude Boys wore more standard black uniforms with the team name emblazoned across their left breasts, someone on the Hostages had gotten the idea to put T-shirts up against a chain-link fence and spray-paint them, leaving the shirts stained with strands of barbed wire. To complete the uniform, players tied yellow ribbons around their wrists. While the Rude Boys looked tall and handsome, like pre-med or pre-law students out for one more fling before getting this "Frisbee" thing out of their blood, the Hostages had a decidedly grubby look, with a minor punk-rock theme running through the team's general anti-establishment motif.

But it wasn't merely sartorial differences that separated the two rivals. There was a distinct Dudley Doright element to the Rude Boys, and they trained as no Ultimate team had trained before. Pushed by Moons, they attacked their infamous track workouts at MIT and ran double sessions in summer. To some more groovy-minded Ultimate players, this was unheard of, almost against the rules. The Rude Boys didn't care for grooviness: They wanted to win. They were not only a large team physically, but their numbers were huge so that opponents had the sense of a swarm of players coming at them in waves. By contrast, the Hostages were a smaller team that intentionally kept their numbers low to ensure camaraderie and tightness, with everybody getting a lot of playing time. During warm-ups, while the Rude Boys stretched as a team, the Hostages were in disarray, some players smoking joints or sipping beers. One Hostage, Jimmy Levine, wore baggy sweats and unlaced workboots right until the game started, and indulged in his own particular psych-up ritual, the pre-game cigarette. When the Rude Boys circled up before the pull, there was the we-mean-business air of a football huddle with Moons outlining the team's strategy.

Meanwhile, the Hostages told dirty jokes and razzed each other, completely disorganized except for their one concession to ritual. Right before they took the field, they would stand in a circle and hook arms and repeat, in unison, "May our passes be linked as our arms are now." Many of the Hostages worked together as stock boys at the Ski Market Warehouse in downtown Boston, and lived together in warren-like apartments, and they seemed to have an almost telepathic communication. Despite the fact that the Hostages didn't stretch or prepare, their passes often *were* linked.

The Hostages were led by David Barkan, a manic whirlwind of a man who popped around the field on pogo stick legs and who, only 5'7", provided every possible contrast to the more staid leadership of Moons. Barkan would sprint wildy from goal line to goal line, eyes full of fire, always ready to huck his backhand long or pump his fist or argue a call. He was also a great thrower, and in this he was not alone.

Tommy Conlon, who played the game with the shambling nonchalance of a scarecrow, could do things with a Frisbee that no one before had ever tried, in his own casual, inimitable style. Jimmy Levine, meanwhile, in cleats, not workboots, but still looking grubby and irritated, was developing into a virtual artiste with the disc, throwing overheads that would tail off backward into the hands of cutting receivers, so that one often wondered if he wasn't growing concerned less with the throw's effectiveness and more with its marks for creative difficulty. At the opposite, more pragmatic, end of the scale was Mark Honerkamp, who would hone his throws with the care of a craftsman whittling wood, and was consistently effective (and jolly) when not sidelined by his occasional dark moods.

The Hostages weren't only great throwers, they were daring ones. They took more risks with their throws, in part because they were a sure-handed team, and the onus was on the receiver to make great catches. The other reason they took more risks was because, against a team as powerful and consistent as the Rude Boys, they simply had no choice.

As might be expected, the Rude Boys and Hostages played entirely different defenses. The Rude Boys relied on their long legs and numbers to wear down teams with an aggressive man-to-man defensive. While the Hostages might be just as fast, their small numbers made them tire sooner, and if they tried to cover the Rude Boys man to man, they would open themselves to severe height mismatches. Instead, they played a zone defense which they tightened like a vise around increasingly nervous throwers. The zone, in which each man was assigned to covering areas of the field, was grounded by the rock solid middle position of Neil Lischner, and aided by the hyperactivity of fronts like Jeff Sandler and the more stolidly active Roger Gallagher. At the center of this communication network, playing deep in the zone, was Steve Gustafason. While Barkan was the team's catalyst and Conlon, if the spirit moved him, could take a game over, Gustafson was the Hostage's best player. Barely six feet tall, he would, as a deep, be required to cover huge distances and engage in sky battles with the much taller Rude Boys. He played the game with a cat's quickness and his throws were absurdly creative and ballsy. Years later, at a reunion tournament, one of his teammates would nickname him "Elvis," because he'd become bloated by weight gain and had the has-been look of the King during his suede suit Vegas years. But during those early years, he was Elvis in his prime, handsome and sleek, with a cocky curl to his lip, possessing a predatory charisma.

The first year of both team's existence was 1981, and Simon and I watched each battle between the two with connoisseurs' delight. It was, we told each other, like having free front-row seats at Celtics-Lakers games. Though our natural instinct to root for the underdog made us favor the Hostages, the Rude Boys were dazzling in their skills, throwing the disc upside down and at sharp angles with great accuracy, and as a whole were better sportsmen than the prickly Hostages. They traded games through the season, but at the Sectional finals the Rude Boys won handily and, going into Regionals, they seemed so strong and well-prepared that they were almost prohibitive favorites. Only one team would emerge from Regionals to go on to Nationals that year, and Simon and I were pretty certain that would be the Rude Boys, a feeling the Rude Boys themselves obviously shared as they had already bought their plane tickets. Harvard had been eliminated before Regionals, and so, for the first time that year, we wouldn't get to see the two teams clash. We considered driving out to Amherst to watch the game, but figured, with the Rude Boys peaking, it might be lopsided and not worth it. Later we'd wish we'd made the trip.

When the reports came back, we could barely believe it. It had been a windy day and the Hostages, making confident throws in the gusting wind, had somehow pulled it off. The game's most talked-about moment had been when David Barkan, almost a foot shorter than Moons, had supposedly sprung into the air and skyed over the taller man. It was a dramatic victory that Simon and I, back in Cambridge, hooted over, listening to friends who had seen the game and then re-creating it with our own words. Even better for the legend, the Hostages characteristically blew off practices in the weeks after their win, drank too much beer, and fell on their face at Nationals. The next year, two teams from our region were invited to Nationals, and the Hostages made it to the national semi-finals. But it was the Rude Boys, methodical and dominating, who went undefeated in winning Nationals and then the first World championship in Sweden.

~

Sometimes I think we choose the things we spend our time doing just because of the difficulty and pain they cause us. A positive way to look at this might be to say we like to "test ourselves," while a more cynical view might hold that we are all, to some extent, magnificent self-torturers.

I'm pretty sure that I chose to become a writer at least in part because I hated to be criticized and rejected. This hatred was due to living with a father, who, for all his good qualities, was a ferocious critic, both in the form of teasing and outright reproach. It was from living with him that I learned to be self-deprecating, a habit that I used as a kind of pre-emptive strike, beating him to the punch by mocking myself before he could mock me. Anyway, given this, you might think I wouldn't choose a profession that would lead to years—decades, really—of outright rejection. You would, of course, be wrong. In this light, my choice to try to become a writer seems equal parts inspiration and masochism.

If possible, Ultimate Frisbee might have been an even more perfect instrument of self-torture. What better way to inspire loathing in my father (and self) than to choose as my other passionate pursuit a game that was considered by most, if they considered it at all, to be on par with tiddly winks and hula hoops. "Is that the thing you do with the dogs?" was a question we got constantly when we tried to explain to people in the normal world what it was we spent all our time doing. That it was a running sport that required real athleticism didn't fly. To go to my father after leaving school to tell him that I was committed to Ultimate was akin to telling him that, having graduated from Harvard, I'd decided to forego traditional careers like banking and medicine and, instead, planned on focusing all my time, passion, and energy on competing in hopscotch tournaments.

In fact, my choice to stay in Boston after graduation to play Ultimate must have seemed almost completely insane to my family. It did to me. But I did it anyway. My literary and athletic priorities set, I left school in June of 1983 for the world my father liked to call "real." In that world, one of my college roommates, Dan Stern, a good Harvard boy, immediately made $300,000 a year working for some rich Texans called the Bass brothers. Meanwhile, instead of heading off for Texas or L.A. or New York, I moved into a cramped apartment in Somerville. I played Ultimate fanatically while also making elaborate vows (and a few outlines) about the novel I would soon start.

There was the immediate problem of money. I found a job as a bike messenger, but that job lasted less than a day. On the way to report to work, I was buffeted by the wind of a truck and slammed into a curb. The next week, I took a job as a security guard in a telephone store in Kenmore Square, which, despite the position's name, was decidedly less dangerous. I sat by the door for eight hours in my guard uniform and watched people shop for phones.

But if my working hours were dull and my writing hours still non-existent, my Frisbee hours were vital enough to lift my life. I was getting better and stronger, my throws sharper, and later that summer I was asked to play on a pick-up team made up of players from both the Hostages and Rude Boys in a tournament in Santa Cruz, California. Usually the two teams treated each other with the type of distrust and suspicion reserved for feuding hillbilly clans, but for some reason they had decided to get together for this one tourney. When they asked me to come along, I could barely contain my excitement.

The drive to California was great, my very first glimpse of the West, but the tournament itself was even more exhilarating, allowing me to leave behind for a while the confusion I felt about my life and my future. I considered it a great honor to play next to the men for whom I'd rooted so long. Our makeshift squad was named *FRAC-49*, after the license plate on a team member's van. I played well the first day, and, the next morning, had an even greater honor conferred on me. David Barkan of the Hostages asked if I would join his team. I didn't say yes right away, and, after our meeting, as I walked around the fields to mull my decision, Steve Mooney approached me. He asked me to play with the Rude Boys the coming fall.

I circled the field again, bursting with pride. My roommate Dan might have turned down Shearson Lehman to go to work for the Bass Brothers for $300,000, but had any young man ever received two such prestigious offers in one day? And, even as pride came over me in waves, I knew that my decision was no decision at all. If I previously had been unclear about my feelings regarding the two different teams, in that moment everything crystallized. My walk became a jog. It was obvious. I would turn my back on the sure thing, the defending National Champ super-team, the Frisbee equivalent of corporate success, and I would play with the scrubby underdogs. Of course, a small ambitious voice nagged. If my father had cared enough about Frisbee to give counsel, he might have reminded me that the Rude Boys represented a better chance for achievement, for fulfillment of my goals. But a louder voice drowned out any nagging, and I didn't hesitate for a second. I would thumb my nose at Moons. I would be part of a gritty band of rebels taking on the powers-that-be. I would become a Hostage.

~

Fall was—and is—the most important season for Ultimate club teams. That fall, my first as a Hostage, I moved out of my dingy Somerville apartment, and down to Cape Cod. That meant I would have to commute for Ultimate practice and tournaments, but it also meant I could work as a carpenter on the Cape and train for Ultimate on the beach. The beach would later become my classroom, observatory, and muse, but that fall it more plainly served as gymnasium. I vowed that I would get in the best shape of my life. Before the trip to California with *Frac-49*, I'd read an article about Herschel Walker, the Georgia running back, and the sprint workouts he did. Walker figured if he worked harder than any of the other players, he would be better, and that made sense to me. I copied his workout exactly, and then did sit-up after sit-up and jumped rope. Better yet, I ran the beach, sprinting repeatedly up a high dune near Corporation Beach, sometimes with a large piece of driftwood strapped on my back for added weight, and then running intervals on the hard, flat sand of low tide. I fashioned a quiver out of an old Dunlop tennis racket cover and some rope, in which I kept my trusty Frisbee. On the way home, I'd toss it into the wind and run it down, or float it out in front of me and dive after it. "First be a good animal," said Emerson, and those words became my motto. I fancied myself a noble savage. When my workouts were done, I'd cool down by plunging into the icy fall water.

Just as my dune work-outs were environmentally inappropriate, so were the ways I occasionally honed my throws, using shorebirds and rabbits as targets. I have no idea what I would have done if I'd ever actually hit a rabbit. Run over and plunged my teeth into its fur? More likely I'd have burst into a sobbing fit of apology. Fortunately, my subconscious screwed with my aim and I never found out. As it was, there were plenty of times that my deepening love of nature combined happily with my work-outs. Sometimes, to vary things, I'd fly around East Dennis on my old ram-horned ten-speed bike, chasing the mobs of starlings that I didn't know the names of yet, a hundred bird-shadows pulsing across the road below my tires. I realized that just by chasing the birds, I could push the shadow mob around over the street and beach and bog, controlling them, painting the land with their shadows.

If it sounds like I'm romanticizing that time, the truth is that I romanticized it even as it was happening. I was twenty-three and my moods fluctuated between supreme confidence and deep insecurity, the insecurity perhaps due to the fact I didn't know what the hell I was doing with my life. To purge my insecurity, I'd work out even harder. "Exorcise through exercise," read a note I'd scribbled on a scrap and tacked to my wall. When I felt afraid, I simply turned around and did hundreds of push-ups and then flexed alone in the shower, admiring myself, cranking the Talking Heads on the boom box while the water burned my scalp. I showered at least twice a day, listening to "Burning Down the House" or "Girlfriend is Better." My hands had never felt more sure and I would toss the soap up in the shower and try to catch it between my thumb and forefinger, like pincers. I wrote myself a note that I still don't understand. "Bodily fluids are crucial," it said. During that fall I had my first "fling" with a girl who came up to me after a tournament. "The world doesn't revolve around you," my father had always said, but now I wasn't so sure. It certainly seemed to: the wind, the salt, the sand, the sex, the leaves, all of it rustling and churning and gyrating and pressing in. *Maybe I brag too much*, I wrote in my journal, *but why shouldn't I brag?* I began to hear messages in the crow's cawing at the beach. "The crows of hope," I called them. Perfect that I could understand the animals now. I was the Tarzan of East Dennis.

~

The Hostages would rise up to have a spectacular fall, suddenly casting ourselves in the favorite's role. Though Steve Gustafson had quit, we had added several other players, and many thought this the strongest Hostage team yet. After a slow start, we began clicking and soundly thrashed the Rude Boys in the two tournaments building up to the all-important Regionals. I loved having fourteen new friends, loved being part of a tribe and pouring my entire self into becoming a great player. The Hostages prided themselves on the number of college drop-outs on the squad and they teased me about Harvard, which, in this Looking Glass world, was a badge of shame. But the teasing itself was just part of the fun of my new life, part of belonging to my new instant family.

I added notes about Frisbee to the rough journal notes I'd begun keeping about birds and plants. Pompous vows about how I would learn to play a "churning, sprawling, wild, unkempt, pounding, relentless game," a game of "raw brag," a game fit for a Hostage. I was still reading Thomas Wolfe at the time and his exaggerated characters had always walked with "earth-devouring strides" and that was how I wanted to run. During the last few weeks before Regionals, my world sped up. It had taken me a while to break into the offense, but now that I had, I was playing better than ever. On defense, I replaced the retired Steve Gustafson as deep in the zone, a position that would require air battles with the tall Rude Boys. Gus had had a cat's quickness, but my own style was more direct and physical, less graceful. Just 5'11", I'd managed to jam a basketball earlier that year, another feat that filled me with delusional glee. I had several flying dreams that fall and once, jumping on the beach with a strong tailwind, thought I might have actually gotten some lift. It didn't seem entirely out of whack with the way things were going that I could learn to fly.

Then, at a party one night, one of the Rude Boy's best offensive players, who I'd been assigned to cover, approached me. After joking around for a while, he turned serious. "I shouldn't tell you this," he said. "But the other night I had a nightmare about you guarding me." That pretty much sent me over the edge. *I was invulnerable!* My already substantial ego stretched even larger. I glimmered with a near megalomaniacal confidence.

These delusions were no doubt aided by the mushrooms I ingested fairly regularly at the time. The residue of those trips—during which I felt I got down to the essence of my animal self, sweating, running, drinking, pissing—spilled over into my so-called normal life. I lived inside a fever that fall. Now, the fever so long past, I see myself for what I was: a scared little boy playing at life. Humans can be narcissists at any age, but there is no narcissism like that possible in one's twenties, particularly one's early twenties. With time, even the dullest of us gets at least some wisdom pounded into our brains, but there is pleasure as well as pain in the time before wisdom. What I really had going for me that fall was the advantage of inexperience. With writing, for instance. I hadn't yet begun and so could still live fully in the fantasy that what I wrote would be brilliant. Unlimited possibility still seems possible before we begin a thing, and before we realize that our bonds define us, that without constraints we have no shape, without limits there is nothing. But the illusion of limitlessness is a drug beside which mushrooms pale.

But in the end, all this moralizing won't do. It's the *feeling* I remember from that glorious fall, a feeling I have never felt since and am quite sure I'll never feel again. I was muscular and strong and full of sap, and, of course, quite deluded. A young Icarus with enough literary training to be pretty sure of where all this was heading. It was hubris plain and simple, but one thing they don't tell you about hubris is how good it feels. In fact, in some ways, though I now know what it will lead to, I still think of that fall as the high tide of my twenties. In some ways, I still think of it as the high tide of my life. Though a happier and better man now, I still miss that time and if there were a way, if granted a wish, I can't pretend I wouldn't run right back and crawl inside that lunatic's skin.

~

Of course, the Hostages lost at Regionals. Lost in spectacular, choking fashion. If the world of Frisbee had become my personal mythology, here was the classic fall from grace. On Saturday, we went undefeated, the best team at the tournament. On Sunday, our usually sure hands deserted us, and the daring that had been our trademark was replaced by a frightened caution, occasionally punctuated by desperate, ill-advised throws. As things started to slip away I felt the icy fear and cowardice only the choker knows. My limbs no longer operated with the confidence that they had all fall; the magic juice no longer flowed through me.

I lurched back to Cape Cod in late October, depressed and defeated, an animal creeping back to its lair. The eel grass had turned the color of wheat and the ocean was grey and frothy. During my career, I have had some painful losses, but nothing to compare to that defeat. The megalomania of fall came crashing down into a winter where I came as close to madness as I hope I ever will. Doubt began chewing into my early certainty about what I'd chosen to do with my life, hollowing out my commitment to Ultimate. Why was I wasting my time playing this stupid sport? It was just too painful, the thought of commiting again only to be burned, of rising that high only to be slammed that low.

The Hostages staggered on for another season, but that loss effectively finished us. We'd always been jokers, sardonically mocking our own sport, but the next year we became pure clowns, pretending not to care. We drank more at tournaments and though we still won some big games and even a couple more tourneys, we were never the same cocky bunch again. A year and a half later, the team broke up for good. Most of the players retired, content to look back on the 1981–1982 seasons as the peak of their athletic lives.

But I wasn't done. I still had a quest to fulfill. I wanted to win the National Championship, something no Hostage had ever done, and I pursued this goal with only a little less seriousness than I'd begun to pursue writing, training for the better part of the year. In fact, over the next decade it was usually left to Ultimate Frisbee to provide what writing couldn't. Working at a series of bad jobs and writing alone at home, I felt, quite frankly, glory-starved. Glory, as my old teacher Walter Jackson Bate has said, is the attempt to "fill the minds of others," and so doesn't exist without an audience. No one cheered me on while I sat scribbling at that stupid little desk or smashed sheetrock with a sledge hammer or, later, rang up customers as a clerk in a bookstore. Ultimate gave me the juice I needed.

I wasn't alone in this. Though Ultimate players sometimes wore beads and funny hats and grew their hair long, I slowly began to understand that there was something else, something decidedly less groovy, going on on those fields that most didn't acknowledge. It may sound strange and oxymoronic, but there was such a thing as "Ultimate ambition." Clearly, people who played the sport wanted not only to win, but to be considered great at what they did, not just in their own eyes but in the eyes of other players. It was the pursuit of fame, really, though a fame closer to the ancient Greeks than *People* magazine, existing only among the bands of players from around the country who, re-telling stories of great players and great plays, created the oral tradition through which the sport was remembered.

Part of the appeal of playing serious Ultimate was that life took on the simplicity of quest, a little like stepping inside of a good science fiction or fantasy novel. There were heroes and villains and wizards and trolls and even a few princesses to impress. There were arch enemies like Kenny Dobyns of the evil New York team (who else gets to have arch enemies these days?) and beautiful exotic lands to travel to, and, to top it all off, Nationals, a great annual quest for the Grail. My father was right when he said it wasn't the "real world." Instead, it was like a game of Dungeons and Dragons and you were in it—right inside it—complete with your weapon and your own special magic powers. A secret world where you were part of a secret tribe.

To keep going as a writer, I needed to pretend that I would one day be great at it, but the truth was, the evidence for that was slim. Here was something I was already great at, something that made me feel full of power and confidence. In the rest of my life I was impotent, a struggling apprentice, but in Ultimate I was *accomplished*. I worked year-round to stay in top shape and loved nothing more than ripping around a field in my cleats. My best weapon was my forehand, which I could throw eighty yards of so, end zone to end zone, in wide parabolas. But my favorite, if not most trusty, throw, was my overhead. The overhead is where the disc is thrown upside down, like a spear, before, hopefully, turning back over and dropping into a receiver's hands. When my overhead was cocked I, like my old teammate Nathan, had a notion.

If the results were erratic, then the truth was that sometimes results weren't as important as the sheer thrill of the thing. One year, Nationals were held on the grassy common in front of the Washington Monument, and, getting psyched for a game, I wandered over to the Museum of Natural History. Inside the museum, I was captivated by an exhibit of a Neanderthal hunting with a spear, and, with that vision still vivid in my head, I went out and threw a half-dozen overheads during the next game. If the results were, again, erratic, the feeling inside me was consistent. For a brief period I felt ecstatic, confident, and strong.

~

Our old rivals, The Rude Boys, had also broken up by 1985. As expected, many of Steve Mooney's teammates were finished with the sport, off to careers and law school. Moons, meanwhile, was busy making a new team, gathering together the best remaining players in the Boston area. I joined that team but felt uneasy lining up next to Moons. After all, wasn't he just a big phony, like the Hostages had always said? Moons was clearly the authority figure on the team, and from the start we had a kind of father-son tension between us. I wanted the team to be called "the Primadonnas," mocking the fact that we were a kind of hand-picked all-star team, but Moons prevailed with "Titanic." I hated the name and, because I knew it irked Moons, made up a cheer that I yelled out before each game: "Titanic, Titanic, our dicks are gigantic!" On Titanic, everything was more structured and less relaxed than with the Hostages; for instance, people frowned not just at my crude cheer but if I sipped a beer before a game. Rigidity replaced wildness, and, reacting to this, I would play my old role of rebellious son to Moon's strict father.

It was a role I would perfect over the next few years. When not fighting beside Moons in an effort to win Nationals, I would fight with him in my role as the team's resident adolescent. In keeping with Hostage tradition, I excelled at idiocy. During my last season with Titanic, after a bitter semifinals loss to New York, I, blind drunk, decided it was necessary to get hold of the microphone that was being used to announce the finals. I merely wanted to serenade the New Yorkers, who were winning handily on the way to their third championship, with a rendition of "We Are The Champions," a graceful and touching concession of defeat in my mind. But the announcers resisted, in part because they foolishly had let me get hold of the mike the year before and I had bellowed my "Titanic, Titanic..." cheer. And so a plan was hatched. The game was being announced, not from a booth, but on the grass beyond the end zone, clearly not a defensible position. Only three announcers stood around the mike, so I put together a small war party, made up of Bobby Harding, my old Hostage teammate who had now joined Titanic, and two other friends, and, after a drunken, Patton-like speech, convinced them to storm the microphone. Or thought I convinced them. Half-way through my charge, I looked back and found myself alone. I could have quit, of course, called off my raid, but what was this if not a chance for another stupid, futile quest? So I charged ahead and tried to wrestle the microphone from the announcers on my own.

Three UPA (Ultimate Player's Association) officials and a policeman grabbed me and pulled me away. I was not arrested, however. Things did not work like that in our Dungeons-and-Dragons world. Instead I was henceforth banished from ever playing Frisbee again in the Washington area, an edict that holds to this day. In the official letter that Eric Broderick, the local representative of the UPA, sent to Steve Mooney, he charged Titanic $300 for damage done to the microphone. He also said that though he understood "that Steve personally tried to help give Ultimate a clean image," this sort of behavior reflected poorly on the team. "This person," Broderick wrote, "who I know only as 'Gessner' was obviously drunk. I'm sure he will greet this letter with howls of arrogant laughter, but this is a very serious offense."

I wish I could say that I was properly chastised, that I began, then and there, to finally grow up, but I'm afraid the truth is I greeted his letter just as Mr. Broderick had predicted I would. Over beers, I showed the letter to my Hostage friends and we howled with arrogant laughter.

~

If I didn't take Broderick's letter to heart, then the events of the next few years would prove a more serious warning shot across my bow. Cancer invaded my family, a cancer I've written about elsewhere ad nauseum, and so won't go deeply into here. The cancer would first scar me and then take my father's life, but, even before I became sick, I began to suspect that it was time to "get serious," a course of action that my father had been urging on me for some time. Ultimate had been a big waste, I decided, aiding if not solely responsible for my arrested development. As proof of this, I had only to look at my college roommate, Dan Stern, who was by now making over a million dollars a year. In contrast, my life was a shambles. Working as a substitute teacher and part-time carpenter, I was fortunate that debtor's prisons no longer existed. Bills provoked panic attacks, and at one point I'd borrowed $1,000 from Dan, money I likely never would pay back. I could only nod in agreement when my father muttered about how I hadn't learned to live in "the real world."

There was no choice but to admit he was right: to step into that real world and out of the Frisbee world. I quit playing for Boston in 1990. My girlfriend moved to Worcester, Massachusetts, to attend medical school at U-Mass, and I tagged along. It was time to put away childish things. By then I had finished a novel that had been rejected by several publishers, and was almost done with a second book. That fall, instead of playing Ultimate, I took a job as a counselor in a homeless shelter and applied to graduate schools in creative writing.

My plans were interrupted, however, by an unexpected event. In March of 1991, a week shy of my thirtieth birthday, I was operated on for testicular cancer. A few days later, I got the good news that I had a stage 1 seminoma. My girlfriend asked me what I wanted to do for my thirtieth birthday, which was the next Saturday, exactly a week after the operation. I said I wanted a party. "Should it be small?" she asked, concerned. "Big," I said. I wanted to celebrate. I asked her to invite all the Hostages and my college roommates and old carpentry friends. She did and they all came. The house was packed.

I knew most of the people there through Ultimate Frisbee and, looking around the room that night at all the Ultimate players, I felt better about all the time and energy I'd put into the sport. Maybe it hadn't been, as my father once contended, "a colossal waste of time." Many of the old Hostages had come, and so had Moons and dozens of players from other teams. While I hadn't achieved my purported goals in Ultimate, I'd gained something else while I wasn't paying attention. I had become part of a second family, part of a tribe, and now my tribe was rallying round me.

For the sake of this essay I could say that it was that night that I started to see how much the sport had given me, like learning the true meaning of Christmas. But the truth is that in the decade since I have only gradually come to see the enormous role the sport played in my life. "Frisbee" may be a silly word—like "boing" or "poodle"—and the sport may not be taken any more seriously than tiddly winks. But that didn't—and doesn't—matter. It's not the object so much as the passion poured into it. What's more, I had gained the strength of working long and hard at something that others considered ridiculous. It was a little like writing in that way. Something we tend to forget, or belittle in our corporate age: that certain muscles can only be built through nonconformity. So what if no one knew what the hell Ultimate was? When NBA players say they "love this game," they also mean they love the money, the attention, and the perks. I loved Ultimate despite the fact it had nothing like that to offer. I loved the pure play of it, the great moments, the camaraderie, the stories we told after. And as silly as it sounds, it is true: Frisbee helped make me.

Which I was just starting to understand on the night of my thirtieth birthday. The party went late with Simon, my arrogant Harvard friend, gloating about schooling some players from a team called The Popes in Scrabble in the TV room. Their game wouldn't end until 4:00 A.M. when Simon fell asleep, drooling right on the board. These were the same Pope players who had once stolen a stuffed deer from a Natural History exhibit while we were playing a tournament in upstate New York, tying it to the top of their car like hunters. Now, before driving off, they took the Scrabble letters and spelled out "Simon is a Greasy Wanker" on the board where Simon slept.

Meanwhile, two of my Hostage friends and I sat in a circle in the living room passing around a bottle of tequila, a beer, and a joint. Each of us would take a hit of whatever was in front of us and pass it along. Sometimes someone would mutter "cannonball it," the silly Bill Murray line from *Caddyshack*. It was crazy to be doing this right after being cut open and losing blood, but if crazy, it was also an appropriate way for my twenties to end. Forget that I still had weeks of radiation ahead or that the prospects for both my health and career were uncertain. For one night it didn't matter. Spring was only a week away and it looked like I wasn't going to be dying any time soon. In fact, within a week I would be walking out at the reservoir, within a month running. This was spring at its most pagan then: Persephone gone to Hades and returned from the underworld.

And on my thirtieth birthday, my cause for celebration was the most elemental of all. I was a strong animal. I would fucking live.

~

Which would make a neat and happy ending except for the fact it wasn't over. A month after my operation, in the midst of radiation, I got into a graduate school in Boulder, Colorado. Boulder was the scene of one of my happiest Ultimate memories. My last highlight for Boston had come two summers before when we won the prestigious Fourth of July tournament in Boulder, against a field of teams every bit as strong as Nationals. In late June, I took a trip out to Colorado to look for an apartment where I could live the next fall. I found a funky blue cabin below the spectacular cleaved canyons of Eldorado Springs, a town outside of Boulder. I also played in the Boulder tournament again, picking up with my old enemies from the New York team. Since I had always played well against New York, they expected a lot of me. But while we won the event, I was a shell of what I'd been, and didn't contribute much. Still, being able to run and dive at all was a victory, coming as it did only three and a half months after my operation and only a month after radiation. I could feel myself getting stronger with each passing day.

The next fall I moved West. In my cabin in the mountains, I felt like a snake that had shed its old skin. Though I hadn't published anything yet, for the first time I defined myself as a writer and not an Ultimate player. I attacked a book about my cancer, writing the first draft straight through. All my efforts before had been halting. The novel I'd tried to write in my twenties came in fits and starts, but this thing, whatever it was, came whole. I began to type as if taking dictation and I didn't stop.

Ultimate had served its purpose, you might think, and it had, believe me, it had. It seemed I'd finally managed to put aside childish things for good. There was a small problem, however. To get to school from my home in Eldorado Canyon, I had to drive past the high school playing fields where the Boulder Ultimate team, called the Stains, practiced. During those days of hard denial, I had no way of knowing that I would play Ultimate "seriously" for five more years, soon numbering some of my Boulder teammates among my closest friends. And I had no way of knowing that I would have a Frisbee afterlife, that while I no longer had the Hostages as my tribe, soon I would have the Stains.

For a week or two I didn't give in, driving by grim-faced, thinking about my novel, trying to ignore the plastic discs describing parabolas or the people running up and down the fields. But by the third week I had a notion, and the notion couldn't be stifled. On the way back from school

I pulled the car over at the fields and dug my cleats out of the trunk. I walked up to the fields casually, cynically even, sure that I wouldn't be suckered in again.

I don't remember which of my new teammates threw me the Frisbee, but I do remember that they overthrew me.

I chased after it like a border collie.

Marking My Territory

Why write about the beautiful if you never acknowledge the ugly? I believe that to fail to give the crude its due is patently false, and I would like to say a word about that most uncelebrated aspect of nature appreciation: urinating in the wilds. It may seem a trite or offensive subject, but to those of us who spend a lot of time in the outdoors it's an important one. And one that has been given short shrift in books, barely hinted at in English literature. By contrast, in real life, I have met few humans (particularly males) who won't, after absorbing a beer or two into their bloodstream, extol its virtues. And why not? "I love all things that flow," said Joyce. Or as Edward Abbey, one of the few high priests of this ritual, succinctly summarized his daily awakening: "Arise. Piss."

We essayists have a habit of leaning on the crutches of quotations, and panic if we can't collect enough of them to bolster our limping arguments. Outside of a couple by Rabelais, Roth, and books of Native American and Yoruban African myths, I find few flowing phrases. Happily my neighbor down the street, the fiction writer Brad Watson, has created a character named Harold, who has said that "he never again wants to live anywhere he can't step out onto the back porch and take a piss day or night." I share Harold's desire, as well as his habit. While I admit it would be a pungent country without toilets, I like to celebrate the fall's exodus of people from Cape Cod by doing something I haven't been able to do all summer: walking out back, whipping it out, and, as the wind blows through the harbor and gangs of swallows spread their shadows over beach and road, at last mark my territory.

This will no doubt be perceived as macho. Perhaps it *is* a case of embracing the brute inside me, as well as my inner canine. And maybe it's a little sexist, too, though I do know a woman who wrote a beautiful essay about living in an igloo, during which she described the chilling daily pleasure of using a snowball as toilet paper. But that seems a bit different and requires some lowering. Maybe it's just that most men, being idiots, enjoy the more mindless pleasures.

But I don't want to pass this off glibly, since it isn't *just* idiocy. I have written elsewhere, and still insist, that there is also something spiritual, or at the very least ritualistic, about the activity. As well as a simple bond between friends, an expression of intimacy, it can also briefly re-connect us to the animals we are, undermining our pretensions, reminding us that we still need occasional relief from theories and thoughts. And it is the relief itself that is a kind of mini-liberation, a liberation often accompanied by the emptying of mind along with bladder. "There is no greater joy to man than relieving a full bladder," wrote Henry Miller. I don't know if I'd go that far, but, ideally, anxiety and clutter flow out of us along with other waste products and, for a second, we can sometimes see what is actually around us: the juniper berries painting the cedar's branches blue, the stars or harvest moon, the light playing off brambles.

Pretty high-flown talk for number one, but I stand by it. "Stagefright" or "shy bladder," the inability to pass water in public (a problem from which I suffered—and still occasionaly suffer), imply the element of performance in pissing with others, though I like to think in terms, not of the theatrical, but the ceremonial. For my part, I prefer the religion of the Hopi Katsina dancers, high fools who alternate buffoonery with reverence for the sun and land. Long ago I knew someone who as a young man would pull up to a particularly beautiful (and private) point overlooking the ocean and masturbate while listening to Beethoven's Ninth. Now *that* was a sacrament. Reg Saner writes about the Hopi clowns: "Especially when Christianizing do-gooders and their high-toned ladies were present, clowns delightedly mimed screwing with spectators, sodomy, eating of excrement, masturbation—strong stuff even now." This reminds the ever-literate Saner of Aristophanes and the way that the ancient Athenian playwright enjoyed showing "how the body's most embarrassing needs undercut our most soulful aspirations." But I wonder if the words "undercut" and "embarrassing" are accurate in this case, at least for the Hopi. These words suggest antipodes, antagonisms, and while certainly the various parts of our nature are often at war, there are other times, moments at least, when the two unite. For instance, here is Don Talayesva, a Hopi sun chief, describing *his* morning ritual: "I walk to the east edge of the mesa to defecate and pray." Personally, I'm always pleased when my best sentences come to me during my breaks behind the house, away from the computer. I don't want to make too strong a case for "oneness," for unity, just to suggest the possibility of occasional glimpses—our best moments—when flesh and spirit unite.

Like a Hopi clown, I have never quite mastered the art of suppressing my own buffoonery, and urine has flowed freely through my creative life. My first artistic success of any sort was a political cartoon I drew in college, a drawing that was taped to not a few dorm walls and sparked debate between the liberal and neo-conservative campus papers. It was a picture of the back of Ronald Reagan, recognizable by his ridiculous pompadour, urinating on an African American homeless man who was sleeping, covered with newspapers, in a gutter. It was called "The Trickle Down Theory."

Not very subtle perhaps, heavy handed true, but it packed a punch. Later, a good friend and I decided to start a small business that would market satiric posters, and for our first effort we chose a real life depiction of this cartoon. For the poster we decided to scrap Reagan and use a generic rich man, played by my friend's grandfather, and my first professional job after college was directing a scene in which one man peed on another. If that isn't enough—and *it is, it is,* I hear you saying—we had originally reached the decision to shoot that poster, and to go into business in the first place, while pissing together down at the bluff on Cape Cod.

While not exactly trying to spearhead a new wave of urinary literature, I have not been shy about relieving myself in my writing. I only made it a page into my first book before I had to go. The word I'd first used to describe this was that ugly spit of onomatopoeia—*pissss*—but my original editor, a man who clearly hadn't seen much of the outdoors, convinced me to use the verb "water" instead. "It seems to grate against the nature descriptions," he said, which of course was exactly the point. I did manage to keep him from hacking the part of my book where my father and I bond over our primitive ritual, walking out on the back deck together to water the bayberries (a ritual that, come to think of it, might explain my continued fascination with the subject). When I first came back East, I chose that section for a reading at the Brookline Bookstore, a reading I believed to be powerful, even rhapsodic, but that the woman who managed the store, an old friend, told me was referred to by the employees as "the pissing reading." Oh well. It's true that the subject doesn't appeal to all.

Ceremony, celebration, provocation. These are a few symbolic uses or urine. Lately I have been preoccupied with other, older aspects: the marking of a place as one's own, the declaration of one's borders, and the implication that one will protect those borders. The pronoun "one" here is pompous, however: I mean *me*. Over the last few years, I have become clearer about just what and where the particular territory is that I am marking. Not just the bayberry behind my house, but the beach below the bluff that juts out where the old Stone mansion stood. Since moving back to Cape Cod I have been fighting a guerilla war with the overlord who lives up on the bluff, who keeps building his home higher and higher, and spreading out further and further, as if his were a castle and the neck his feudal lands. The bluff has long been the last wild place in our increasingly tame neighborhood, and the incursion of this and other oversized homes strikes me on a personal level as a violation, especially now that there is no place to stand on this rocky point where you can't see a house. I have tried to fight this growth by civilized means, attending conservation meetings and attempting to communicate with the homeowner through correspondence. But the owner never replied to my letters and refused to shake my hand after a spirited disagreement at town hall. As it stands, my only recourse has been to roam the rocks below the bluff, marking them as my own in a way quite different than a legal document.

It is still strange to me to think that someone else could possibly "own" this wild spit of land. Urine, you see, isn't the only thing that flows from me below the bluff. Since returning here I have looked to this place as my source, and I often feel compelled to write when I am here. Words, ideas, sentences, whole essays keep popping up, looking for me when I was looking elsewhere, undermining set plans and projects. If these thoughts seem the idle considerations of an aesthete, let me say that, in my life, they are quite sound and practical. Words are my business and I found my words here on the edge between water and land. This shoreline below the bluff is—once again in very practical terms—my source. This is the place where most of my writing comes from, a place where, with great regularity and reliability, I can go and collect sentences as if they were driftwood or sea glass. Here words spill. The bluff is an old but ever-exciting lover around whom I can't keep my mouth shut. Like any lover, she elicits poems. Often I can talk an entire essay into my tape recorder as I walk on the rocks below the bluff. Historically, the essay is an ambling genre, sentences and walks strolling hand in hand, and it is here that I rediscovered that truth on a personal level, learning just how perfectly the two activities fit. I used to run, bike, lift weights for recreation. On the bluff, walking became my sport, my pleasure, my pastime.

And it is here also that I often feel batted back and forth, like a mouse tortured by a cat, between ecstasy and rage. The other day, I clambered down to the beach by the juniper tree that I'd seen fill up with cedar waxwings the winter before. On the beach, I stared at hudsonia blooming bright yellow while above me six common terns flew through the fog. The next day, I experienced a particularly painful moment when my neighbor began plowing rocks down on the beach. Meanwhile, up top, old brambled fields have been torn up and a golf course–like carpet of grass rolled out, and, recently, a section of the bluff was shaved back so that he could erect a $250,000 statue of a sounding whale, apparently untroubled or unaware of the irony of destroying nature so that he could put up a tribute to the same.

Just last week, I woke up straight from a dream and had a cold realization. A man like that, who needed to control the wild, would also need to control the night. That is, he would soon have a spotlight spraying its beams down on my beach. It was five o'clock in the morning, but I couldn't sleep, so I decided to walk by the ocean down to the bluff. It was then, after pink began to splotch the sky and the world filled with an unreal golden light, that I, feeling particularly melodramatic, waved my fist and declared war on the house and its owner. Later I would write another essay about the house, check on the restrictions with the planning board, and meet with the town's environmental officer to fight light pollution. But at that moment I needed a symbol of my martial declaration, something more than flashing my middle finger toward it (which I'd also been doing a lot of). So I climbed the bluff and, cutting through the old path between the poison ivy and pitch pines, arrived at the house itself. The molten ball was just rising over Brewster, and the workers hadn't arrived yet. I marched over to the house's foundation, unzipped, and made a symbolic and watery protest against the man and his bullying building. It was juvenile, I know, and illegal, and, ultimately, pointless. But it felt good and right to leave my signature splayed and splattered across the concrete. It was the first shot in a battle, heard, if not around the world, at least around the town of Dennis.

Later, when I got back home, I immortalized the morning's events in my journal.

"You have marked my territory," I wrote. "And now I have marked yours."

A Polygamist of Place

I begin with a confession. While it's true I have only one wife and no hidden mistresses, I am a polygamist of place. The writers I've always admired most, from Thoreau to Colorado's Reg Saner, have made it their habit to wedge into one place, to know that place well through long association with the land and people. In this way, they learn things that will only reveal themselves after a relationship of good, hard duration.

I'm more fickle. My first book was a paean to the beauties and wonders of Cape Cod. The book ended with my father's death, and concluded with these words: "Like my father, I know where I'll finally settle. He has committed to Cape Cod. I will follow him." I wrote those sentences while typing in a study that stared out at the front range of Colorado, two thousand miles from the Atlantic. Not long after, I completed a book about my love of Colorado. I penned its last line in an attic room overlooking the white breakers and deep blue waters of Cape Cod Bay.

This division of devotion has caused me no small amount of anxiety, not just for moral but for practical reasons. In these competitive and crowded days, writers, like everyone else, tend to specialize. Nature writers in particular carve out their little fiefdoms, niches to claim as their own, and, as a rule, these niches keep getting smaller and smaller. Years ago Edward Abbey wrote of how every place now has its own Thoreau, critics calling one nature writer the "Thoreau of the Rockies" or the "Thoreau of New Jersey" or the "Thoreau of Arizona." In the time since Abbey's death, it's only gotten worse: now we have the "Thoreau of East Providence" and the "Thoreau of Mexican Hat." But as others industriously settle their territories, I find myself charging from coast to coast like an adulterous husband in a madcap sixties movie, passionately declaring my love for one place before hurriedly packing my suitcase to rush back and proclaim my love for the other. This is not a stable position for an essayist to work from, particularly one who is prone to lecture, at the slightest provocation, about how good writing should grow from local ground.

Even more unsettling is the fact that two of my literary heroes, Wendell Berry and John Hay, have made "marriage" to their chosen places a primary metaphor in their work. Hay has lived in the same house on top of Dry Hill on Cape Cod for over half a century, while as a young man Berry returned to settle the land he had loved as a child. In contrast, I am a typical rootless American, of no place and of many places, nervous if I stay still for too long. On the one hand, I am what I once heard John Hay call another Cape Cod writer: "a flibbertigibbet." On the other hand, still not having recovered from a high school encounter with Thoreau, I can't quite give up on the idea of having my own Walden. So far the closest I've come to a base camp is this house on Sesuit Neck in which I now type, a house that I do not own. This isn't marriage of the sort that Hay and Berry exemplify; my affair with the Cape has not been wholehearted and exclusive. And if that fact causes me guilt, what about the fact that I have other lovers—Colorado only most prominently—to whom I am almost equally committed? Is there something wrong with me?

The truth is that all this talk of settling and geographical marriage makes me uneasy. I'm not ready yet to say a forever "I do" to one town or county, and, despite the pressure of my nature-writing forefathers, I'm not sure I have to. For all Berry's agrarian bullying, his is only one way to be in the world. "Firm ground is not available ground," wrote A. R. Ammons, and so it is for me. I won't go as far as to say that I am more comfortable with chaos, just that chaos is what life has dealt me. It would be nice if my world centered on one local place, but it does not. So I need to find another way.

But if marriage to a place is something of a strange metaphor, it's also a fairly natural one. Having spent more time on this small neck of land on Cape Cod than anywhere else in the world, I can see how the idea that I will be here forever appeals. Practically speaking, a long-term commitment to place means you are more likely to undertake a long-term study of place, of its woodchucks or terns, say. And even if you don't undertake anything systematic, you will begin to notice things over time—they will come to you. But of course you can know a place over time without being monogamous to that place, which the marriage metaphor still, hopefully, implies. Marriage, as a cultural institution, seems too limiting a metaphor for our love of place, particularly since we are the ancestors of creatures who roamed the world over.

~

But, as always, I am nervous going it alone. And so in hopes of support for my own polygamy, I turn away from those literary settlers and toward other heroes. Specifically, I turn to those two monumental Westerners (and closet Easterners), Wallace Stegner and Bernard DeVoto. Though both were raised in the West, they moved to Massachusetts as young adults, and took an almost giddy delight in their new homes. DeVoto called himself "an apprentice New Englander," but if he was an apprentice, then it was of the most passionate sort. He threw himself into the East, specifically into "the hallowed ground" of Harvard and Cambridge, with the passion of a convert. Stegner was no less effusive. "Cambridge was our Athens and our Rome," he'd say later. While both would work long and hard to debunk stereotypes of the Westerner as rube, and the East, specifically the Northeast, as the country's center, their own attitudes and actions at least mildly mimicked the same stereotype. They wrote and acted as if they'd emerged from the dry Western desert and could now gulp down a cold glass of Eastern culture and sophistication.

DeVoto was particularly guilty of this. For all his bristling toughness, he never stopped angling for a full professorship at Harvard and, had it been granted him, one imagines he might have reacted like Sally Field getting her Oscar: "You *like* me . . . you really *like* me." While his words often travelled West, after his childhood he spent surprisingly little time there, much of his field work the result of hurried road trips before rushing back to "civilization." Stegner, on the other hand, would ultimately return to live in the West, but, like a man sipping a bottle behind the barn, could never stay away from the East for too long. Perhaps, after he had been ensconced as the Dean of Western writing, there was even an element of guilty pleasure in summering in New England.

Unsettled by my current crisis, it's heartening to see signs of inconstancy in these two icons. As I sift through their lives for clues to put to use in my own, I keep coming back to the fact that both Stegner and DeVoto first wrote powerfully of the West after settling East. It makes me feel less guilty about having written about the wonders of Cape Cod while staring out at Boulder's flatirons. Of course, my own journey was in the opposite direction. Raised in Massachusetts, I worked hard to make sure I attended Harvard myself, at least in part to please my powerful father. Living in New England for seven years after graduation, I experienced feelings of claustrophobia, of clutter, of judgmental puritan eyes upon me. I could never put words to these vague feelings until I finally moved West at the age of thirty.

In heading West, I lived out an American cliche. I moved to Colorado to get healthy and start anew. I don't remember if I ever said it out loud, but I knew that in my own small way I was living out our national myth—tossing off old burdens and moving Westward to experience renewal and regeneration. The strange thing was, it worked. If DeVoto felt inebriated stepping onto the hallowed ground of Cambridge, I was no less so hiking the mountains of the Front Range. Feeling ever stronger and healthier, I interwove these associations with my new place, a place that I believed was helping heal me. I became an apprentice Westerner. Fittingly, my new Western friends gave me a nickname that all but replaced the name my father gave me (a name that I also shared with him). Though Cape Cod was my first love, the West became the object of my affection and, as with any loved one, I revelled in it both physically and symbolically.

And then, when my love was strongest, something even stranger happened. I started writing well about the East. Like Stegner and DeVoto, I suddenly had the advantage of looking at a place from somewhere else, defining, as we always do, by differences. It's common to speak of "needing distance" to write about something important to us, and that distance can be literal as well as emotional or chronological. The thing that people who remain stuck in one place perhaps can't see is that America, for all our malls and McDonalds, is still a remarkably regional country with remarkably regional differences. Stegner himself might have remained what he most feared being—a "regional writer"—had it not been for his mental and physical straddling of the country. Perhaps to know and love a new region is to see the old region more clearly.

It may be true that transplanted trees don't always take, but one thing that I've found does transplant fairly well is the capacity to love a place. The tools you develop in one place—the bird books you skim through, the questions you ask and the people you find to ask them to—work well, with some slight adjustments, in other places. I've always been partial to Erich Fromm's take on love: love as the exercise and development of certain muscles. If the ability to love is a skill, that skill also allows us to love new places.

And here, trumpets blaring, I could tie things up neatly were it not for the facts. I'm back East again, here to promote the book I wrote in the West about the East (though, fortunately, it looks like the Western book I finished in the East may be published so I can move back West.) Hopefully, I'll soon settle in one place, or, at least, determine that one place play the role of steady wife, the other as mistress. I can see my two options in my two heroes. Stegner took West as wife and New England as summer fling; DeVoto made the opposite choice. Undecided still, I squat on Cape Cod while my books and belongings remain in a storage locker back in Colorado, a promise to myself that I'll make it back. I remind myself that Thoreau's time in the cabin was a passionate affair and not a lifelong marriage (though he certainly loved the place his whole life). In the meantime, like any good polygamist, I'll take Steven Still's advice and love the one I'm with. If the model of polygamy may no longer be a practical one for physical love, for love of place I embrace it. As Stegner and DeVoto remind us, we often see what we love most clearly from a distance.

II.

Getting Personal

I am hungry to make myself known,
and I care not to how many, provided it be truly.
—MONTAIGNE

The Apprentice

The other day I was standing in line at the East Dennis post office, minding my own business, when an old family friend, a man in his late sixties who has grown progressively more addle-brained over the years, approached me and grabbed my arm.

"David!" he said. "I was just thinking about you."

I asked him why and he told me that the other night he had been watching the play *Brighton Beach Memoirs* at our local playhouse, a well-known theater mostly featuring has-been TV stars.

"While I was watching I kept thinking 'David should do this!' It's true! You could write something like that. You've got a real way with words. You could really reach people that way! And make some money!"

I gave the man a polite smile and thanked him for the suggestion.

"I'll think about it," I said. "But the truth is I'm probably going to keep writing the way I write until I die."

What nonplussed me a little afterward was how non-nonplussed I was by the encounter. I understood that there was the implication in the man's words that what I had done so far, the books I'd written, didn't really matter much, or affect many people, but for some reason it didn't bother me. What would have once provoked rage or outrage, or at least insecurity, now seemed merely funny.

I guess that over the years I've learned that being a writer means constantly getting unsolicited advice about your work. I remember sitting next to a man on a flight when I was in my late twenties, who, after I admitted I was trying to write, offered up this little pearl regarding literary craft:

"You know how to keep them reading?" he asked. Then, before I could say anything, he answered the question himself: "Show a little tit every few pages."

~

Fifteen years ago the simple question "What do you *do*?" could make me completely lose my composure.

I don't think I'm alone in this. It occurred to me recently that it would be so much easier if they just handed out "APPRENTICE WRITER" cards. Then when some fat, self-satisfied burgermesiter approached you at a party and asked what you "do" you could just flash your badge and he would mutter, "Well, yes, you're legit . . . Carry on then." People would understand—and perhaps more importantly *you* would understand—that nothing very productive, outside of reams and reams of unpublishable paper, would come from you. People—and you—would understand that the good stuff would come later.

They don't give out cards, however, and they don't brief you on what you're in for, especially if you start young, right after college, for instance. In that case, you kind of look around in a daze as all your fellow graduates get jobs, some pretty good jobs, and you wonder what the hell to do next. Surprisingly, it turns out there are no listings in the classifieds for "real writers." What you do—unless you are extremely lucky or resourceful or talented—is what almost every other person in your situation does: You get a shitty job so you can write.

As I look back on my own illustrious career as a cashier/security guard/carpenter's apprentice/bookstore clerk/substitute teacher, I try to resist the middle-aged tendency to say, comfortably, "it was all for the best," viewing what was then misery as inevitability, or worse, as a necessary difficulty leading to my current comfortable position. It *wasn't* all for the best; the fact is that I wish I'd found a better way. As much as I believe that our calluses define us, that is, I believe that there is a strength gained in banging one's head against a wall until either the head or wall give, I also believe that much of the angst and fury of many young writer/poet/actor/artists, is justified.

~

"I'll give you all the advice you need in one word," my father said to me at one point in my twenties. He then spelled out that word for me: "W-O-R-K."

I resented the comment, of course, in part because I felt I had already

W-O-R-Ked plenty. The truth was, I'd gotten to know a world of work my father had never known. When I was around twenty-five, for instance, I became a carpenter's apprentice in Boston. "I was a terrible carpenter," I wrote in my first book, and it was true. But I did have some strengths, and one of them was strength. While I couldn't build things very well, I was great at destroying them. Our job was demolishing old apartments in downtown Boston and then gentrifying them, and while I could barely turn a screw, I proved a solid demo guy. For eight hours a day, I smashed down walls with sledge hammers, tore up lath with a cat's paws, pried up floorboards with crowbars.

I came home covered with dust and grime each night and steamed myself in the shower until I felt human again. I hated the job, but it felt good to collect a pay check, and already I was beginning to see carpentry, as I saw everything, as a symbol for writing. At nights and on weekends I sat down at my little desk in the corner of the apartment I shared with my girlfriend Rachel, vowing that I would approach my work the way my boss Dennis seemed to approach carpentry: calmly, easily, building things slowly and well. Not a great plotter or planner, Dennis would simply scribble down plans on the back of the shingle, and his ease seemed like a possible antidote to my constant intensity. "Write a little every day without hope or despair," was the Isak Dinesen quotation I taped above my desk. Following this dictate, I wrote the first sentences that I was proud of.

The strangest fears can get hold of adolescent minds and, working calmly at my book for two hours a day on the weekends, I sometimes worried I was becoming "too reasonable." "I need to be wild to write," I scribbled in my journal, echoing Thoreau. The truth was I was already plenty wild, and adding a little reasonableness to the mix couldn't hurt. One reason for all of my balking was that growing steadier was hard work. I had plenty of things to worry about at the time. Being too reasonable wasn't one of them.

~

For two years, I kept slogging away at carpentry, though it soon began to seem more like a sentence than a job. During my last winter, our crew gutted an old slum apartment in Roxbury. As a rule, we worked hardest during the winter months, since we had no heat in the building except an occasional space heater. I spent most of January and February of that year in the dirt basement of the tenement, shovelling so that the base floor level was deep enough to start putting in wood flooring for an additional yuppie apartment. My work mates in the basement that winter were Eric and Larry, two black guys from the neighborhood we were working in, who my boss Dennis had hired on just for the dig. Eric was crazy and could go off about anything at the drop of a hat, but big Larry was steady and funny. When Eric was there, he entertained us with monologues about various government conspiracies, but often enough he didn't show, so it was just Larry and me in the cellar for the better part of the winter. Larry was a big friendly man, young, about my age, but with a kid and a wife. He spoke with a vaguely southern accent but though we told each other everything about our lives, I don't remember much about him, and I suspect he doesn't remember much about me either. The reason for this is simple: We were stoned all the time.

"Hey Dave, you bring the cheeba today?" he would ask.

I would nod or ask him if he had. We took turns more or less.

We smoked in the morning and then shovelled all day. We usually got stoned off a tightly rolled joint first thing before shovelling and then got stoned again and ate danishes and drank tubs of coffee at break before shovelling until lunch. Our job entailed scooping shovelfulls of dirt up onto a creaky old conveyer belt that then transported the piles up to an open window in the cellar wall, a small square of sunlight that was our one view of the world outside and that soon began to look a whole lot like freedom. At lunch, we got stoned again and then shovelled till the end of the day listening to bad rock, WBCN and WAAF, turned up loud to block out the chugging of the conveyer belt. Two orange-caged extension-cord lightbulbs that hung off nails in the side walls were our only light, other than the small window, and our shadows stretched around the room. We were like trolls down there in the near dark. I had a minor heart condition and thanks to the pot and coffee my erratic heart trilled and skittered through the winter.

"How come they don't rent a fucking backhoe to do this?" Larry asked me once.

"We're cheaper," I told him. It was true. Dennis had figured it all out, factoring in our pay rate versus the cost of renting a tractor.

Larry was 6'1" and neither of us could stand up straight without hitting our heads on the ceiling when we started digging. But over the course of the winter, the floor fell as we dug, and the little window of light became higher up and further away. The other, more skilled carpenters on the crew occasionally popped their heads in to make sure we were still alive. Every once in a while, when there weren't other projects or on Friday afternoons when the whole crew got stoned and drank beer and were therefore reluctant to operate power tools, everybody would come down to the cellar and we'd have a shovelling party. But for most of the winter it was just Larry and me.

One time, when we were standing there taking a break with our shovels at our sides, Larry sucked in a hit and then gestured with the joint at the conveyer belt. It was at a steeper angle now, chugging up to the window and out, dumping a huge pile of all we'd dug outside in the lot in back of the apartment.

"How the fuck you think they're going to get rid of that pile out there?" he asked me.

And he was right. Shovelling that pile into a truck would be our early spring job.

The basement story would have a kind of funny ending, at least for Larry and me. Once we'd dug down deep enough, a lot of things were left up higher than they usually are in a room. One of those things was the old oil tank and the pipe that ran into it from the outside. I asked Dennis what to do about it and he had me cut off the pipe with the Sawz-All (the Sawz-All being our universal solution to any thorny problem). The oil tank itself, once disconnected, lay on its side like a dead elephant, until we knocked a hole in the wall, and had the whole crew drag it out. We did nothing with the outside section of the pipe, however, the part where oil would usually be pumped in. The next winter, when the cellar apartment was finished—wood-floored and fancy—the oil man unknowingly pumped a hundred gallons from the outside right into the unconnected pipe, filling the apartment with a sea of oil.

~

Soon after the winter of digging, my hand quit working. And then I did. I had carpal tunnel syndrome, and could no longer dig or bang nails, or write for that matter, and so I left carpentry for a career in retail. Out of money, and still paying off loans, I needed a job right away. I must have thought something like this: I love books so why not work in a bookstore? It's a trap many young people fall into, I suppose, forgetting that working in a bookstore is about *selling* books, not reading them.

I took a job in a chain bookstore on Cape Cod, and not long after I started working I was promoted to night manager. I liked being night manager, mainly because it made it easier to steal. Desperate for money, always in a panic about bills, I decided that "the man" wouldn't miss a few dollars here and there and so embarked on that great American tradition: stealing from work. My scam was foolproof. Magazines were the only untaxed item, so when a customer bought one I would hit the "No Sale" button and the drawer would pop open with a ring. I'd put the money in the drawer but write down the exact amount of the sale on a bookmark. Later, when I balanced the drawer, I'd pocket the surplus amount. Usually no more than twenty bucks, enough, in my mind, to correctly bolster the seven dollars an hour I was making. It all seemed justified by my attempt to survive and, more importantly, to write.

I made a point of making most of my profits off of pornography. We claimed to be booksellers, but we were, more accurately, porno-venders. It was strange, but in that old Puritan fishing village we sold a veritable potpourri of porn. The people in Orleans might not have liked to read much, but they sure liked their *Hustlers, Jugs* ("Home of the D-cup") and *Legshows*. One guy in particular, a prominent local businessman, always made a big show of picking up the raunchiest magazines and leafing through them right there in the open, then waving them all around on his way to the register, even greeting little old ladies by flashing pictures of naked women. In Olde New England, he might have been thrown in the stocks, but here, people, including my manager, a chipper old Yankee lady, only smiled and shook their heads as if to say "what a character." To make my confession about that bookstore a full one, I will say that on top of petty cash I also occasionally lifted some porn of my own. It wasn't just Henry David Thoreau that got me through those cold Cape nights. Mostly I stole *Penthouses* but once indulged myself in something a little more perverse and fingered a copy of *Dominant Secretary*.

I hated the job. It is a plain fact that there are some people who should never work retail and I was one. The position of clerk, which involved a lot of bowing and scraping and fake politeness and "yes sirs" and "no ma'ams," managed perfectly to stoke my feelings of inadequacy and, therefore, naturally, my fury. Thoreau wrote of shopkeepers and others who work inside all day: "I think that they deserve some credit for not having all committed suicide long ago." More impressive, to me, is that they don't commit murder. Working as a cashier, bloody thoughts are never far from your head.

In retail, you learn to hate customers for lots of different reasons. With some, it's just the way they hold their money. My particular peeve—or the most intense of my many peeves—were those who purchased their goods with credit cards. Back then, we still had the clunky credit card imprinters that you had to run—*rooock, rooock*—over the card before filling in the tiny boxes on the inky form. Though I'd say nothing to the customer, I'd give off clear signals of my rage, letting them know that this was something that *I*—David Gessner—shouldn't be doing. I'd rip the imprinter over the card with all my strength, trying to break its rugged plastic spine and rip the logo off its face. Then I'd fill in the stupid little boxes ever so slowly—the expiration date, the price, the tax, the date, the items—slowly enough to get the customers tapping their fingers. If they dared express irritation, I'd slow down even more. Choking the pen tightly, I'd proceed at a snail's pace until I finally offered it up for them to sign. "Can I please have an address and phone number above your signature?" I'd ask, just as trained. I'd snap apart the carbons crisply, as if tearing out a tuft of hair from a small animal, before handing them their bag and singing out "Have a nice day!" Though those were my words, we both understood that that wasn't my meaning. "I hope you die in a car accident," was closer to it.

~

The whole reason I was working at these crappy jobs in the first place was so that I could write, but that wasn't going particularly well either. It turned out that writing a book wasn't quite as easy as I'd first anticipated. Beginning is terrifying business, particularly terrifying if you have invested the thing that is to be begun with enormous quantities of hope and expectation. In my mind, I was already wearing a laurel crown with Keats, while in reality I hadn't even tried to start a short story. The truth was that the thought of setting pen to paper scared the shit out of me.

For weeks I would stare at my writing pad with no words coming. While I was still convinced that, deep down, I had something profound to say, I didn't have a clue what it was or how to say it. None of the things that are now habit were in place back then. Little details plagued me. What time should I start in the morning? Should I write with a clock in sight? Did I eat breakfast before I started? Should I have a set number of hours to aim for? And how could I even try to write when I had to spend all this time working retail?

Gradually, grudgingly, the sentences started to come. A plot emerged, or what passed for a plot in my mind. But if I sometimes managed to work in the reasonable manner that Issac Dinesen advocated, more often the writing came in erratic, unsustainable bursts. The words would gush out, followed by periods of intense doubt. Back then, creativity was a lot like drinking for me, the incredible highs followed by the hard depressions.

Isolation was part of the problem. I didn't show anyone a word of my writing, and if Rachel came near my desk I'd hunch over protectively. I was worried she would think my words, and therefore my self, imperfect. My creative world, like the world of most young writers, was an intensely solipsistic one. There is an insanity to showing one's work to no one, to spending hours whirling around in your own narcissistic universe, an insanity that would build in me over those hard first years.

~

At twenty-eight, I moved back to Boston. It was then that Rachel and I, still broke, became involved in an elaborate sitcom-like ruse, posing as husband and wife so that we could live for free as dorm parents at a Boston prep school. During those two years, we wore fake rings and ate free meals in the dining hall and told bad, bald lies when asked about our wedding or honeymoon. Despite our obvious discomfort and our blushing, people seemed to believe us, and why not? (We certainly fought as if we were married.) The kids even called her Mrs. Gessner for a while until she began sharply correcting them: "It's *Ms. Rulf.*"

To support myself, I took a job at a bookstore in Brookline, commuting to and from the prep school. I held the job for a year and a half before being fired. The day that led to my firing, not long after I had gotten a batch of form letters rejecting my first novel, I went into work hungover. I had already built up a fairly healthy head of resentment— snarling at customers who interrupted me while I tried to scribble down notes for my *next* novel on our complimentary bookmarks—when a guy in a seventies-style Adidas running suit approached the registers. He didn't walk up to my register but to Kathleen's. I had a crush on Kathleen and felt protective of her, and looking over I could see right off that Mr. Running Suit was trouble. While I helped someone else, I watched their interaction out of the corner of my eye. He drew an American Express card like a sword from a little velcro side pocket on his suit. Kathleen politely explained to him that we did not take American Express, but he treated her as if she wasn't a native speaker and simply hadn't understood. He tried again, speaking more slowly, as if to an imbecile, explaining that he had "jogged down to the store" and only had the one card with him. When he persisted, I finally butted in. I said something like, "I'm sorry, sir, but you have to understand that we can't suddenly take a credit card we don't accept." Reasonable, but apparently said with enough of a sarcastic spin to provoke his ire. He turned his attention, and building outrage, from Kathleen to me.

"I don't like your tone, young man" he said. "I want your name."

Happy to be engaged in an actual, not imaginary, battle, I handed him a bookmark and a pen. I began to spell my name out, letter by letter.

"D-A-V-I-D—That's David. G-E—"

But apparently I even spelled too sarcastically for him.

He'd had enough, and that's exactly what he said: "I've had enough!" He pounded the counter with his fist and started to turn away to leave.

And that might have been it. A small victory for the cashiers, maybe, a funny story to tell the other clerks. Might have been it, were it not for the pen. In turning to charge off, he made one last angry gesture. He tossed the pen and the bookmark he'd been writing on up in the air. He probably just meant for the pen to skitter across the counter, but in fact it cartwheeled slowly through the air and hit me lightly in the chest. It didn't hurt, not at all, but at that moment, as that ballpoint binked my chest, something *binked* inside my head.

It was the final indignity, the last straw. As if some gate had opened and all my frustrations over *serving* people for all those years came pouring out. In that second *he* was the one making me work at that job; *he* was the one stopping me from being a real writer; *he* was the one calling me a failure.

I came down off the dais and caught up with him right at the store's entrance. He was between the two magnetic sentry devices that guarded the door and he turned around and glared when he saw me coming. Having no idea what I was actually up to, I stopped and stood in front of him, face to face, shoulder to shoulder. Already sneering at me, he twisted his face into an even more condescending look and asked the question I didn't know the answer to:

"Just *what* are you going to do?"

He said it with a syrupy certainty. After all, he was right, what could I, or any sane person, possibly do? He was sure that the answer would be "nothing," which it likely would have been had he not posed the question. But the question itself proved his downfall. Something in his snotty tone and the implication of my impotence called forth a daemon that had been slumbering inside me for almost a decade, a daemon that the jogger would soon wish he hadn't conjured. He had unwittingly unleashed all the rage of my miserable twenties. I acted before I could stop myself.

We were about the same size but he wasn't running on ten thousand amps of adrenaline. Before he could defend himself, I'd grabbed him by the collar and thrown him into a self-help display, knocking over most of the books. He lay splattered along with M. Scott Peck and Leo Bus-calgia for only a second before I was on him again. We wrestled on the floor for a short while until he managed to scramble to his feet. Running out of the store, he yelled back, "You lunatic!" This last word describing me must have seemed entirely accurate to anyone who had watched what had just transpired. Then he added: "I'm getting the fucking police!"

Which he did. Fortunately for me he was every bit as pushy with police officers as he was with cashiers. He stood in front of the store hectoring them and demanding quick (and, if possible, brutal) justice, and by the time they took me to the back office to interrogate me they were clearly sympathetic with my situation, maybe even tempted to administer a little beating of their own. Sitting at the shipper's desk now, I was shaking all over, intensely apologetic, amazed and appalled by what I'd done, and, as always, confessing my sins. One of the cops put his hand on my shoulder and spoke to me in a compassionate voice.

"Don't worry, son," he said. "Just tell us exactly what happened."

I did, completely and honestly, convinced by the time I was done that I'd be looking at ten-to-twenty. But the avuncular officer assured me it was not so, and then he told me exactly why not.

"If he charges you, you counter-charge him," he said, no doubt acting unprofessionally by coaching me.

"With what?" I asked.

"Assault with a deadly weapon," he said. He smiled. "The *pen*."

It turned out that rather than get involved in that particular mess, Mr. Adidas sued the store. While his running suit may have been outdated, he had a contemporary love for libel. The store decided to settle with him, part of their settlement being, of course, my dismissal. But those last two weeks were the best of my young working life. The other cashiers, rather than being appalled by what I'd done, saw me as a kind of hero in the war against the enemy. After all, I had fulfilled their darkest, deepest fantasy. I had struck back at the customer, our common foe.

~

Thus ended my career as a cashier.

There were other jobs, of course. A fairly meaningful stint as a residential counselor at a homeless shelter, where I worked with the children of the homeless, especially the boys, playing ball and taking them for hikes. And then, on the other end of the meaningfullness scale, was my year or two as a substitute teacher. Though there were plenty of lowlights during my twenties, perhaps working as a substitute was the lowest of all lights. "Who are you today?" the other teachers would ask in the hall, and I'd feel as if they were in on my secret, questioning my fragile identity. "Mr. Lemay—Geometry," I'd say. Or "Miss Rogan—Gym." My answer didn't matter. To the real teachers, I was barely visible, living in my little fuzzy sub-world.

But the kids could see me, that was for sure. Let anyone who dares proclaim idealistically the general goodness of children try their hand at substitute teaching. That will cure them. Having done it myself, I'd consider subbing an acceptable defense in a murder trial. Kids, otherwise nice kids, become hateful little beasts trying their best to push you over the edge of sanity (not knowing, in Mr. Gessner's case, just how gentle a nudge that would take). And each one a little container of germs, too, as if it were thirty petrie dishes I had in my charge. I was always catching their miserable colds, despite washing my hands as frequently as Lady Macbeth.

Sadly, that's not all I did in those faculty washrooms. Each day served up a half-dozen potential Lolitas. Rachel was in medical school by then and had no time for me that fall, and so I resorted to fantasy. I sat there tapping a pencil on the desk while the kids half-heartedly scribbled down some rote assignment their "real" teacher had left them. I scanned the room, spending a good part of my time imagining what the girls looked like naked. I did nothing technically wrong while subbing, but I, like Jimmy Carter before me, often lusted in my heart (though I don't know if President Carter privately followed through on his desires with quite my frequency and fervency.) Did those seventeen-year old girls, happily cleaning the erasers just as Mr. Gessner had asked them to, realize that they were also being stored up in Mr. Gessner's sick mind? I was, I understood, despicable.

~

What do I make of it all now, more than a decade later? My attitude toward that time is prejudiced, prejudiced by the simple fact that it is now over. For all our retreating to the past and reaching toward the future, we all live in the perpetual present. Who wouldn't want to have dramatic—even miserably dramatic—things happen to them once they are over? These things are, at the very least, good material. During my twenties, Rachel and I travelled through Europe, and I remember marvelling at the system of grants and support that was set up for young artists and then, returning to the states, cursing the American "system," or lack of one. Now, with that time over, our way seems superior. Struggle must be more than mere metaphor. It is, I believe, a very real part of what we do when we sit down at our desks.

On the other hand, sitting down at a desk isn't so easy when covered in sheetrock and dust. How much sooner would I have gotten through my apprenticeship if I'd had time to churn out the bad pages? Both question and answer are moot. My route is my route, and there's no changing it. By saying "my way was the right way" I'm slipping into just the sort of nostalgic backwash I was hoping to avoid: "It was all for the best," and all that garbage.

I like to tell my students the story about the young Hemingway. How his wife took the train down to Spain to greet him, a suitcase filled with his early short stories on the seat next to her. The suitcase was lost on the trip, devastating the young Hemingway (though he claims, of course, to have responded calmly). "Lose the suitcase," I exhort my students, trying to get them to shed their earliest writing skins. But even this advice is two-sided. For while we tell young writers to let go, there is no more important tool of the trade than that of hanging on. "There is no doubt that creative work is itself done under a compulsion often indistinguishable from a purely clinical obsession," writes Ernest Becker in *Denial of Death*, "In this sense, what we call a creative gift is merely the social license to be obsessed." Amen. The advice then is complicated advice: *Let go, but, by the way, also hold on. And hold on obsessively.*

Of course I don't remember ever using the word "apprenticeship" when I was still inside it. We aren't aware that what we are doing is just a warm-up act, and that's a good thing. How could you ever muster up the necessary intensity, the necessary obsession, if you thought what you were doing was merely a prolonged exercise? Delusion about the importance of what we are working on *now* is a necessary tool.

What would I say to that arrogant, spoiled, insecure boy if I could go back in time? I'm not sure there's much advice I could give that would really help. I wouldn't tell him to "W-O-R-K", he already knew that. I might sit him down and have a long talk with him, trying to explain the nature of this apprenticeship thing, all of it, that is the hard and necessary work of getting better, of becoming an artist, but I'm not sure he would get it. Or I might reveal his future to him, but while he would be pleased to know he would get a book published, he wouldn't want to hear about his father's death or other family tragedies. No, about the only worthwhile thing I might have been able to say to him is what the spirit-guide elder says to the novitiate at the beginning of an initiatory peyote trip:

Hold on, son, I would tell him. *Just hold on.*

To the Fatherland

With minimal effort I can still picture him: bald, heavy, with a malleable mouth instantly shifting from the cherubic to the stern. It's only a little harder to set him in motion: Here he is throwing a football with that tight lefty spiral and scolding my nine-year old self when it skims off my fingers: "If you can touch it you can catch it." Or I can move him ten years forward and see him thrusting his arms over his head as he steps off the bus to the company outing, bellowing "Guess who won the betting pool?" not letting others know until later that the pool—a wager on what time the bus would arrive at the picnic area—was fixed when he bribed the busdriver. These flashes of memory, as well as his more full-bodied return in my dreams, provide me with pictures for sustenance, but all the while I know that I provide a more serious function for him. My father may be dead, but he remains alive in me.

Today I choose to conjure up another time. It is December of 1991, and we are driving a rental car across the border into what has been, until only recently, East Germany. This makes me thirty years old, which means our relationship, never easy, has been strained for the past ten years or so by my stubborn refusal to live in what he calls the "real world." This refusal manifests itself primarily in my insistence, despite lack of evidence, that I am a writer. But just as great changes have been in the air in Germany, a warming after a long frost, so our relationship is beginning to evolve into something else. One reason for this is that I have finally done something concrete about my airy plans: I am now in graduate school, and while it is, admittedly, a school for writing, school is something he can get his head around. Another reason is that, nine months before our trip, I was diagnosed with testicular cancer. After a period of uncertainty and radiation therapy, I began to recover, and at a check-up right before we left for our trip, I was officially declared "clean." Not long before, my father was also deemed cured of bladder cancer, and this has forged a new bond between us. What we don't know as we approach the former border is that a new tumor, a secret uninvited guest, is already growing inside of him; what we don't know is that he has only two and a half years to live.

But let me stop right there. This essay is not about the fact that he will soon cease to be, as much as it is about what he will achieve before that abrupt deadline arrives. Because one of his life's proudest accomplishments is right around the corner, and before he dies my father will become one of the first Americans to purchase and own a company in the formerly Communist German state. He will delight in this as he tends to delight in accomplishments, but he will particularly delight in the way his family history dovetails with world history. The word "industrialist," though outdated, suits my father perfectly, but for all the pleasure he takes in the sport of business, a part of him always remains the history student he was in college. Buying a company in Aue, the ancestral home of the Gessners, binds together these two passions.

On the plane I was kept awake by the monologues of my neighbor, an overweight frat boy from Boston College who ranted on about how he was going to "pot-ty on good beer in Germany." After the flight, I met my father in Frankfurt and exhaustion washed over me once I settled into the passenger seat of the rental car. But my father was wide awake. Feeling obviously boyish and excited, he filled me in on details about the town of Aue and the company that his great-grandfather had long ago owned, *Ernst Gessner Textilmaschinen*.

"The surprising thing about Textilmaschinen is that their machines are all world class. Varsity machines."

I nodded. Varsity was my father's word for good; J.V. for not so good.

"They supplied machines for the Eastern block and Russia, and the quality is right in the same ballpark with our best. It's the management that's suspect. They never had to play in the big leagues, never had any real competition. That will change quickly."

Despite his obvious excitement, his voice hadn't had such a soporific effect on me since he'd read me the *Mother West Wind* stories as a kid. My head bobbed forward as he spoke until I finally gave in and dozed my way through Western Germany. An hour or so must have passed. Then, just as we're about to leave the West, my father roused me by grabbing my shoulder.

"Wake up, David. You've got to see this."

I woke in a strange, almost drugged, mood, the warmth of blood collecting in the ridge above my eyebrows. Since we'd left Frankfurt a cold rain had been drumming on the rental car's roof and I'd barely been able to glimpse the slate grey sky through the fog, but now the fog lifted. We were on Route 4, approaching Eisenach, the old border, and tall erector set constructions rose on the horizon, sprouting from the frozen yellow ground.

"Gun towers," my father said.

We passed through no-man's-land. Then beneath the deserted towers and buildings where suddenly not so much as a passport was required. The sound of hammering echoed. Workmen converting barracks to rest stations.

Driving into East—now *Eastern*—Germany, the architecture underwent a dramatic change. Smokestacks and steeples jutted out of the rolling hills while ugly Bauhaus-box apartment buildings, like bad college dormitories, muscled in on ancient villages with dirty red roofs. As we drove across the German plain we passed onion-domed steeples next to car dumps, the remains of castles littering the hills right next to cone-shaped piles of strip-mining waste.

"Get a good look," my father said. "Because in a year it'll all be changed. The other Eastern block countries are in for a real struggle. But just watch the fucking East Germans go. They know the meaning of the word *work*. Right now it's a mess: forest's are dying and you can't walk through the cities without feeling a burning in your throat. But these bastards will clean it all up. Then, in a few years, they'll pass Japan and the West Germans. They'll be the ones with the newest computers and equipment and machines."

Looking out at the dismal landscape this was hard to believe (and as it turned out my father's faith in all things Teutonic was misplaced), but as much as pondering any prospective changes in the German countryside, I found myself marvelling at the volatile mixture of sentimentality and hard-headedness in the man sitting next to me. As we drove on, I thought about his peculiar love for Germany. Though he hadn't been born there, and had lived his whole life in the United States, he blatantly romanticized what he liked to call "the Fatherland."

This was not in itself strange as his own paternal roots were solidly

German. His grandfather had moved from Germany to the United States before World War II and established a textile machinery company in Worcester, Massachusetts. This first American Gessner was, by my grandmother's account, an effective businessman, but also a domineering lunatic, who lorded it over his company, home, and those unfortunate enough to attend his Sunday dinners (dinners filled with long, monologue-filled sessions where no one spoke but David Sr.) His son, in contrast, was an eccentric n'er-do-well who ended up puttering around in his father's garden and collecting statues of elephants, statues that I later discovered in our basement. That son, my father's father, was also named David Gessner and his short, unsuccessful life ended while he was still in his thirties. My father was only six when he lost his father. Shortly after, the elder Gessner died too, and the company slipped out of the family's hands.

It had been up to my father to reclaim the company. This alone, and his fatherless state, might have led him to romanticize the country those lost men had come from. But early in his career the company was purchased by Germans, so that he was frequently required to fly to Germany on business, and, cramming in Berlitz courses, had taught himself the language, which he occasionally spat out at the dinner table. He liked German efficiency, German punctuality, German beer. I remember that he would sometimes bring us to attention at the table with commands of "Achtung Bitte." I also remember that when I first watched *Hogan's Heroes* as an eight year old, I recognized Schultz's "Ja wohl, mein kommandant!" as my mother's sarcastic response to his commands.

His Teutonophilia had always had a strange and playful edge, but after the Berlin Wall came down it intensified. He began to indulge in his own whitey version of *Roots*, seriously exploring the possibility of buying back his great-grandfather's textile company. Before our trip, he had already made several visits to Aue, tracing the Gessners back hundreds and hundreds of years to the goatherders in the surrounding hills. The company executives first greeted him with suspicion, but soon began to see him as the great American savior for their nearly bankrupt textile factory and its employees. At that point, many—if not most—East German companies were going under, and thousands of employees were losing their jobs. Perhaps the most telling moment for my father came the spring before when he was standing on the catwalk above the Textilmachinen factory floor with the company's acting president. The two men were pausing briefly on the elevated walk after a morning spent inspecting machines, when all of the sudden the machinists and press rollers stopped working and looked up to where they stood. Facing my father, they started clapping and then chanting his name.

"Gessner, Gessner, Gessner," they chanted over and over, louder and louder, "Gessner, Gessner, Gessner."

Apparently Germans hadn't quite gotten over their peculiar love for charismatic authority figures. As they chanted, he stood there above them, waving like Evita, and, knowing him, basking in it. When he told me the story he wore a broad grin.

On the other side of the border the road became rutted and rough, and smokestacks, larger than any I'd ever seen, belched orange clouds. We passed dozens of sputtering cars as they struggled down the highway. These cars, both on the highway and in the frequent random dumps, were the small box-like Trabinis, or "Trabbies" as my father called them. We drove through Gotha, Erfut, Weimar, and the city of Gera, where rugs hung over the balconies of the ugly dormitory-style rooms. Enormous crows sauntered along the road. We cut through the middle of Schneeburg and I stared out at the grimy, sooted brick and the soupy layer of film covering the Schneeburg River. The homes were flat, grey rectangular slabs and the roads in the middle of town were cobblestone. It might have been a scene from another century if the inverted cups of satellite dishes hadn't graced almost every one of the red slate roofs. Leaving Schneeburg, we drove up a long hill and then, at last, down into the valley that held the city of Aue.

"There it is," my father said. "The home of the Gessners."

The town was surrounded by hills, hills that I would soon learn were amazingly effective at holding in the clouds of pollution that had resulted from years and years of coal burning. Giant smokestacks, larger even than those I'd seen an hour before, shot up.

"Land. That's the secret," my father said. "The company is right in the middle of town."

He had a predatory look in his eyes, as if he were coming down into the valley not just to visit, but to devour it. He jabbed his forefinger across my face, pointing off to some buildings on the right, explaining to me that they were once Gessner employee housing.

Studying the dark orange buildings, I picked out an unusual detail. Black cast-iron candle holders stood in almost every window. I would later learn that these were traditional miner's candles but to me, at that moment, they looked a lot like mennorahs, and I noted this excitedly.

The thing is, my father wasn't the only one in my life who romanticized a country. As we were driving across Germany, Rachel, my girlfriend of seven years, was boarding a plane for Israel. It's hard to convey the intensity with which Rachel pined for and glorified Israel, the country in which she had been born. Just months before, world events had become entangled with *her* family history, and we stared at the television in horror as Iraqui missiles dropped on her grandmother's town. Over the next days, we learned that her beloved Softa, at eighty-eight, had to barricade herself in a sealed room, don a gas mask, and urinate in a bucket. Softa had survived the war and Rachel visited soon after. Softa had never been very fond of me, given my lack of Jewish credentials. This lack, and Rachel's desire to eventually move to Israel, were two of the great stumbling blocks in our plan to get married.

But Rachel had a secret theory that made at least one of those obstacles moot. The theory was woven together out of equal parts fact, wishful thinking, and the drunken spouting of one of my mother's best friends. The facts were that David Gessner, my great-grandfather, had always travelled back and forth from Germany and the United States, but had moved permanently to the states in the mid-1930s, mysteriously losing control of the German company at about the same time. Out of this, and out of what she saw as my father's overcompensating need to prove how German he was, she had concocted the theory that the Gessners were actually Jewish, a theory that was bolstered over some drinks one night when my mother's oldest friend told Rachel she had always believed the same thing. I doubted it, but must admit I liked the idea. It made perfect sense to me that I was Jewish, as were not just Rachel but so many of my friends. Something was so right about it, and of course it eliminated one of the major barriers between me and my lover.

I had little time to digest the strange fact of the menorahs, however, as my father was now pointing out the Ernst Gessner company. It stood in the center of town as he'd said, its cast-iron gate spanning two unassuming grey buildings. Behind the gate was an enormous factory with the words *Veb Textilmaschinebaus* on a sign bolted to its front.

"Herr Gessner," my father announced to the man in the guardbox. The heavy gates swung open.

We drove down a brick road that opened into a large circular courtyard. The factory stretched on and on beside a sickly yellow river, the buildings extending and elongating, a twisted vision of nineteenth-century industrialism. An old clock tower rose from the building next to the courtyard; ducts and walkways and pipes ran overhead. My father parked in front of the main entrance, directly below the largest stained glass window I'd seen anywhere outside of a church.

We walked up three flights of stairs and then along a dingy, unadorned hallway that turned into a kind of catwalk above the factory floor. We stopped and stared down at the enormous room where the machines were built, a room that a football field, goal posts and all, could easily have fit inside. Below were rows and rows of shining silver-colored textile machines and black rollers. Dozens of men in blue full-body uniforms worked around and on the machines, some bending over drafting tables with plans unrolled before them, some cutting metal surrounded by flying sparks, but most simply standing around kibitzing, apparently untroubled by the set-up that allowed their bosses to spy down on them from above. I realized that this must have been where my father had stood while the workers below chanted his name.

We walked down the catwalk into a dark corridor; our next stop was the current president's office.

"He worked as a front man when the Communists were in power," my father said to me in a stage whisper before we went in. "He's a bit of a bullshitter, but he's okay."

The office inside looked as if it had been decorated with hand-me-downs, bare florescent lights illuminating card tables and cheap chairs of the type used in junior high school. Radiators and pipes jutted uncovered and tacky brown curtains hung in the windows. Immediately after we'd announced ourselves to his secretary, Herr Henke came bursting out of his office, cigarette in hand. He looked surprised, even shocked, to find us standing there.

"David, my good friend!" he said to my father. He shook my father's hand hastily while patting him on the shoulder, the ashes from his cigarette falling on my father's raincoat.

"Ah, and the young Herr Gessner! Such a handsome young man!"

He grabbed for my hand and pumped away, bobbing his head like a doll. He was lanky with an ill-fit, chalk-covered coat, and he held his low-burning cigarette protectively, as if afraid someone might try to tear it from his hand.

"We have much to talk about. But you are tired. And more important, hungry."

He spread his arms magnanimously as if it were a great feast, not his drab little room, that lay before our eyes. Then, with a jerky spasmodic movement, he rushed back into his inner office and returned with a raincoat and umbrella.

"We will walk, yes?" He began to nod vigorously again, answering his own question. "Tomorrow we talk business and show young Herr Gessner the town where his family is originated from. But tonight we eat!"

The restaurant was right across the street, only a hundred feet from the gates to the factory. The rain pelted us, and Herr Henke, unable to decide whom to protect with the umbrella, jerked it back and forth above himself, my father, and me, so that, despite the short walk, we were all cold and wet by the time we got inside. The host greeted us at the door wearing a tuxedo, but the room was spare and almost entirely unadorned. We were alone in the restaurant and sat at a large card table set with supermarket paper napkins. The only decoration on the walls was a brown mat of fur.

"The skin of a pig," Herr Henke explained. "A wild pig with big teeth."

"A boar," my father suggested.

"Yes! A *boar!*" Henke's small eyes shone with excitement at the word.

We shook off our coats and hung them and as soon as we were seated, Herr Henke hurriedly set to translating the menu for me. As he translated, I began to understand that every one of the offerings was one sort of *schwein* or another, which would be pretty much the case for the entire trip. Eastern Germany, I was learning quickly, was a land where pig was king.

My first course was a small albino sausage. I stabbed at it with my fork but it squibbed out from beneath me and off my plate. When I reached to pick it up, I found it remarkably slippery, jumping out of my hand as if alive, landing on the floor. I glanced over at Herr Henke, worried that I was offending him by soiling the pork, but my father and he were now engrossed in conversation. I gave the sausage a little kick and let it rest in peace under the table.

The sausage was followed by Scweinschnitzel, greasy but good. Far more intriguing to me than my meal, however, was the conversation between Henke and my father.

"What we need is a game plan," my father was saying.

"Strategy, yes."

"We look like we're worried. That's bad. Scared, you understand?"

"Scared," Henke echoed.

On the ride, my father had explained to me that a government trust called the Treuhand would oversee the land deals as Eastern Germany opened up, and that the Treuhand would ultimately decide on the company's new owner.

"I want you to go in to the Treuhand and tell them that I'm balking," my father said. "Hesitating, right? I want you to quote them a lower figure."

"But there are other offers for the company."

"But we have everything going for us. You represent the present management. I represent the historical owners. The Treuhand *wants* us to own the place."

"That, Herr Gessner, I am afraid I am not so sure of."

"*I* am sure of it. You quote them the lower offer. Tell them I won't budge. Make me the heavy."

"But if there are higher offers."

"They'll bring me in to talk. I'll take it from there. You just make me the bad guy and get me in there."

"I am not so sure of this."

My father jabbed the air with his finger.

"It'll work out. But we've got to let the bastards sweat."

Herr Henke replied in his own language, and, to my disappointment, the conversation continued in German. Even in English I'd been only half-aware of what was going on, and now I was completely lost.

But only for a minute. As I listened more closely and watched their faces, the fact that they were speaking a language foreign to me actually began to help me understand what was going on. Herr Henke, waving his thin arms in front of his chest, was obviously frightened for his job. My father, on the other hand, grew more and more aggressive. In German his speech sounded even blunter, slurred and guttural like a Klingon's. Watching him in action, sighing, jabbing, grunting, I became vaguely aware of an alien sensation bubbling up inside of my chest. It took a while, but by the time the bill arrived on a five-by-eight-inch piece of lined yellow notebook paper, I recognized that sensation as pride.

When we first got together, Rachel had quickly noted my father's love for all things German. Particularly incriminating was the plaque that his employees, well aware of his fascination with the Fatherland, had given him on his fortieth birthday. It was a small silver rectangle inscribed with the word *Geschaftsfuhrer*. My father decided to display the gift prominently, bolting it into the wall of our front hallway. I tried to explain to Rachel what my father had patiently explained to me: *Geschaftfuhrer* was simply the German word for "business leader," which my father clearly was. It was meant as an honor.

Rachel would have none of it. She couldn't believe he had allowed the plaque in the house, let alone hung it on the wall. On seeing it, she'd been unable to focus on anything but the last two syllables. Her grandmother, Softa, had barely escaped Germany for Israel before the war, one of the few in her family to survive. The sight of the word *fuhrer* in the hallway of the home of her beau—no matter how well disguised within another word—didn't exactly warm her heart.

I had trouble with the word, too, though for different reasons. It was the *Geschaft* as much as the *fuhrer* that bothered me. I always thought that the recent problems between my father and me were due to the fact he didn't respect me for trying to be a writer, and I neglected the fact that I didn't respect him much. Like *Geschaftfuhrer*, the word "business-man" didn't hold a particularly bright place in my cosmology, paling beside the lives led by my literary heros. My father was a smart man who had told me more than once that he would have liked to have been a history professor. Instead, this supposedly tough iconoclast had docilely followed the line of earlier David Gessners into the thrilling world of textile machinery. "You need to have balls," he'd always bluntly counseled me, but had his own course taken balls? It seemed awfully *safe* to me. I was the oldest of four children and for a while there had been the silent assumption within our family that I would be next in line, the heir to the company. But I'd soon made it abundantly clear that that wouldn't be the case. To anyone familiar with the previous cycle of Gessner history, my interest in "writing" (to say nothing of Frisbees) would have been a clear warning sign. For a while it was starting to look like I would repeat the previous generation's cycle: Hadn't I, too, frittered away my early potential? Hadn't I chosen a profession so impractical and ethereal—a profession so unlike the solid family production of textile machinery— that I might never make a single cent at it? Once again, a dictatorial industrialist father was faced with the prospect of a flakey n'er-do-well son. It was my turn to play with the elephants in the garden.

But things were changing, and not just in my father's feelings toward me. As it turned out, our porkfest with Herr Henke wouldn't be the last time I experienced a feeling of pride for my father during our week in Germany. It would bubble up again and again. In fact, that week may have been the first time I began to understand something that seems obvious to me now. During my twenties I'd been so busy with the brutal business of breaking free of my father that I had been blind in some ways. But at thirty, I finally began to see—or more accurately *see again*, since I'd worshipped him as a child—that it had indeed taken balls, and brains, to run his company and to run it in his own way in his own style. The man across the table from me, spitting out commands in his guttural Klingon, was a man who had found a way to be in the world, a man who had his own voice. He was a hard-headed gambler, part romantic but all realist, and I felt like a little kid, proud again, listening to him tell

Heinke how they would "stick it" to the Treuhand. And no one listening would have doubted that this bullish man would have done just that. If need be, he would *stick it* to them.

We stayed at the Hotel "Blauer Engel," only a two-minute walk from the factory. The first morning, I walked out into the cold rain. "Feel that spitting," my father had said to me the night before, "It does that all winter." I walked behind the hotel through the town's main square, staring up with pride at the corner street sign. The square, which for the last fifty years had been named Karl Marx Platz, had now been returned to its original name: *Gessner Platz*.

I walked around Gessner Platz for a while but it was so cold that it seemed preposterous that it was raining, not snowing, and soon I dipped into the town post office to warm up. As I entered, a young man walked up to me and spoke to me in German.

"I don't understand," I said.

"Ah, English."

"Yes."

"That surprises me. You have a face that could be from here. From the Brunlasberg. The mountains."

The stench of the place overwhelmed me as I walked back through town to the factory. The waste from years of coal burning sat in the valley, and the exhaust fumes of trucks wafted up into my nostrils. Smoke also poured out of the Rathaus chimney, then died and dropped, the taste of last night's pig mixing with the pollution, an odd and unpleasant mingling of pork and smoke.

At the factory I found Herr Henke, who led me up to a small room on the top floor.

"When I first came here they didn't even acknowledge the Gessner name," my father had told me. "But the last time I came back they'd put a room aside as an archive of Gessner family history. They even have an employee who's a curator for the room."

There was no curator in sight but I didn't need one. For an hour or two, I rooted into my family's history. It seemed a pretty straight line from goatherding to textiles but I was happy to note the small sidestream of artists and composers. I skimmed through textile patents signed by the king, Franz Joseph, and the musical compositions of Heinrich Traugutt Gessner and Ernst Gessner's journal. In one box was a paper that I unfolded carefully. It was a family tree that went back to the 1500s, to George Friedrich Gessner.

Later I told my father about it.

"They've got it charted even further now," he said. "The curator claims he can verify it back to the 1400s. Back to sheep and goat herders outside of Lossnitz."

"Where's Lossnitz?" I asked.

"Only about five kilometers away."

Twenty minutes later we were riding down the main street of Lossnitz in the rental car. Lossnitz offered little more than a shanty town of tin corrugated houses with green roofs through which Aue's dirty river ran, but we stared out at the dingy houses and little side streets like spellbound archaeologists. This was, after all, the holy seat, the birthplace of the Gessner clan.

"This is history, David," my father said, shaking his head in wonder. "*History.*"

I watched a goat skitter out of an alley in the rain, and thought that it was also a bit of personal history in the making. For the first time, I didn't feel like either cowering in the corner of my father's car, as I had so many times during my twenties, or conversely, rising up like a berserker to smite him. Instead, I felt exactly like what we were: two adults talking.

"Does it ever bother you that I didn't go to work for the company?" I asked, my own question taking me by surprise.

He glanced over at me quickly, then back out the front windshield. He seemed to be chewing on his own lip, studying the rain.

"It doesn't bother me at all," he said. "Textile machinery is a business from another time. A dying business. Not for young people."

His voice was matter of fact, but he might have kicked me in the stomach for all the blunt impact those sentences had. With a few words he'd overturned an assumption I'd clutched to for the better part of a decade. What came next surprised me even more.

"There's only one real regret I have," he said quietly. "That I don't have any grandchildren."

I stared over at him, at his beefy face and bald, slightly freckled head. He looked more like a kind, oversized infant than the villain who'd stalked my subconscious throughout my twenties. If he'd confessed to me that he was leaving the company to start an orphanage I wouldn't have been more surprised. I wondered if he planned to elaborate, but as he turned the car back to Aue, he said nothing.

The next day, while my father took care of business, I returned to the archive room. This time the curator was there, a slight ghost of a man who, in broken English, took me on another journey into the lives of Gessners past. When he was done, I thanked him and asked him if he could give me directions to the cemetery where my ancestors were buried. He offered to accompany me, but I said I preferred to go alone. He drew out a simple map on the company stationery.

Before we'd flown off on our respective trips, Rachel and I had playfully created a fantasy scene. In our joint daydream, my German trip would focus on my search for my Jewish roots. I would work diligently, interrogating the citizens of Aue but, after four days of fruitless questioning, I'd be ready to give up. Then on my last day, dejected, I'd walk for hours, ending up in a strange and run-down part of town. There an old crone, hair twisting down her back, would clatter her walking stick and call after me in a screeching voice: "Herr Gessner. Herr Gessner." The old women would take me aside and, over ginger tea, tell me stories of my family, stories from before both wars. Then she would point a long gnarled finger, like the twisting branch of a locust, directing me to an old abandoned cemetery on the outskirts of town. As rain began to fall, I would search fruitlessly for the graves of our ancestors, searching and searching but finding nothing. Finally, looking for a private place to piss behind a stunted oak, I'd stumble upon a half-dozen unkempt graves. I would kneel down and clear away the overgrowth of years of weeds and brambles, and discover the name of Ernst Gessner. I would read the dates out loud. *Geb. Dec. 19 Juni 1826—gest. Den 28 April 1897*. While I read the names above, I'd continue to clear dirt off the stone until—lo and behold!—the truth was revealed. There—larger than life—would shine out the Star of David. I'd stare down in shock, the Gessner family secret revealed, and then, the rain pouring down on my ancestor's graves, I'd embrace the glorious truth. Later, returning to the hotel, I'd call Rachel with the wonderful news. From Germany, my father and I would book a flight to Israel, where we would meet Rachel and I would receive her grandmother's blessing. We would be married by a Rabbi in Tel Aviv with my father and Softa each holding corners of the *chuppah*.

As it happened, my trip to the cemetery was decidedly less dramatic. I walked for a half mile, a steady climb past butcher shops and a vivid dark orange stone church with a green steeple that shot up into the air like an arrow. The front gate of the cemetery was open and I had little trouble finding our family's plots. Far from unearthing a crumbled weed-covered stone in the corner of the cemetery, the Gessner's gravesite was prime real estate, right in the yard's center. On that land, the Gessners, wanting to make their mark, had modestly erected a shrine that might have housed Lenin. The monument stood twenty-five feet high and twisted and turned outward for twice that length again. "Ruthestaette Der Familie Ernst Gessner," the scrolled sign across the top announced. Below, in gold lettering emblazoned into dark slate was a roll call of various dead Gessners. I dutifully scribbled all of the names into my notebook and then, starting on the left, sketched details of the grave. I already understood that Rachel and my fantasy about my roots had been just that, but, twenty minutes later, as I reached the far right side of the tomb's face, any remaining hopes I had regarding my family's Judaic heritage were snuffed. I noticed the relief of a face protruding near the top of the right battlement. The face was unclear and I climbed on top of one of the vine-covered lower steps to get a better look. Standing on tip-toe, the face still wasn't very clear, but the long hair and crown of thorns gave him away. There, where Rachel and I had projected the Star of David, was good old Jesus himself.

If I hoped that my vacation was going to yield any great revelation, I knew now that it would not be the uncovering of my Jewish roots. But that isn't to say the trip was without its strange discoveries. Chief among these was the behavior of my father. From the first night, he bristled with energy, his eyes lit by the kind of sparkle I'd come to associate only with red wine or vodka. The convergence of history and business obviously excited him, and I hadn't seen him so ready to charge ahead, so full of bull-like energy, in years.

There was something else at work in our changing dynamic. He'd never been able to fathom the series of jobs I'd taken to support myself as a writer. "My son, the cashier," he moaned. Or my son, the carpenter. Or, more than once, my son, the bum. The one time I asked him for advice, he'd replied: "I'll give you all the advice you need in one word. W-O-R-K." It frustrated me that he couldn't see just how hard I was working, not just to scrape together money to survive, but at my writing. Neither of us really understood that what I was going through was a long and hard apprenticeship.

He hadn't said much when I'd gotten sick. Like him, I was a skeptic and later I admired the way he died without ever dropping God's name. Everyone else had stupid theories, but my father was about the only person I knew who didn't volunteer a "reason" for my sickness. The truth is, I preferred his silence to the babbling of everyone else around me.

In Germany, I felt a sea change. My father had always loved anything to do with school, and was happy that I'd gone back to get a Master's degree, even in something as flimsy as writing. But more than that was the simple fact that it was becoming apparent that I wouldn't give up on my stubborn career choice no matter what he did or said. I was going to keep calling myself a writer until I actually was one; I would bang my head against the wall until the wall gave or my head was crushed. Of course, the things he'd taught me were exactly why I refused to quit and exactly why we hadn't gotten along for so long. Not exactly a stunning revelation in the father-son business, more like standard fare, but news to the young me.

He loved words and books and would have loved to see a book with my name—and *his* name, the name I got from him—on the spine. But he never saw me publish a book and neither of us were the sort to imagine that he is now up on a heavenly cloud somewhere looking down at me. On the day he died, I sat in the corner of the living room, next to his hospice bed, when he suddenly snapped awake from the morphine haze he'd been in for days. He looked over at me where I sat in the room's corner scribbling in my journal. His eyes were fierce.

"Make sure you get the facts down," he said.

And I listened to him. I got the facts down. As it turned out, my first published book was about his death, the son making his name on the father's corpse.

On the last night of the trip, we got drunk together in the small tavern next door to the Blauer Engel. It was called Zum Teufelchen.

"The Devil's Den," my father translated. "And they've got a varsity beer selection."

The bar was dark, flames blazing in the fireplace at its center. Appropriate satanic trinkets decorated the walls, like the sculpted devil's mask that jutted from the dark chocolate beam above us. He drank a pilsner while I gulped down a Wiessbeer that bubbled up in my head. Shadows from the fire skittered across our long oak table as I listened to my father summarize his business dealings.

"Herr Henke's okay, Dave. The trouble is, he's been trained to fear. To not take risks. He wants to bring another buyer in from a West German company to make the deal more secure."

He tilted his glass back and let the golden liquid slide into his mouth, his Adam's apple bobbing. He swallowed, grunted, and pinned a beer coaster against the table with his thick forefinger.

"I think we should go it alone. March into the Treuhand and offer less. If they don't take the lower price, I'll threaten to pull out."

He slid the coaster across the table toward me like a puck.

"The way I see it, we can sell the Treuhand on this."

He smiled a wide smile that twisted across his red shadowed face.

Our next round of beers arrived. We mirrored one another, drinking at the same greedy, gulping pace. I noticed that his eyes soon began to glaze over, at the same time lighting up with their habitual glassy twinkle, and I supposed my eyes were doing the same. After a while, we stopped talking and settled into silence. It wasn't like the old silence between us, however, a silence that had always made me want to scream. This was the relatively comfortable silence of two people, both brooders, who were working their way down personal alleys of thought.

After a while, my father lifted his glass in the air.

"Here's to your health," he said. "The main thing now is that you're healthy."

I clinked my glass, a long slender bugle, against his stein.

He inhaled, puffing up his cheeks. Moods always stormed across his face, his internal weather there for all to see. Now he exhaled and his face seemed to sink, the red mottled skin drooping from below his eyes, his cheeks deflating and chin sagging.

"I don't know how it was for you," he said. "But when they cut me open it scared the shit out of me."

I often wonder how the night would have proceeded from there if we'd been left alone. Perhaps, I've imagined, we would have talked about our cancers and forged an even stronger adult bond; perhaps unspoken thoughts and feelings would have gushed out in some kind of overblown father-son Robert Bly love fest.

We would never know. Just then, the waitress appeared. By her side was a tall thin man with a prominent bulging forehead. His wispy hair grew in grey patches above his ears, and he smiled an obsequious smile. He held a gin and tonic.

He bowed and gestured, speaking rapidly to both the waitress and my father. My father responded in his guttural German and the man sat down with his drink at the far end of our table.

"The tables are full," my father explained. "And he's asked if he might join us for a while."

My father stood up and shook hands with the man. He gestured over at me and I stood up, too.

"David, this is Dieter Baumgarten," my father said.

I shook his hand and sat back down.

It was immediately apparent that Dieter wasn't shy. He moved a seat closer to my father and began to talk at a great clip. I watched his pale pink lips flap up and down, understanding not a word. When our food, a flaming pork fondue, arrived, he eagerly took up my father's offer to help himself. He stabbed at a pink scrag with a toothpick.

"He knows the Gessner name," my father told me. "He knows about our family."

I nodded. My father bought another round of drinks. A beer for me, a vodka for himself, and another gin and tonic for Dieter. Our guest rambled on while my father listened. Apparently, in recompense for the drinks, Dieter had decided to treat us to his life story, and he leaned in closer to tell it. I watched the two men's faces in the firelight, my father's a slightly brighter shade of red than his guest's. After five minutes had passed, my father stopped Dieter's narrative by holding up his thick index finger.

He turned to me.

"You should hear this. It's fascinating. He's drunk and his accent's a little tough, but what I can understand is some pretty serious stuff."

He turned to Dieter and said something to him. Dieter nodded emphatically and tipped his drink toward me. He smiled and I noticed a single shining gold tooth.

"From what I can make out," my father said. "He's had a tough life. His mother was Jewish. Before the war, she moved them all to Austria. But right after they moved, Germany invaded. I can't quite make out how, but it seems the family got hold of some papers and managed not to be uncovered. The father landed in the German army. He says his mother and brother died during the war."

My father turned to Dieter who immediately launched back into his narrative. He became even more animated, occasionally touching my father's shoulder as he spoke. He spoke rapidly, faster and faster, and then stopped suddenly. He pointed at me as if to say: *Tell him what I said.*

My father relayed the tale as another round of drinks arrived.

"After the war, he says, his father had an important position with the GDR. But then, in the early sixties, he disappeared. Dieter himself was something of a gadfly. He had a lot of trouble with the state. Particularly with a man named General Hoffman. He tried to escape, though his story isn't completely clear to me. His sister had made it and he tried in '81. He talks about barbed wire, snow, dogs. He was caught. Put in prison for eight years. From 1982 to 1990. In 1990, he began rehabilitation. But then reunification came. They have tried to re-pay him for some of his trials. They have given him a place on the Landstrat—"

The choppy story was interrupted by Dieter, who now grabbed hold of my father's arm and squeezed. With his other hand, Dieter made a fist and began thrusting it in the air. He spoke urgently and then began to yell one word over and over.

" 'My life has been one long hardship,' he says. But he has learned to fight."

Dieter was yelling his one word over and over like a crazed cheerleader.

"What's he yelling?" I asked.

" 'Fight! Fight! Fight!' " my father said.

Dieter interrupted again. He spoke rapidly, pausing only to drink down half of his gin and tonic. He removed his glasses and wiped his eyes, paused, then looked over at my father and again pointed dramatically at me.

" 'We will not quit,' he says. 'Germany, yes, but this part of Germany in particular. The strength of Saxony is strength. We were once the industrial capital of the world and when the Communists are swept away, we will be the capital again. Saxony's strength is strength. We will persevere and become the strongest part of Germany once more. And you will help us—you from the West—you will help us regain our place.' "

The next day was our last in Germany. That afternoon we drove out of Aue through the usual grey drizzle, the near-freezing rain. Lotto signs dotted the highway. We were both hungover. My father's face was grim, jowls hanging low, as he stared at the road.

"I talked to Herr Henke about our friend Dieter," he said. "It turns out he spends a good deal of time sponging drinks in the Devil's Den."

"He seemed like a nice enough guy," I said.

"Henke says he's something of a town drunk. A clown."

I stared out at two kids by the side of the road who were shovelling large hockey pucks of coal into the bed of a truck. I figured that that was my father's last word on the subject; he had never had much tolerance for moochers or "bums." I belched—the taste of the morning's pork rising up in my mouth—and was surprised when my father spoke again.

"But you know, Henke says that Dieter's story is true. He's had a hard life, one long fight of a life. And even if he's a clown, he says some good things."

I nodded. We passed a rest area. Porto-potties and patches of litter.

"He's right, you know," my father said. He spoke quietly now, as if talking to himself. "If you don't quit, you always win. No matter what they throw at you. You win because the other guy eventually quits. You can't ever quit."

I nodded in agreement at what was essentially the family motto. *You can't ever quit.*

At the time, these seemed words to cling to, and to some extent they still do. But of course my father would quit, or at least his body would, less than three years later when he was only fifty-six. During the time that remained, his great pride would be the purchase of Ernst Gessner Textilmaschinen in January 1993, just a year after our trip together. The Treuhand accepted the forceful, though somewhat low, offer made by a coalition he headed, the coalition that included Herr Henke and several other communist managers whom my father dubbed "instant capitalists."

After my father got sick, I often found myself thinking about our trip to Germany. For the first thirty years of my life, I played the child to his adult, but during his last weeks, when he was restricted to his hospice bed, our roles were reversed. I became the parent, helping him to the bathroom, emptying his urinal, hand feeding him grilled hotdogs (the one thing he could stomach after chemo), finally lifting his emaciated form off of the bed so that we could change the sheets.

Both of these phases have the disadvantage of unevenness, of one figure being relatively powerful and the other relatively helpless. But what I'm thankful for today is that there was another phase, a phase that began on that trip to Aue, a time when we were as close as we'd ever get to being on even ground. Sometimes when I get melancholy, I imagine what might have been: a period of years, not months. But if that time didn't last long enough, I'm thankful to have had it at all. Thankful to have been, however briefly, my father's equal, or at least his near-equal, and, for a short while, something like my father's friend.

On Creating Nonfiction

1. Going Home Again

When my wife and I returned to Cape Cod in 1997, we were returning not just to a *landscape* I'd written a book about, but to human beings I'd turned into characters as well. "Congratulations on your novel," friends would say and I'd nod and take it as a compliment. My book was meant to read like a novel, after all, and I'd hoped to use novelistic techniques to show how the narrator—who just happened to be me—had changed over the course of an earlier year on the Cape.

But there was one catch. The book *wasn't* a novel. Rather it was, theoretically at least, nonfiction, which meant that my "characters" were based on actual people: friends, family, neighbors. Of course I had taken the memoirist's usual license with other people's lives, twisting and turning them to fit my purposes—"You nonfiction guys are the biggest liars," says a novelist friend of mine—but given that, I had tried to write as honestly as I could. During the months after our return, I would learn some lessons about honesty as an actual policy. And about sensitivity. "If you write about people and say they are beautiful, smart, and wise, they'll be okay with it," observed my wife. "But if you write about them and say they are beautiful, smart, and wise, and occasionally get in bad moods, they'll hate you."

Even before we moved back, there was the problem of my mother. She had never read a word of my writing before the book came out, and though I was apprehensive because of the book's portrayal of my father,

I was also excited to find out what she thought of it. The day the book was released, she bought it at a store in North Carolina and read it straight through in a night. This I would learn later. I didn't find out immediately because she didn't call me. For two days I waited until the phone finally rang. It would turn out that she had been very affected emotionally and has come to love, or at least like, the book, despite its warts-and-all portrayal of our family. But what I heard coming through the phone line that day was the kind of qualified, restrained praise that my writerly (read: paranoid) ear knew as criticism. And, after a general heaping on of half-hearted compliments, she did let it slip that two things bothered her. Expecting a scathing critique of my filial disloyalty, her actual complaints surprised me. First, she was angry at me for having transformed her beloved summer home into an overgrown shack. Relieved, I prattled on about "poetic license" and how—since the book was called "A Wild, Rank Place," after all—I couldn't very well appear to be living in the lap of luxury. (I would have thought that this would have been a relatively minor objection, confined only to the homeowner, until my aunt told me about her surprisingly violent reaction to my description. She had spent summers in our house as a teenager and had romanticized the place and didn't want anyone editing her dreams. She threw the book across the room three times on her first reading.)

My mother's second complaint came from my comparing her to Walt Whitman. I wrote:

If my father was the mad Ahab of this house, trying to instill his vision of order as he ripped out roots and mowed the lawn, my mother is our Whitman, loafing on the grass and singing a song of physical pleasure.

Like Whitman, she loves to brag.

"Have I talked to you since my check up?" she asked me once before my father got sick. "My doctor said, 'I can't believe this. You're so healthy. You've got ninety-nine percent good cholesterol, and the blood pressure of a baby.' He's right, you know. I'm as healthy as a goddamn horse."

Hers is a strange sort of bragging—happy and unselfconscious. It makes people like her.

I thought this was a tribute to my mother. Her response: "I never said 'I'm as healthy as a goddamn horse'—you make me sound like a truck driver." My sister later testified that she had heard my mother use that phrase at least sixteen times, but no matter. What my mother said next really caught me off guard.

"I can't believe you said I was like that airhead Whitman," she complained.

That airhead Whitman. I had somehow imagined that being compared to America's greatest poet was a compliment.

As I say, my mother has come to appreciate the book—which makes me very happy—but there were other problems. Houses again got me in trouble. I had written honestly about some of my neighbors, specifically about what I thought of the buildings they lived in. The truth was that I was fond of most of the people on Sesuit Neck, just not some of their choices in architecture. It didn't help matters that my mother's hobby, when she returned for the summer, was telling everyone she met just which houses I had been referring to, like a cryptographer decoding that which I'd so carefully coded. Still, other than a couple uncomfortable moments at the post office, and a few overly hardy handshakes and fake smiles, there were no incidents, which is to say they didn't chase after me with torches and drive me out of town. I did hear several direct complaints about the title, however. People objected to my having used a crude word like "rank" in a title describing their beloved Cape Cod. To those I responded defensively, and still do, challenging anyone to come down to my house at low tide and not have the word pop into mind.

There were problems closer to home. In my wisdom, I had chosen to write about our enormous and occasionally violent neighbor, Todd, an ex-boxer. I liked Todd, and still like him, and I hoped that that affection would show through in my writing so that, if he ever read it, he would choose not to kill me. His was one of several names that I decided to change at the last minute and so, in my efforts at disguise, I kept the physical descriptions, as well as the fact that he lived next door, exactly the same, while cleverly changing his name to "Seth." "That'll fool him," said Nina, rolling her eyes. Todd, for his part, remained perfectly friendly, though he had read the chapter. But during our first weeks back, I, over-reacting in characteristic fashion, was verbal enough with my own fears to scare my poor wife half to death. One day when the lights went out, I spent far too long bumbling with the fuses in the basement, long enough for her to create the following fantasy in her head: Todd had killed me, and, leaving my corpse down in the cellar, was coming after her next. When I walked back in the front door my petite wife had a hammer cocked back over her head, ready to smash it down on my skull. I pointed out that Todd was easily four times her size and she pointed out that the first weapon had been only a decoy. If he'd come at her, she planned on faking with the hammer and then striking with the ice pick, which she then brought from behind her back with the other hand. Despite these paranoid dramatic flourishes, we continued to get along with our neighbor as we always had, which is to say, well. I have long been grateful to Todd for singlehandedly lifting my red AMC Spirit out of a snow bank during a blizzard back in '86, and, as I must stress again (particularly if you are reading this now, Todd), he has always been a good neighbor.

Squeezed between Todd's house and ours was another. "I thought your book was honest," the woman who lived there said one day when I walked by as she gardened. "You may not like houses like mine but it was honest." Fair enough, I thought. The truth was I didn't mind her house and its finely manicured gardens at all, and when they built they had been considerate enough to plant a row of trees to maintain the privacy of our front yard. I walked on, wondering what she had thought of the book's third chapter, the one where the narrator (me again) ate psyche-delic mushrooms and roamed the marsh like a stray dog, salivating and grunting and muttering to himself. Nestled between me and Todd, she must have felt quite secure.

Another "character" (and the word is entirely apt in this instance) whose name I changed was Dickie Buck. In part, this was because I suspected that no one would believe his real name, though my last-second fictional creation—"Sammy Mack"—wasn't much more believable. Like Todd, I had portrayed Dickie in what I felt was a positive manner, but hadn't been shy about showing a few of his warts. Dickie was our town's trickster, and the second day back I saw him in his Corvette holding court in front of the post office. I hesitated, nervously wondering if he'd seen the book, but then decided to do what I'd always done. "Dickie Buck!" I called across the parking lot with a wave. He heard my voice and turned a glinting, mischievous eye my way. "That's *not* your name for me!" he yelled back. And so I called out his fictional name: "Sammy Mack!"

Dickie's typically over-the-top reaction to being made into a character was to turn himself into more of one. Well-muscled but small, he must have been closing in on sixty by then, but he still had a young man's bounce and swagger. Perhaps it was in hopes of having his praises sung in print that he loaned us the woodstove for the winter, or perhaps he was just generously doing the sort of thing he'd always done for me. Whatever the motivations, he brought my friend Hones and me up to his "shed," a full bay of a garage jammed with an assortment of tools, toys, and parts: cars, half-cars, a one-man submarine, chain saws, a dune buggy, a Sunfish, scuba gear. When he met us he was just back from driving a client to Boston in the limousine he rented out and was wearing a suit and tie. But he quickly pulled a Superman in reverse, draping his mechanic's overalls on top of the suit, and helping us with the impossible task of getting what seemed a two-ton woodstove into the back of my little rusty truck. If it had been up to my wholly impractical mind, we would be up there still, but he ran about like a manic elf, laying down boards and running the stove up into the truckbed on a dolly. As usual, he spouted a running monologue spiced with wild but accurate facts of local and universal interest. It was only when he started quoting Robert Service poems that I began to suspect he was laying it on a little thick for the sake of the local author.

I had first met Dickie when I was about thirteen, just after I became friends with the Schadt family. The Schadts had been the subject of a one-chapter hagiography in my book, in which I had deified both Heidi and her son, Danny. This presented a whole different problem, as their main reaction seemed to be one of embarrassed pride. Danny actually was pretty straightforward, and I think he liked being inside the pages of a book. But Heidi could never quite get around to letting me know how she really felt, even after a few drinks, though she kept threatening to tell me all summer.

Today, writing this essay, I chew over some of the old Wolfian questions about going home again. I don't have any answers yet, but for me these are interesting issues to consider. When is it right to be honest? Is my loyalty to actual people or to my "art?" What about being a good person versus a good artist? Of course you can see from what I've written already that I'm fairly unrepentant. "You seem like such a nice guy," a student commented in class the other day, "How can you write this stuff?" I assured her that one of the prerequisites of writing good nonfiction was being at least part asshole.

2. Making a Name

The truth is, the hardest character for me to write about wasn't one who was going to confront me, that being because he was dead. It was no great coincidence that *The Brothers Karamozov* was my favorite novel in college, as patricidal fantasies were never far from my mind. To me, the scenes in that book seemed only a minor exaggeration of my own life. Here, for instance is one of my Oedipal confrontations, my home movie version of the Karamozovs, this one occurring when I was seventeen, maybe eighteen:

I am young and strong and drunk and so are my Cape Cod friends. It is the end of a night of drinking and we all end up back upstairs at the Cape house. I challenge my friends. Sober I mutter into my chest, but drunk I'm Muhammad Ali. "I'll do one hundred push-ups," I crow. For every push-up fewer than one hundred I will give each of them a dollar, for each one over one hundred they will each give me a dollar. There are five or six of them and the way I figure it, if I can do a hundred and ten, then I'll make sixty bucks. We shake on it. My sister Heidi is my coach and she gets a cassette player and cranks the theme from *Rocky*. I start high on adrenaline but a hundred, it turns out, is a lot of push-ups. Soon there is heckling: I am not dipping down far enough or coming back up all the way. I push on despite the jeers.

I am well into the eighties, doing half-push-ups by then, when my father bursts through the thin oak door. We didn't hear him coming because of all the yelling and the blaring *Rocky* theme, on its third loop by then. He is in his underwear and T-shirt, and he is enraged, a heavier Stanley Kowalski. Like me, he had been drinking earlier, and has been woken from a deep sleep. A bad combination in anyone, but particularly in my father. He yells and I yell but I still try to keep doing the push-ups, intent on getting to one hundred.

The next thing I know he has taken a full swing with his leg and is kicking me in the gut and I am being lifted up off the floor. I yell in pain but don't retreat. Instead, fired by endorphins and alcohol and adrenaline and youth, I leap to my feet and then, before I know it, before I can believe it, I grab him by the collar and throw him—*my father!*—up against the wall. *In front of my friends!*

We are off and running through the house (this was real, not a nightmare, though typing it it has the feel of one). I forget who was chasing whom, but I know that we end up in the woodshed—the actual not proverbial woodshed! There he grabs me and shakes me and yells at me like I've never been yelled at before. I have assaulted the father and brought down his full wrath.

Skip ahead a few years to a summer night sometime after college where I get to once again witness my internal Oedipal dramas played out on an external stage, like a spectator in a dream. This time it happens at the Dennis Yacht Club, an oversized barn-like shack where the neighborhood WASPs, including my parents, gather. Somehow I agree to join the rest of my family, which means a night of repeatedly answering that question that every young would-be writer abhors: "So what do you do for work?"

"I'm a bookstore clerk," isn't much of an answer, but I prefer it to "I'm a writer," which inevitably provokes the next question: "What have you published?" I usually settle for a more honest, "I'm trying to write."

By the time I drive down from Boston, it is late and everyone is drunk, which means my father is drunker. A thick rope has been hung from the rafters and people gather around it in a circle. The game is to climb up the rope and ring a small bell that has been nailed to the crossbeam. I watch as a dozen middle-aged men, wearing silly pants with boats or ducks on them, try, one after another, to monkey their way up to the bell. Some succeed, some fall short, but either way my father heckles them mercilessly. The game is pretty well played out when my father himself, to the accompaniment of great jeers and cheers, makes his way over to the rope. He looks bleary-eyed and stewed, and I feel more than a tingle of apprehension. It should have occurred to me that he would try—of course he would try—he was too competitive not to. He'd been a jock once, not a jock the way my mother was, naturally gifted, but a scrapper, the only lefty shortstop in the history of South High in Worcester, and a gritty guard on the basketball team. But now he rarely lifts anything heavier than a beer, and his gut bulges over his belt.

He holds the rope in one hand and tests the tension, then looks up to the far-off ceiling in his great, comic, exaggerated way, as if he were about to climb a beanpole. But his face changes entirely as he grabs the rope with both hands and launches himself off the ground. He makes it up about one arm's length, enough so his feet don't touch the floor, but that is it. Some people hoot and hiss; others cheer. He pulls on that rope and he pulls but he can't move upward. His arms, and even his considerable will, are no match for his bulk. But he, being who he is, won't let go. If he isn't going to move up he certainly isn't going to go down. As he strains to hold on, his round bald head turning tomato red, the cheering and jeering stop. Everyone grows uncomfortable, then silent, in the presence of this raw, bald effort. "Dad, let it go!" I want to yell, but say nothing. Finally, he makes one last desperate effort to reach up and what has been melodramatic becomes obscene. He falls hard and backward, and hits his back and head on the wood floor. People gasp and run to him. I get there first, pretty sure he's dead. But then—just as he had after being hit with Nathan's Frisbee—he jumps up and brushes himself off to show he is okay. Soon his hands are wrapped around a Schlitz.

The rope game is over and the space around the rope, which before was a circular stage, fills in with people. With a beer in my hand, I walk over to the rope and test the tension, just as my father had. I know it would take me all of three seconds to pull myself up to that bell and a part of me wants to do it, to show him up. But of course I don't.

By the time I finally got around to writing about my father, our relationship was much more stable, even loving. Still, my grandmother never forgave me for my portrayal of her son. In my defense, I thought about it long and hard, and sweated over it, before committing him to paper. In the end, my first book centered on my father as much as it did on me. My father died just as I was finishing the book, and I wrote the descriptions of his funeral almost as it happened. And this is where writing about real people was most challenging. The book was dedicated to my father and a big part of what motivated the writing was trying to preserve my memories of him, but I didn't see much use in preserving dishonest or watered-down memories. Yes, I wanted it to be a fair portrait—after all, he wasn't there to fight back—but I didn't want to do a milquetoast portrait or a sappy cancer book, a kind of Gessner-Lite, and, I've convinced myself, he wouldn't have wanted that either. My father would have sneered at the line on the book's jacket describing Cape Cod as a "sandy, wind-swept enchantress." I doubt my father ever thought of Cape Cod as an enchantress and I've never thought of it that way either. In fact, that's one reason I called the book by its much-maligned title. That title came from Thoreau: "It is a wild, rank place, and there is no flattery in it." I like the no flattery part and thought my father would have, too.

In the end, I tried to take what he had taught me—his humor, his bluntness, his honesty—and use it to describe him. In fact, if, as I suggested before, the narrator of the book changes in a novelistic fashion as the year on the Cape progresses, I think the change is that his own voice becomes less effete and literary and more blunt and straightforward. More like his father's. Finally, I think my father would have seen something Oedipaly appropriate about my making my name over his dead body.

There was one last sticky issue about telling the truth, or at least, my version of the truth. While my book was often shelved in the nature sections, it was distinct from its neighbors there in the fact that it had a lot of drinking in it. There was no getting around the fact that my father drank, and to de-booze his story would have been to leave out one of the often troubling, and occasionally delightful, aspects of his personality. One difference between my Western friends and my Eastern ones was that my friends out West never had the chance to know my father. By "know," I mean they never had a chance to be out on the back deck of the Cape house while the wind swirled around and he pontificated and told blunt jokes and philosophized and drank vodka and red wine. I felt I had to include this in my portrait of him—and I did. While I knew that it would offend my grandmother and upset my mother, to *not* include it would have been to give a dishonest portrait of an essentially honest man.

Regarding this, I'll mention one final detail. *Publisher's Weekly* ran a review in February, long before anyone in my family had gotten their hands on the book. It was a good enough review, but it frightened my mother. The review described my father as "fastidious by day, refulgent by night." None of us knew right off exactly what refulgent meant, but we of course assumed it was being used as a synonym for "drunk."

In fact—and I quote from my *American Heritage Dictionary*—it means "Shining radiantly, brilliant, resplendent."

I now like to use the word "refulgent" in conversation.

3. *Creative Nonfiction, Inc.*

The book I wrote about my father, and the stuff I still write—essays, memoir, nature writing, and usually some mixture of all of these—has come to be called "creative nonfiction." The phrase has been commodified to the extent that you half expect some writers to say that they work for CREATIVE NONFICTION, INC. But if I chafe at the way it has become a professional category (even more than nature writing), I have also both benefited from and been reassured by the "invention" of this not-new but newly named genre.

Like most ambitious young writers, I set out to write the great American novel, and for a decade after graduating from college I slammed my head against that particular wall. Rather than go directly to writing school, I used a template from an earlier century. Retiring to my garret, I wrote three novels in solitude with no audience except the publishers—or more likely slush-pile interns—who rejected them. It wasn't until I was thirty that I took a writing workshop, and I think the class helped me despite the sadism of the professor. By finally showing my work to others, I learned that my sentences were not as precious as porcelain. The day my first story was to be discussed, I went into class proud, sure that what followed would be a confirmation of my deepest beliefs, forgetting once again the lessons of hubris that life seemed intent on teaching me over and over. I was lifted up even further when a woman came up to me before class and said she "really liked" what I'd written.

What I'd written was a thirty-page, single-spaced, autobiographical piece that I hoped would be funny. What I didn't understand yet was that the program I'd stumbled into favored "experimental" writing, and turned its nose up at the faintest whiff of plot or character. The teacher, who was about to pass judgement on my work, was a bitter little man with a bad complexion named Steiner whose own "experimental" work was read by at least six or seven other people, most of them also experimental writers, all around the country. It would turn out that Steiner was heir to a cleaning-detergent fortune and would retire to Nevada to write his obscure masterpieces, but at the time he hadn't inherited his money yet and was angry about having to teach. He took out that bitterness on his students.

He asked the class what they thought of my work and they started in gently. Phrases that I would soon recognize as standard workshop fare like "What exactly is the character trying to say here?" Usually this could go on for some time, but Steiner abruptly interrupted the students. "How old do we think this protagonist is?" he asked. The class looked at me and figured rightly that I was about thirty, and so guessed my character was also thirty. "I would say younger," Steiner decreed. Someone guessed "twenty-eight" and he said younger still. They seemed ready to quit at "twenty-five" but Steiner pushed them. "Decidedly younger," he said. The game of workshops is to guess what the teacher wants and now the class was on to it. Like a crazed reverse auctioneer Steiner drove them all the way down to "seventeen."

When that was done, he cleared his throat and made his pronouncement.

"I would have to say that for thirty single-spaced pages we are trapped in the mind of a seventeen-year-old self-obsessed adolescent boy."

He launched into a lecture about how this sort of autobiographical writing wasn't really writing at all, just soiled, pathetic confession. After he was done, my classmates, as they were trained to do, turned on me like a lynch mob. The torture of workshops is compounded by the fact that you are not allowed to speak and defend yourself, but I had nothing to say anyway. I opened myself to what was happening; it was all I could do not to throw my arms out as if on a cross. When the class ended, I was still fighting back tears.

But I didn't start to bawl and I didn't punch Steiner in the mouth either. Instead I walked up to him where he was sitting after everyone else had left. "Can I ask you one question?" I said. He looked up at me and nodded yes.

"I know you didn't like the piece much," I said. "But did you think it was funny?"

"What?" he asked.

"Did you think what I wrote was funny?"

He looked at me as if I were speaking a language he didn't understand.

"Yes, I suppose," he said finally. "It was funny."

I thanked him and left.

After eight years of hiding my work, I had had my first real taste of criticism.

To my credit, I think, I went right back to work, completing the novel that the piece was a part of. It wasn't until I had begun my next book that I considered switching genres, and I'm not afraid to admit that some calculation factored into my crossover into the field of creative nonfiction. The unpublished manuscripts were starting to stack up, when another teacher, whom I greatly respected, suggested I might consider writing the new book as nonfiction. This was partly because he thought my material was better suited to it, but also because he knew nonfiction would give me a better chance of actually seeing my work in print.

"Our motives are always mixed," said Samuel Johnson. Whatever nudged me toward nonfiction, I felt remarkably freed by the genre. It was like coming home. It let me cut to the chase, get to the root of what I'd been circling around. Suddenly, looking back, there was a certain ugly duckling feel to my years writing fiction. And I realized that the writers I admired most—from Montaigne to Samuel Johnson to Thoreau to Emerson to Walter Jackson Bate to Ed Abbey—had been primarily writers of nonfiction. I'd always had a sweet tooth for biography and autobiography, garnering hints on how to live from the lives of others, and I found that, not surprisingly, I liked writing the same stuff I read. Kurt Vonnegut once wrote something to the effect that when he tried to write nonfiction his words were wooden, but when he wrote fiction his imagination was set free. For me the opposite was true. I imagined more in my nonfiction. As I wrote about my father's death, I began to see him for what he was: a blunt, no-nonsense businessman whose credo was "no more bullshit." That became my credo, too. And, as my father forever lost his voice, I found that my nonfiction voice began to sound more blunt and powerful. A voice suspiciously like his.

4. My Left Nut

A dismasted man never entirely loses the feeling of his old spar, but it will be still pricking him at times. —MELVILLE, *Moby-Dick*

At the same time that this "new" genre has come into vogue, it has simultaneously come under attack. Over the last decade, more than a few self-styled cultural thinkers (i.e., magazine writers) have decided that the rise of memoir signals the end of civilization. These critics (like any dogmatist who denigrates an entire genre of writing—who says, for instance, that the novel is dead or that poetry has outlived its usefulness or that he is "sick of nature") usually make their attacks out of a desire for attention, not as the result of real thought.

There has been much fretting. Take, for example, James Wolcott of *Vanity Fair*, who a while back launched a broadside against my genre. Using the lingerie- and perfume-filled soapbox of his own magazine, he decided to pick on a small literary journal called, appropriately enough, *Creative Nonfiction*. While he mostly spared the name writers who appear in the journal's pages—Annie Dillard, John McPhee, Tobias Wolfe—he made a point of bravely attacking the young, unknown writers who sometimes share the pages with the big shots. In short, he saw these newcomers as whiny narcissists, navel-gazers who wrote about victim subjects like child abuse or cancer or watching their fathers die.

Of course, as one of those whiny navel-gazing narcissists, I take offense. At the time Mr. Wolcott's article came out, one of the highlights of my fledgling literary career had been the publication of a piece in *Creative Nonfiction*, a piece, not incidentally, about recovering from cancer while watching my father die from the same. Since I am the sort of creature who apparently haunts Mr. Wolcott's pure literary nightmares, I thought it might be worth indulging in some self-examination—in a fashion characteristic of my kind and sure to make him cringe—and seeing if I am guilty as charged.

If I were to serve as a prosecutor and attack myself—the mealy, little memoirist—I would center my case around the defendant's obsession with his own missing testicle. I would point out that, in his first two books, the defendant has gone on and on, ad nauseum, about the gonad in question. Having lost said testicle during a relatively minor bout of cancer, the defendant has since shaped it into a thousand metaphors: from a fleshy boulder he was forever doomed to roll like Sisyphus to a crystal ball in which he saw his cancerous future. "I sing a song of myself," the accused once wrote, "Of myself and my testicle I sing." And, "I want to do for testicles what Melville did for whales." Furthermore, I would argue that the defendant clung—and continues to cling, as this essay demonstrates—to his testicular security blanket, leaning on it like a soft crutch. All so that he can play the oh-so-poor victim.

I would also charge that the defendant is guilty of an even more crass and vile crime. That is, he used his illness, and his father's, to gain a foothold in the literary world. That, being an unexceptional white male in his thirties, he knew he needed an "in" as a memoirist and so fashioned an identity as the "cancer guy," all in hopes of being published. Being one-balled, it turned out, was almost as good as being lesbian or Chicano.

I plead guilty to the charges. But only partly.

Yes, the possibility of being published might have somewhat affected my choice of genre and subject matter, but this is as it has always been. "Not in my day," I can hear the old guard grumbling. "Back then we didn't have these fancy writing schools and new-fangled genres—you had to learn your craft down in the writing mines." Maybe. I'll grant that forty years ago many of today's bad memoirs would have been bad first novels. But contrary to Mr. Wolcott's belief, today's young writers don't just slap together a whiny spiel about their problems and hand it over to publishers. In fact, though there are more outlets than ever before, it could be argued that it has never been harder for a serious literary writer to achieve *significant* publication. While in the past apprenticeships could often be worked out in print, now most of the apprentice work is done behind the scenes, in the years before the first book comes out. For instance, I had already submitted my three novels to publishers when I began my first memoir. Those novels may not have been great works of art, but I'd be willing to put them up against most any first novels of the good old days.

The same goes for writing about testicular cancer. It might strike the genre's critics as adolescent that I spent so much time writing about my sickness, my "victimhood." But I decided that there might be something valuable about turning my developing art directly toward the problem of my own mortality. Maybe I was too glib in writing about the testicle itself, but at least I wasn't squeamish. And I wasn't trying to over-dramatize. At that point, at thirty years old, my cancer was the pivotal event of my life: it caused me to re-evaluate, break from my own life, move West, and begin a stronger, healthier life. "Whatever returns from oblivion returns to find a voice," writes Louise Glück. I thought that telling the story of this time, an honest account, might be valuable, and not just for me.

The question isn't whether my subject matter qualifies me for full status in the victim sweepstakes. The question is rather what I chose to do with that subject matter. What I chose to do was work it, over and over, molding and re-molding, and letting it re-shape and finally harden over time, hoping it would affect others. It is a process that I suspect most novelists would recognize, and a process not unfamiliar to many of the current crop of fine young nonfiction writers.

5. All About Me

I understand the impulse to attack memoirists, because I share it. Despite having written almost exclusively about myself for the past few years, I have an oddly ambivalent relationship with the first person. If my father was a blunt man, he was also reserved: He didn't tolerate whining or the airing of dirty laundry. The one time I tried to talk to him about my personal troubles was after the break up of a relationship that had lasted throughout my twenties. I called him and let it all out, the words tumbling forth in a cathartic burst. I don't remember exactly what I said, but it was personal and revealing, and by far the longest speech I'd ever delivered to my father. When I finished, there was dead air on the line. Finally, I asked him what he thought about what I'd said. There was another long pause before he spoke.

"Do you realize how many times you said the word 'I' in the last ten minutes?" he asked.

One of the reasons we are so quick to despise "memoir" is that we are still in many ways—despite our love of the violent, lewd, and lurid—a Puritan society. Like my father, we frown on the "I." To write about ourselves is to have our Puritan forefathers, sometimes disguised as Mr. Wolcott, ask us questions like my father asked. And it's a valid question. When a child of a famous writer whines about his or her life in a memoir that is only published because he or she is that famous writer's child, I am as disgusted as anyone else, probably more so. I can level the same criticism at myself: that I have exploited my own illness and exposed my father to the world, making my name over his dead body. We live in a time of memoir mania, the reign of St. Augustine, where confession is king, and creative nonfiction can be seen as another part of a national orgy of public admission, of sin and redemption both in the pages of books and under the TV lights.

At its worst, memoir is just another room at the orgy, a room where everything is okay as long as you later confess. But that is at its worst. Because if the genre sometimes borders Montel Williams and Geraldo, it also, at its best, borders Montaigne and Thoreau. We can take the very same personal materials and fashion something powerful out of them. It comes down to intention, and to the use of grace, humor, and craft, the things we talk about when we talk about art. Rather than attacking a whole category of writing, Mr. Wolcott and other critics might consider the more difficult and intellectually strenuous task of peeling things apart, of trying to see what distinguishes truly good writing from bad. I think he would find that, if there is value in the work, it is because of the art of it, not because it belongs to a certain genre. What separates good nonfiction from bad is exactly what separates good and bad fiction: honesty, artful writing, discipline, wildness, humor, empathy, and distillation over time.

Maybe it pays to remind ourselves that we are not the first to wrestle with these issues. "I should not talk so much about myself if there were any body else whom I knew as well," said Thoreau on the first page of that fine piece of creative nonfiction *Walden*. Bristling with both defensiveness and braggadocio, Thoreau's sentence reads almost like a direct reply to my father's accusation. Or we can go back even earlier and look at Montaigne, who, when not examining every minute detail of himself, spends many pages rationalizing why it's okay that he is taking himself as his subject. He does this with charm and humor; if he didn't, we wouldn't read him. The truth is, we have always indulged others their self-indulgence *if* they pull it off. That's the big *if*—the crux of art—and I'm sure someone could write a tome entirely about their belly button lint if they had enough imagination and talent.

Who are these people who don't want anything of the personal in personal essays anyway? They must be pretty dull. And proper. They never want to reveal anything or hear anything revealed. They have *rules*. In the end, essay writing is like conversation. Too much or too little self bores, and part of the game is entertainment. To reveal not simply to be revealing, or to blurt out out of compulsiveness, but to mold what is blurted into a story. With all the story's usual purposes: to illustrate, educate, communicate. And to have fun. It is the nature of prudes and prigs to judge dogmatically. To want to keep things neat. But here is the thing with art: What works works, what doesn't doesn't.

It's simple, really. A truly fine memoir must have the emotional resonance of a great novel, must in fact be a nonfiction novel. "Creative nonfiction" is a straw man; bad writing is the culprit. The word "autobiographical" has for too long been wielded like a cudgel by critics. Wallace Stegner denied for a long while that he wrote and rewrote his own life before reaching this admission: "Sure, it's autobiography. Sure, it's fiction. Either way, if you have done it right, it's true."

In the end, it doesn't really matter whether some magazine writer wants to get attention by stabbing the straw man, or whether it's now fashionable to bash a genre that has itself become fashionable, or even whether it's moral for a glossy magazine (that sells itself by exposing Demi Moore's breasts—and pregnant belly) to bully a tiny literary journal striving to build a small readership and carve out an intellectual niche. What really matters is whether the writing is good or bad. Nonfiction or fiction, what matters is if the writing is, in Stegner's words, "true." What matters is if it's art.

6. Home Again

Having come home again to Cape Cod, I feel comfortable working in what some see as a "lesser" genre. Part of that comfort comes from the historical reassurance that there is nothing lesser about it, that long before someone came up with the newest name people were making literature out of truth. Another part is that it fits me comfortably, like the pair of sweats and flannel shirt that I write in every day.

For the time being. Grand statements, like resolutions, tend to inspire contradictory acts, and having proclaimed myself a nonfiction writer I feel the sudden urge to scribble down notes for a historical novel. But while I'll resist becoming a lifer at CREATIVE NONFICTION, INC., for now I'll see what I can make out of the essay form. Updike called nonfiction "hugging the shore" and maybe it was for him, but then again, James Baldwin's essays are more daringly out to sea than anything Updike ever wrote. A genre is only as bold and wild as its practioners make it. One of those early practioners, who as best I can tell never wrote a short story, said: "In literature it is only the wild that attracts us." It is both the tradition of the old and the wildness of the new that recommend we take this thing seriously, whatever we call it. Let's break it out into new territory and see if it thrives there.

Being Theo

1. Talking to Ourselves

We are brothers. Peter lives in Florida; I live on Cape Cod. We both spend a good part of our days alone, talking to ourselves. In Gainesville, staying the night in his uninsured car or a temporary apartment or the homeless shelter, Peter keeps up a muttering, soft-spoken monologue. Coffee and cigarettes help fuel, and sometimes quiet, this monologue, but it runs on in his head almost all the time, even when the words aren't formed out loud.

Meanwhile, a thousand miles to the north, I walk the beaches and stare out at harbor seals strewn across the low-tide rocks. Occasionally my brain quiets and I really *see* the seals, but more often I'm busy with a monologue of my own: speaking my ever-profound thoughts into a Sony M-527V Microcassette-corder. When I get back to my cottage I type these notes furiously into my computer. Then I send them out to people who put them in their magazines or make them into books.

2. Hearing Voices

When Peter first broke down, I flew to Gainesville to take care of him. In Florida I found chaos. "Sometimes I feel as if language has control of me," Peter told me during that first night, and I nodded. He tried to explain his world, a world where people communicated telepathically and where he was being judged, punished, and sentenced. "I feel like I need to stop thinking," he said. "I need to work at a construction job, or hard labor, for a while." Speaking quickly and urgently, he paused only to gulp coffee and puff on his cigarette. I opened the fridge in search of a beer but found instead a scattering of old chicken bones and a dinner plate heaped with cigarette ashes.

The apartment was unbearbly humid. It was also five miles from the airport and every few minutes a plane flew overhead—a frighteningly large noise. Sometimes when the planes passed, Peter would whip his head around and up. Not two days later, I would listen to a psychiatrist explain that one of my brother's symptoms was "aural hallucinations." These began to manifest themselves during his internship in Poland. When Peter rode the bus to work in the mornings, he would hear the Polish workers speaking directly to him in English, discussing intimate details of his life. These voices continued when he returned to the United States.

One thing they don't tell you about mental illness is that it's contagious. I will think this when I return to Cape Cod after my trip to Gainesville. Walking the beach, I'll feel qualities of Peter's life slosh into mine, like water over a sea wall. We're brothers after all; we contain each other.

I have what most people would consider a healthier relationship with my voices. I put them to work for me. For fifteen years, family and friends said I was crazy to spend so much time and energy fashioning forms around these voices, but now that I've begun to trade my stories for dollars, they no longer complain. Still, I write, not entirely by choice, but—as many writers say—"because I have to." Before Peter got sick, I would joke with friends about my "muse." My muse, I'd say over a beer, was not a silk-clad beauty playing on her harp and beckoning from the reeds. My muse was more like an aggressive homeless man who accosts me in a public washroom, chattering and jabbering nonsense no matter how I try to avert my eyes and get away, following me out of the restroom and down the street, forcing me to listen.

In fact, I go to great efforts to convince myself that voices don't just "come" to me. I've always put a heavy emphasis on the word *work*, telling myself elaborate stories about my own industry. These stories are merited for the most part. I'm disciplined and regimented: getting up every morning before dawn and stretching my back, making and drinking my tea, heading right for my desk. I don't live alone, but sometimes my wife suggests that I might as well. On our honeymoon in Taos, I brought along a prescription of Valium so that when my body woke at five, ready to run for the computer, I could drug it back to sleep. When not eloping, I never miss a day of writing. The momentum of this activity allows me to accept the words as a given, but sometimes I wonder: What if I did all the same things, went through the same routine, and the voices didn't come?

Because, for all of my love of the word *work*, there's something about this dear fiction that I don't want to admit. For all my discipline, the voices still have to *come*. This, if I'm honest, is something very different from work: It is *grace*. And grace is a frightening thing, something beyond my control and quite unconnected to effort.

After visiting Peter, I spent a lot of time thinking. What if the voices still came, but they were different sorts of voices? "The right voice can't lie," is a writing maxim that I keep on a notecard over my desk. But what about the wrong voice spoken insistently?

3. *Structure and Empathy*

In his Pulitzer Prize–winning book, *The Denial of Death*, Ernest Becker calls schizophrenics "failed artists," artists of nothing but themselves. He describes how their internal symbols take on the potency of a waking dream or a great work of art, except that there is no objectivity to those self-symbols. They make sense to no one but their inventors.

My brother spends hours filling spiral notebooks with words. Sometimes those words spill over onto his hands and arms if there's no paper handy. His handwriting is small and cramped, and looks like it's being blown over itself by a tailwind. As a teenager, he drew elaborate maps and kept statistics for teams that played each other in a game that involved rolling dice over and over while he bucked up and down like a pecking hen. Though undisciplined, Peter showed early brilliance as a student, and even as a teenager could carry on impressive lectures about arcane historical subjects. Everyone praised him as the most imaginative child in the family.

Now Peter's maps and words are twisted, as elaborately convoluted as the thoughts they reflect. During the last days of my father's battle with cancer, I found myself writing about him in the past tense. Now I often write Peter *was*, not Peter *is*. "The death of a living child," was how one psychologist described schizophrenia to my mother. As young kids, Peter and I shared both a room and a sense of humor, and I, four years older, would put on imaginary slideshows on the bedroom wall, describing ridiculous scenes until I had him giggling uncontrollably. Now the only time I see a flash of his old self is when he makes a joke. Sometimes his jokes become twisted along with the rest of his words, but every once in a while he'll tell a good one, and I'll feel something lighten inside me. When I was in Gainesville, he read me a poem he'd written in his notebook:

Everyone is floating in space,
Especially the Astronauts.

But Peter's old self only comes in quick flashes, always leaving me empty. I have to watch how I feel. Empathy, I've learned, is a tricky thing. Open the tap too much, let Peter into my life too fully, and everything I've built begins to fall apart. I become flooded with Peter. And that's something I can't afford—financially, emotionally, and most of all, artistically.

Thinking about Peter leads me to thinking about the chaos of my own life. "You're crazy," my father told me when I was a teenager, "But good crazy." In my work, I draw on the chaos of my own life, but I have constructed, as well as books and sentences, a web that holds me above the chaos. One of the main strands of that web is writing: Though I often write about myself, my art insists on a degree of distance and objectivity. Other strands are my routine, my work-outs, my beach walks, my reading, my drawing. But the strongest strands of all are those intertwined with others: my wife, family, friends. When I think about all these necessary supports—from the strongest to the weakest—I slowly begin to understand that my brother hasn't managed to construct even a single strand.

When I last saw him he cautioned me against romanticizing in my writing.

"I re-read *On the Road* when I was in a homeless shelter in Texas," he said. "I hated it. Kerouac was *playing* at being a bum. He doesn't know anything about it."

For the same reason, he can no longer listen to Tom Waits. He wants nothing to do with work that glorifies being poor and drifting.

4. A Physical Thing

As a child, Peter, was an imaginative introvert.

I, by contrast, was a part-time extrovert and an athlete. I was constantly frustrated by Peter's unwillingness to play sports, and often bullied him into competing. The thing that drove me crazy was that he never seemed to be able to muster the necessary *effort*. I remember the time he let a basketball roll out of bounds down into the hole by the briars without even pantomiming hustle, and I remember even more clearly how I reacted with disproportionate rage, chasing the ball down myself, throwing it at his head as he scurried back to the house. "Can't you at least fucking try?" I yelled after him.

But while enough incidents like this occurred to paint a fairly unflattering self-portrait, I don't find it difficult to hold guilt in check, at least too much guilt. These are the usual battles during the war that is childhood in almost any family with more than a single child, the battles that we try to bury under the thin, civil crust of supposed adulthood.

My father was aggressive, too. Though a smart and good man, he had a volcanic temper. He romanticized intensity. When he talked about working very hard on something he said he was "going crazy" on a project.

"I grew up in a house with two angry men," Peter told his psychiatrist when he first broke down. Though I suspected that my bullying was part of what had driven Peter over the edge, the doctors assured me that Peter's illness was not the result of losing a basketball game, but a physical thing, like having a bad kidney or heart. Except that with Peter it wasn't his kidney but his brain.

This has been a hard concept for me to swallow, my father having weaned me on notions of work and free will and self-determination left over from an earlier century. But now I at least partly believe the doctors. And I have partly convinced myself that what happened to Peter is no more my or his fault than if he had a bad kidney.

Of course, if your kidney's bad it doesn't start talking to you and telling you to hurt other people. Peter has become increasingly angry and violent. Not long ago, he turned on my sister while staying at her house, frightening her and her two year old. Most frustrating of all for the rest of the family, Peter refuses to take his medication. He insists that he isn't sick and that the medicine takes his real self away. I, as someone who makes a living putting my own idiosyncratic self on display, understand this to a point. But I can't help but see the damage he does, particularly to our mother, who has had to handle the loss of a husband and son within the last few years. Why can't Peter at least glimpse the damage he's done? Why can't he at least *try*?

I still spend a lot of time angry at my brother, and part of that is the most basic sibling rivalry. He may have lost at basketball, but in some ways Peter has won childhood's real game. That game is called getting attention. The quietest child now dominates the family. When my sister or I call home, the talk is always of one subject. I don't doubt that if I told my mother I'd just won the Nobel Prize, she would say "that's nice," and turn the talk to Peter's latest problems. This sounds petty, I know, but we never stop being our parents' children and it is a daily fact of our lives.

While I half believe the doctors when they say that "willpower" has nothing to do with Peter's illness, another part of me wishes that I could inhabit Peter's body for a month. Like a marine sergeant, I would whip that physical thing, brain and all, into shape. I would cut out the constant coffee and cigarettes and take the body on long runs (on which the brain would come along). I would will the diatribes into stories, unkink the paranoid spiels and iron them into essays. I would force his fingers to dial up old friends and talk to them instead of himself. I know this is simplistic. But for all of modern medicine's insistence that all you need is pills, a part of me has to believe I could fashion something out of my brother's chaos.

5. Being Theo

We all have crazy selves. As a young man, one of my forms of madness was an incipient megalomania. I had arrogant, secret dreams that I would one day become a Van Gogh of words. After I graduated from college, I moved to Cape Cod, where I found a landscape that reflected my own internal, swirling vision. That fall, I walked into a world of gnarled trees and violent storms and salt winds, and thought, yes, this looks familiar. I worked with intensity, ferocity, and single-minded determination. "Going crazy," as my father would say. I experimented with psychotropic drugs, as would my brother. Since we both thought too much, we both romanticized thinking's opposite—the animal emptiness and seeming clarity that drugs brought. During that first year on Cape Cod, in part thanks to the hallucinogens, I suffered intense depressions and minor hallucinations, aural and otherwise. But, wrapped in the romanticism of adolescence and taking Van Gogh as my role model, I told myself that it was the price I had to pay for my "art." Mine would be a raw, driving, virile art, and if I had to go crazy for it, so be it. My megalomania surged.

Looking back, I can see many similarities between my own early life as a writer and my brother's current life. Lack of structure, lack of support, lack of money. Both of us spent much of our time knocking around inside imaginary worlds, trying to explain something that no one else seemed to understand, and both of us were angry about not being understood. But over the years, slowly, gradually, I began to fashion those strands that allowed me to live just above the chaos. If in some ways, my art—the art of talking to myself—is still close to my brother's, in many ways it's just the opposite. Something I didn't understand during those first years on Cape Cod was the vital importance of control and discipline, of looking outside of myself.

I now grip tight to the idea of control, to an almost burgermeister's notion of work. I take solace in activity, understanding that, for reasons of both health and art, the mind is better off not spending too much time focusing on its own processes. But more and more, it's my brother who dominates my subconscious and artistic worlds. He hijacks essays, stories, and whole novels; he stalks my dreams. Sometimes it feels as if I have a real-life bogey man, a doppelganger of chaos always ready to raise its head if things go too well. During my early Cape Cod years, I had an almost manic confidence, riding the highs of my work, but now my attitude is more calm and craftsman-like. A quote I keep above my desk is this one from Donald Hall: "Only depressives make a golden age; or maniacs create a golden age because the dark brother lurks behind the barn." I try my best to temper my own wildness, giving up that stage for my brother. Over fifteen years have passed since I first came to Cape Cod, and in some ways it's fair to say that I've achieved my dream of becoming a Van Gogh. The only trouble is that the Van Gogh I've become is Theo.

For all the stories I tell myself about work and discipline, for all the construction of strands to support myself, I understand that my brother's situation requires not work, but grace. Three nights ago, I had a dream. In it a young Peter, barely ten, was playing on the Cape Cod beach. He was building sand castles with a shovel and bucket when I walked up to him. He looked tan and thin and had such a healthy, goofy smile on his face that I swept him up into my arms. I became excited. "You're okay, Peter, are you okay?" I asked. "Yes, I'm okay!" Peter said, "I'm okay!" I'm not a blubbery type, and I wasn't crying when I woke up. But I was somewhere close. I lay there for twenty minutes and let myself bask in the memory of a healthy brother. It's easier to control the tap of empathy in life than in dreams, or in art for that matter. I haven't let myself go back to Florida, but in many very real ways, Peter is always with me. We are brothers after all. We contain each other.

III.

Back to Nature

The most alive is the wildest.
—THOREAU

Dungo in the Jungle

Now the spoiler has come.
—ROBINSON JEFFERS

They were poaching deer and drinking dark rum out of a decapitated spring water bottle, Dungo and his friend. In the front seat were two shotguns: Dungo's 12-gauge—he'd rewelded the barrel himself with bronze—and his friend Lilpo's 16-gauge that looked like a Civil War musket. In the back of the truck lay two rusted machetes (pronounced with two syllables—ma-*chet*—in southern Belize.) Lilpo thought he saw a light far down the trail and so Dungo drove in further over the bumps and ruts, though he didn't see it himself. But as they got closer, they were sure they made out two or three flashlights.

As it turned out, we were the ones waving the flashlights. They stopped twenty yards from us and called out.

"Jake?" I yelled back. Jake was the name of the man who ran the research station we'd been scheduled to hike into that day. We'd been lost for several hours, so I thought he might have come looking for us.

"No, it's not Jake, man," Dungo yelled, already laughing. He pulled the truck up to where we stood.

I later teased my wife that she ran up to them as if they were AAA rumbling up the interstate: "Oh, thank God you're here! We're Americans, we have money!" My friend Mark, for his part, greeted the truck's arrival by lying down in the mud on the side of the road, the last of his energy spent. By default, it was up to me to play the part of the paranoid; I wasn't quite so sure that we were being saved.

"You want a drink, man?" the driver asked me, holding out the rum.

I declined and began to explain our situation. The driver was a black man of medium height who told me his name was Edward, but that out here he went by what he called his jungle name: "Dungo." Dungo had the distinct look of an Australian aborigine—"What I am they call a 'Coolie' around here," he explained to me later when giving me an ethnic sketch of Belize; "Coolie" being a term for anyone with East Indian blood. He had a ready but wild smile, and a quick laugh. His friend Lilpo was taller—"A Creole," Dungo said the next day—and more stoic, but his Rasta hat seemed to hint at pacifism, despite the jutting gun. I offered them twenty bucks American to drive us back to the nearest hotel, and soon Nina, Mark and I had all piled into the bed of their truck.

~

What we were doing out there in the first place was another story. Stick to the road, our host had told us before sending us off on our adventure, and so we stuck to the road. Stuck to it when it suddenly veered south, parallel to rather than into the jungle; stuck to it when it meant wading through knee-deep water and waist-deep grasses, despite all the snake-warnings we'd been given; stuck to it when it began to weave crazily in and out of the jungle itself, despite the increasingly obvious evidence that it was leading us nowhere. "Snakes love leaf litter," our long-gone guide had warned us, but as the afternoon wore on leaf litter, specifically the perfectly snake-colored dead palm fronds, was all we walked over. It said everything you need to know that when a six-foot diamond-patterned creature the thickness of an engorged firehose lay in our path, we quickly dismissed it as "only a boa constrictor," shrugging off the largest uncaged reptile I'd seen in my life as if it were a gray squirrel.

The three of us were hiking into a biological research station in the most remote jungle of Belize—me, a momentarily displaced New England nature writer, my wife Nina, also a writer, and one of my closest friends, Mark, who, it was slowly dawning on me, wasn't quite the young, Ultimate Frisbee–playing jock I still imagined him to be, but was, in fact, an out-of-shape middle-aged man with pale skin never meant to be exposed to the equatorial sun. In other adventures—lost and water-less in the Utah canyonlands, carrying a burning crib (really) full of newspaper and kindling out of our home on Cape Cod—Mark had acquitted himself quite heroically, and he was by far the most survival competent of the three of us, having been given instructions by our former guide to "watch out for Nina and David." But this would not be his finest hour. By mile two of our hike into the Bladen Nature Reserve, the brown jays scolding down at us, he was already grumbling and stumbling across the pine savannah, the rain forest still some ways off, the Maya Mountains shimmering in the West. When we veered south, he began to mutter about the idiocy of the trailmakers. In fact, he was sensing correctly that we were going the wrong way, but I just wrote off his warning as more griping. He did perk up briefly when he saw the seven-inch jaguar print in the fresh mud, pulling a camera from the knapsack that held twenty-five pounds or so of photographic equipment that he wore like a papoose hanging off the front of his chest. But, by the time we started wading through the muddy water, he was all but finished, not even reviving when, after three hours, the track finally seemed to begin heading in the right direction. In retrospect, I understand that he was suffering from heat exhaustion, and having since been leveled by it myself, understand what an effort it took to move those many miles while sick, but at the moment I thought him a slacker. More and more, Mark began to take unannounced breaks, lying down right on the trail, even on the dreaded leaf litter itself.

My own reaction to his condition, and our predicament, was a fairly perverse one: I was transformed into one of those fanatic conquistador-type characters out of a Werner Herzog film, complete with crazed eye gleam, convinced that we needed to push further and faster into the jungle despite the growing evidence to the contrary. The dynamic between Mark and me had been similar for a while near the end of the time we'd been lost in Utah, when I, pumped on adrenaline, had waxed poetic about the glorious rising full moon that seemed to be leading us home and he had snarled back: "Fuck the Moon." In the jungle, he barely looked up when I pointed out the swirling tornado of white and yellow—both pale and bright yellow with delicate white outlines—butterflies. He did manage to snap a shot of the boa constrictor, which, after posing for us, slithered politely off the trail, but when he sat down to rest again I decided foolishly that Nina and I should charge on without him. After another couple of miles, the jungle closed in, the cahoon palms canopying overhead and the chatter of strange birds reverberating. The straps of our backpacks cut into sunburned and bug-bitten skin, slipping on a pool of sweat and slime. Nina called back to Mark and I blew hard on the whistle he'd given me, but there was no response. It was now past four o'clock and the sun would set at six. Nina, the youngest and fittest of us, was also the voice of reason. "We can't just leave him back there," she said.

"This path is going nowhere." I had one last surge of Herzogian energy and charged ahead for another mile to discover that she was right. The path simply stopped, swallowed up by green.

It was around this time, the sun starting to drop over the mountains, that we remembered that the most deadly of the snakes we had been warned about, the fer-de-lance, was nocturnal and was likely just yawning itself awake. Later a herpetologist would assure us that the fer-de-lance, or Tommygoff as it was known locally, was not "aggressive," as the guide books all claimed, but was in fact merely territorial, but at the time we knew nothing but what we'd been told. Nina and I turned around and began to backtrack out of the jungle with a new and desperate energy. As it grew dark, we walked even faster, crunching over fallen logs and occasionally tripping, leaf litter be damned. By the time we got back to Mark, it was clear he was not merely malingering: he was sick, a case of heat exhaustion at the least, and I'd never seen him so lifeless. We lugged him to his feet, and Nina took his camera pack, divvying the contents up between the two of us. We set short-term goals, the first and most urgent being to get out of the jungle before dark. When that was done, we briefly considered setting up camp, and began gathering wood and taking our packs off, but that idea was squelched by the look on Nina's face and the notion of spending a tentless night with the jaguars and fer-de-lance, not to mention the bugs. So the forced march continued, the next goal being to get back to the water we'd hiked through. In a day full of worst moments, my very worst might have been sloshing through two feet of brown water in the dusk, smacking a large stick in front of me to ward off snakes, while my boot was sucked off into the muck. I dug the boot out, and we plowed through the water, but once we got to the other side, we all collapsed in the hump of mud between two deep tire tracks of water.

On the back of Nina's pack, she still carried the pineapple she'd strapped there that morning. We considered slicing it open, but finally decided to save it for dinner. By that time, we'd been hiking seven and a half hours and were out of water, but Mark's bottle of warm Coca-Cola gave Nina and me new life as the light faded and dozens of swallows carved up the insect-filled sky. At the point where we'd made our wrong turn, we stopped and listened to the wild mockery of laughing falcons, a noise that my field guide rightly described as being like "maniacal laughter."

It was dark by the time we'd turned back West, with three miles to go to the highway. "Highway" here is a loose term to describe a bumpy dirt road with little traffic. That morning, we'd been driven two hours from the biological camp where we'd been staying and dropped off at the sign for the Bladen Reserve. We had no assurances that getting out to the road would be our salvation, or even a particularly good idea, trading the reptilian threat for the human one, but Nina was now sure of one thing: She wasn't sleeping outside, at least not in this place. So we trudged on, our flashlights reflecting back the eyeshine of our audience, the many animals watching us from the sides of the trail. With the sun down, Mark mustered a new surge of life and was now moving at a steady clip. I walked out front, smacking my stick on the trail, channelling some ancient tribal song meant to ward off snakes—"Snakes begone . . . Snakes go away . . . We kill snakes"—and singing loud, bad renditions of "Rumble in the Jungle," "Jungle Love," and, for no particular reason, "I Want to Rock and Roll all Night (and party every day)."

It was in this tattered, ridiculous state that we suddenly thought we saw a light, suspecting wrongly that we'd made it out to the highway. After a second of readjustment, we realized our mistake. The light was coming down the trail itself—headlights, we saw now. An old, battered truck was rumbling toward us.

~

We must have looked ridiculous as we lay there in the bed of Dungo's truck. It was a scene I later tried to draw. Mark lying down flat, all 6'4" of him, his head by the tailgate resting on his pack, next to an uncovered cooler full of fish, snappers that Dungo had caught in the Monkey River earlier that day. Nina up by the cab unknowingly leaning on Lilpo's machete as we bounced out along the trail, with me next to her, sitting on a bag full of corn and leaning in the window to the cab, keeping up a steady stream of conversation with Dungo, still not entirely sure if he was friend or foe. Maybe I'd read too much Hemingway as a teenager, but I slipped Mark's fillet knife out of his pack and under my belt as I crouched and leaned into the small window. We discussed the various hotel options and then Dungo said: "We just got to go drop Lilpo off at his farmhouse first." They talked in Creole for a minute while I tensed, imagining a long dirt road and our executions by shotgun. I suggested we head to the hotel first instead.

"No man," Dungo said. "It's right on the way."

And it was. After we'd dropped Lilpo off and continued down the Southern Highway, I relaxed and gradually began to see Edward for what he was: a generous and exceedingly gregarious man. I took the pineapple we'd carted in off of the back of Nina's pack and sliced it with the fillet knife. You haven't eaten a pineapple until you've eaten one in the tropics, and this might have been the greatest pineapple ever. Mark, Nina, and I ate it all, slice after succulent, dust-covered slice.

We drove to Independence, a small town of dirt roads and shacks with corrugated tin roofs, many of them blown off by the hurricane back in October. A scrawny dog with low-hanging teats jogged down the middle of the road as if interested in a game of slow-motion chicken, swerving out of the way after Dungo hit the horn. We pulled up to a cinder-block building that didn't look like a hotel, but Dungo took care of us. Soon he'd helped us carry the bags upstairs, helped me cut a deal for less than the usual price, and told us we could find him later at the bar across the parking lot. Even before we got lost, our trip hadn't been a very touristy one, mostly involving hanging out with ornithologists and botanists, but now, in a perfect counterpoint to the day, we discovered that the "Hotel Hello" was the single most American place we would stay. The room had two queen-sized beds; it was air-conditioned with cable TV and, for the first time that trip, hot water. Mark lay still but shivering in one of the beds for a while, but began to stir after drinking about a gallon or two of water. I brought up a plate of fried chicken and soon we were lying down on the beds, admiring our torn-up feet, and gorging on chicken, watching *Blind Date* and *Rendez-view* on the tube.

The bar I found Dungo in was equally modern. Five Belizean and one white English Banana sales rep were staring up at Schwarzenegger in *True Lies*, cheering on the preposterous closing helicopter scene. A poster called "Ten Ways a Beer is Better than a Woman" hung on the wall. Dungo slapped me on the back and began to tell his barmates about our escapades. I admitted that I hadn't been sure at first if Dungo was there to kill us or save us, and everyone laughed. Over the next hour, I bought us each three Belikins, the national beer, and soon we were retelling our jungle adventures with the over-hearty air of drunken camaraderie. Like me, Dungo was a talker, and he knew everyone in the bar. Soon I'd learned about his career as a truck driver who sometimes drove up to the United States, his days as an apprentice in the bush, his plans to expand his home for rentals, and the hurricane's disastrous effect on those plans. In the course of that hour, I asked Dungo if he would be our guide for the rest of the trip, and he agreed for a reasonable price.

We were in business.

~

Nina and I took a walk through Independence the next morning. On blistered feet, we followed the dirt road down to the river. The water flowed dark green and wide. An old rickety shrimp trawler, with an outrigger and huge winch, was tied to a collapsing dock. On the way back to "Hotel Hello" we passed "SHADZ Cool Spot," where music was already throbbing from the jukebox at 9:30 A.M. "Cool Spot" was the name of many of the bars and refreshment stands throughout the country.

Our first task of the morning was talking Mark into going back into the jungle. To his everlasting credit, he agreed fairly easily, despite the disaster of the day before. He did this despite the fact his feet were in tatters and his energy still low, and he did it with a stoic, barely grumbling manner, even before he realized how much we could learn from Dungo. Dungo himself showed up while we were eating breakfast, around ten, as promised, and began to talk and backslap his way through the hotel restaurant, most of the patrons being Belizeans who were working on the building. Dungo wore a black T-shirt with white lettering reading "Kentucky Derby Winners," the winning horses listed across his chest. After breakfast, we piled into his truck, Mark and Nina in the back, and me in front. On the way out of town, we bought lots of water and then stopped by Dungo's house. It was a cinder-block one-story that had briefly been a two-story, its top floor blown off by the hurricane. Dungo explained that no one was rebuilding in the old way, with bay palm fronds, since the hurricane, but they were all opting for metal roofs. I climbed out of the car and checked out the old dory and older outboard motor that lay in the dirt, and told him I might be able to find him a cheap motor on Cape Cod. Dungo's wife Maria came out to say hello, carrying their baby daughter Lasaria, named after Maria's grandmother. Through the open door we could see two other young girls, illuminated by the blue haze of a television. "I get cable now for twenty-four Belizean a month," Dungo bragged.

Once we were on the road, Dungo and I started talking and didn't stop. He began by telling me about his own heritage—East Indian, Guatemalean, a little Spanish, a little English—and how his grandfather had once owned a huge banana farm a little north. Then he broadened his lecture to include a full ethnic history of Belize.

"It's all a mixture down here," he said as I stared out at the dusty road through the cracked windshield with the Toyota decal across it. "You got some Coolies like me and then you got the Carib people, with their music and their drums that they beat every November nineteenth. Then you got the Creole and Mestizo, and the Kekchi Indians." I noticed that Dungo slowed down and talked to almost any car coming the other way, and gave the country's characteristic two-fingered wave to people walking along the street. Then, after we passed, he had me look back through the rear view to study the people while describing their backgrounds. "There are some pretty Kekchi girls, man," he said, and then pointed to a small Mayan village, a rundown dusty place with scrawny dogs jogging up the streets and a single sign: "Fanta: Taste the Fun."

"They used to live from the soil—they planted corn and beans—but now they go hunt jobs. They go drive tractors to pave the highway or whatever, man. Their old tradition is gone."

"Hunt jobs," was an expression I would hear again and again, a small part of that gone tradition preserved in language.

We pulled off the highway near where the workers were flattening the road to be paved. The paving of the southern highway would open up the South in predictable ways, bringing in all things American. But for now the road was still rough and wild. We bounced and jarred along in the Toyota, down the Bladen Trail, past where he'd found us the night before, and a little further, before Dungo declared the road unpassable and pulled over. He lent me his machete and insisted on piling some of our stuff into his makeshift knapsack, a fertilizer sack with straps called a *mactay*, the same kind of bag, he explained, that "the old *chicleros* used." I asked about the *chicleros* as we began to walk.

"They got further up into Bladen than anyone, all the way up to Esperanza camp and beyond. They went out to search for sapodilla trees. Then they took long bags, cloth bags they'd brought, not like this one, and they bled the tree and they made those cloth bags into rubber bags and tied that rubber bag on the foot of the tree. And then they drilled into the tree."

"Like maple syrup," I said.

"Ya, and then they climbed up the tree with their spurs on their feet. And as they climbed they chopped grooves as they went up and then the milk drained from the grooves to the bag. If they get to where they can't chop any more, like they reach a limb, well some of them are very good climbers and they cut the limb off and keep chopping. And then they climb down and wait an hour or maybe two and when the tree stops draining the milk, they tie their bag up and they take it to the town. Then they got a way of balling it until the milk is a rubbery lump, a block. And they let it cool off and take it to market."

He shook his head. "A whole lot of work for fucking chewing gum," he said.

Soon we were heading down the very familiar dirt trail and when we got to the wrong turn toward the water, Dungo pointed and laughed. We laughed, too, heading the right way now, into the jungle. We were in good spirits, in large part thanks to our guide, who was almost single-handedly transforming what had been a vacation into something more. Dungo knew the name of every bush, bird, and tree, and when he didn't know them he made them up. "We call that the yellow-tailed bird," he said when an oropendala flashed past, "Of course there are lots of other yellow-tailed birds so maybe it's not such a good name." "Pyam pyam," he called the brown jay for the noise it made, a good and logical name. "Tiger" or "red tiger" was the name for jaguars, and he was sufficiently impressed when Mark showed him the tracks we'd seen the day before. Later he pointed a stick at the trail of a *bocatura*—a turtle—and showed us the tiger tracks behind it, and he acted out the drama told in the dirt, how the tiger turned the turtle over and "ate it all up."

Nina had always wanted to see a howler monkey, locally called "baboons," and Dungo found her one, up in the top of a cahoon palm. It hunched over the leaves it was chewing and looked—just as my field guide said—depressed and glum.

"There aren't so many baboons after the hurricane," Dungo said. "It blew their trees down."

As we walked deeper into the jungle, the leaf litter increased, and the talk naturally turned to snakes. Dungo looked for a certain tree and pointed it out. "You cut deep into it and it's good snake medicine," he said. "You drink that down and you can go for three days without dying and get help."

This led to other things that bite.

"If a scorpion bites you, you kill the scorpion and put the guts on the wound," he said. "But worse than the scorpion is this hornet we got. If he hit you, man, you dig as deep as you can into that mud right there and eat it, then put that mud on it and you relax a little and you'll be all right. But if you don't believe it and don't do it, you're going to suffer for a long time."

Mark mentioned the more pedestrian threat of ticks, which an earlier guide had warned us about, suggesting we bring along a roll of duct tape for extracting them.

"There's another way to get rid of them, too," Dungo said. "You get in that cool green Monkey River up there, man, and you sit there and let these little fish called billum come over to you. They're related to piranhas, but they're not as mean—they're gentler. They come over to you—hundreds of them—and start nibbling at whatever you got on you: ticks, botflies, other bugs. They clean you right up."

Then he told us how the Mayans got revenge on the nibbling billum.

"They would catch baskets of them and then when the sun is hot like now they laid them out and season them with pepper and sauce and dry them. They put them in cornmeal and dry it up. They use it for protein and they sprinkle it on their beans when they put it in their tortilla.

"They take a bottle of that dry fish with cilantro and a couple pounds of tortillas and some beans and they go to the jungle for a week. We need to pack all this stuff in if we hunt for three or four days and all they take is this little bottle and some beans and that's their food. They sprinkle it on everything."

We walked for a while in silence. Mark had his old strength and long stride back. Nina felt some small apprehension that had nothing to do with snakes or scorpions. Our destination was the Belize Foundation for Research and Environmental Education, or BFREE, a small biological camp across the Bladen branch of the Monkey River begun by an American couple seven years before. A friend of mine had put us in touch with the couple, and arranged for our stay there, and when he had e-mailed the couple's information to me, Nina had recognized the husband's name from high school. He had been Nina's boyfriend's best friend, and she hadn't seen him for over sixteen years. His name was Jake Martin and Nina explained he'd been known as "Jake the Snake" back then due to his enormous collection of poisonous snakes.

While Nina wondered how her reunion would go, I thought about Dungo. I already understood that our guide wasn't an entirely romantic figure, something of a clown at times, and a scammer by necessity, patching a living together with a poached deer here and a lost tourist there. In fact, he reminded me of certain Cape Cod characters, who cobbled together livings off odd jobs and tourists and schmoozing. But if I'd been suspicious of Dungo the night before, I now believed he was essentially good-hearted and obviously generous. He was a man caught between cable TV and sapodilla trees, and it was apt that he had two names: one for the jungle and one for the city. He existed on the edge between older jungle ways and emerging Americanism, something he knew well from his days spent trucking in the states. In his late forties and well past prime shape, he also reminded me of myself, not just because of his wear-and-tear and loquaciousness, but in the way that the land—that is the jungle, as he called the rainforest—seemed to wake him up to a better, younger self. The focus of my life over the last several years had been becoming intimate with the land where I lived, but I felt like a beginner next to Dungo. As we neared the river, I asked him how he'd learned so much.

"From older bushmen. From *chicleros* like Artruro and Santiago. They are old now but they used to lead expeditions up the Monkey River for scientists and archaeologists. I came up here with them when I was young and strong."

I nodded. In many ways I was in Belize because of an older man, a mentor. During the past year, I had been working on a book about my relationship with John Hay, the dean of New England nature writers, who had spent the better part of his eighty-six years rooting down into the sandy soil of Cape Cod. It was John who had put me in touch with the ornithologist Alan Poole, who had set up our trip to Belize.

"Artruro and Santiago hunted tigers," Dungo said. "They got serious faces. Not like my face, man. Like tigers. Hunter men. You don't play with guys like that. I don't know where Artruro is now, he cut his fingers off working at the lumber mill, but you should come down to Monkey River Town and talk to Santiago."

I laughed and told Dungo that on the plane I'd unfolded Mark's map of Belize and pointed to Monkey River Town and said, "That's where I want to spend my birthday." I would turn forty-one in two days.

"You should do it," he said. "You should come down and meet Santiago."

"We have reservations in Sittee River," I said. "Maybe next time."

We hiked across a shallow section of river with our pants and shoes on, and up the opposite bank into the camp of BFREE.

~

Nina had her reunion with Jake and we were soon all soaking in the river, with the billum—those gentle piranha—picking and biting at us, my peeling sunburn and Mark's moles their particular favorites. Jake told us that when they'd first lived there in tents, the little fish had grown increasingly aggressive, until Jake and his wife had begun to bring stale tortillas down to the river, which they tossed far out like Frisbees to distract the fish while they bathed. Dungo didn't swim with us, but he stayed until late in the afternoon, talking about hiking in the next night to play guitar with Jake, and agreeing to meet us at a set point on the trail Friday morning. I mentioned to Jake and Dungo that I'd been thinking about writing a novel in which the protagonist hiked all the way from Bladen over the Maya mountains to Caracol, the largest ancient Mayan settlement found in Belize.

Jake laughed, and said "They'd die," but after thinking about it a while, added: "Obviously you'd have to do it during the dry season. You'd have to stick to the river beds, follow the Bladen to Snake Creek up into the mountains."

"Artruro or Santiago could do it when they were younger," Dungo said. "You'd take a one-man tent and shoot partridges and gibnuts along the way."

After Dungo left, we unpacked our gear in the bunkhouse. The only other person inside was a German ornithology professor who taught at Cal Davis, but nearby, in a tent, lived Rose, a biology student with a deep southern accent, who had been in the bush for months, studying the effects of the hurricane on the bird life. That night we all gathered in the dining hall, its roof a massive cone of woven dried bay fronds, and ate a fantastic meal of whole snapper and pinto beans prepared by Candelaria, the Mayan cook.

After dinner, we lay in the hammocks bolted into the beams of the dining hall and Jake handed me a thin bound manuscript, tattered around the edges. "This might help with your novel," he said. The manuscript was called *Up the Monkey River* by Bruce "Sleazeweasel" Morgan. I read: "The watershed of the river above the Southern Highway is uninhabited and has been since the Mayans left approximately one thousand years ago." The book was an account of Morgan's wild adventures in the early 1990s as he and his guides tried to penetrate as deeply as they could into the unknown territory of Bladen, discovering all sorts of Mayan ruins along the way. It was fascinating reading, and I noted with interest that Morgan's chief guide had been "a tough old tiger hunter." His name was Artruro.

The next day passed in the strange jungle world of the biological station, hiking and swimming and watching birds. We paddled a canoe down the river below a terraced hillside of cahoon, ferns, and vines that had once been a Mayan settlement, the Maya mountains shining blue further upriver through the clouds. We watched a kingfisher skim low over the water with a metallic blue flash and studied a rufous-tailed jacamar that seemed to stop and pose for us on a branch ten feet away. The jacamar looked like a giant hummingbird, malachite green on top and orange below, and when it finally took off we thought we saw a flash of turquoise on its back. Sleeping in the bunkhouse was hard at night due to the wild cacophony of hoots, whistles, and shrieks: the laughing falcons, the gurgling turkey whoops of the toucan-billed oropendala (or yellow-tailed bird), the cicadas sounding like they were playing recorders in a high school band, and then, a couple hours before dawn, the deafening grunts and barks of the howler monkeys that made us feel as if they were yelling down to us through a reverberating oil barrel.

The next day, bleary from lack of sleep, I went along with Jake while he worked on a new building on the south side of the settlement. I nervously walked the same jungle paths that his young daughter and son ran down barefoot. When we got to the new house site, two Mayan workers, Sebastian and Vincente, who had successfully "hunted jobs" from Jake, were lifting massive beams of Cortez wood into place to support a water tank. Despite the fact that the men were at least four inches shorter and fifty pounds lighter than me, when I tried I couldn't lift my half of the beam.

While Jake worked, he told me the story of their first coming to the jungle, with Kelly five months pregnant. "When I first met Kelly she wore high heels and dresses," he said. "It took a little talking to convince her to live in the jungle." Despite her initial reluctance, Kelly worked alongside Jake, hacking out a clearing with machetes. During the whole enterprise, the couple relied heavily on the help and wisdom of local Mayan guides. Of course it wasn't easy. Being pregnant at the time, Kelly would grow so hot at night that she would have to dip into the river while Jake shined his flashlight into the eyes of the neighborhood crocodile, warning his wife when the eyes disappeared as the croc dipped into the water.

Why had they done this? For adventure, sure. But theirs had also been an effort at preservation. "Now the spoiler had come," wrote Robinson Jeffers of humanity's chronic tendency to ruin paradise. You saw the early signs all over Belize. The first place we had stayed, the Sittee River, hadn't had electricity until a few years back and now there was talk of a condo development and golf course near the mouth of the river. The encroachment was subtle and not-so subtle: from golf courses to Fanta signs to Schwarzenegger on TV.

Jake was there to fight the spoiler. He had the confidence of a true believer and he needed that confidence to have done what he had done. BFREE bordered one of the most remote patches of rain forest left in Central America, one of the few to contain mountain rainforest as well as relative lowland. As impressed as I was by the Martins' fight to preserve what was left of the Belizean rainforest—to fight poaching and overuse and depletion of the area's resources—I was even more impressed by the originality of their enterprise. The place they had built looked like a magnificent Swiss Family Robinson of the jungle. Out of the rainforest the couple had carved a camp of several houses, a dining hall, a huge garden, and a classroom for their children, a kind of sane version of *The Mosquito Coast*. But for all that, this was not the obsessive variety of manifest destiny/white man's burden. After years of struggle, BFREE was now an official wildlife sanctuary, a classroom for environmental education, and a important player in the attempts to conserve the remaining rainforest of Belize. Though the Bladen Reserve theoretically was preserved rainforest, the government had done nothing to protect it, not even assigning a game warden, leaving Jake and Kelly to be the land's unofficial protectors in the face of logging and rampant poaching and the despoiling of Mayan ruins.

Back in the States, I was always amazed at how so many people seemed incapable of having their imaginations stirred by anything except money. Was it simple cowardice, or a failure of imagination, that kept people from building daring, beautiful lives? Jake, I thought, was someone who had taken a daydream and made it real and who was living out the environmental convictions that many of us half-heartedly spout. BFREE was his exotic, well-managed Walden.

I found Jake fascinating. His love of snakes, for instance, was not a teenage affectation; he became a noted herpetologist in his early twenties, accumulating an enormous collection of rare, poisonous snakes. (He has kept in close touch with poisonous snakes in his new home, as they slither across trails that his young daughter and son walk down.) On our last night, I learned that Jake was also the reigning ping-pong champion of Punta Gorda, the largest town in Southern Belize. I also learned that ping-pong is different in the jungle. We played on a finely crafted ping-pong table in the open area below his stilted house, and I tried vainly to give him a match. When the ball rolled off into a cinder block on the edge of the bush, I went to reach for it, and Jake yelled sharply, warning me to watch for scorpions.

After the game, I was slathered in sweat, and we all sat around and got drunk, the residents of BFREE trading beefworm stories. Beefworms are transmitted by mosquitoes and laid inside people, before popping out like the creature from *Alien* and eventually becoming botflies. The idea of these parasites seemed to delight our hosts, or maybe they just delighted in shocking us. "You know you got one when you feel a kind of prick from *inside* you," drawled Rose, showing us her taped-up elbow. We had noticed that all of the station's inhabitants were covered with bug bites and it turned out that everyone, even the kids, had had several botfiles. We listened as Rose and Jake debated the best way to smother the beefworms: Vaseline or duct tape.

On the morning of our last day, Dungo showed up for breakfast. When we had walked in together he had stopped at one point and, looking thoughtful, said: "I used to do it, you know. I used to wander around in here in the jungle all the time. I used to take it like a Mayan. Taking my chances with snakes and things. I used to do that when I was younger. I would camp in there and stuff. Now I don't want to walk more than I have to in here."

But apparently he could still occasionally "take it like a Mayan," especially when fortified with rum. To meet us for breakfast, he had begun his hike in at four in the morning. He had even wandered down to explore the trail where we'd made our wrong turn, and said: "I can't believe you guys went way down in that swamp." We told him the story Jake had told us: The week before, a group of high school students and their parents had come to BFREE, and that some of the kids had made the same wrong turn, which explained the bootprints that led us to feel we were on the right track. A few of the kids hadn't been rescued until 1:30 A.M., when Sebastian and Vincente finally found them on the logging trail. Jake laughed about how the parents had been "freaked out" when their kids turned out to be missing. Before we left after breakfast, we politely suggested that BFREE invest in a sign.

We hiked out to the truck with Dungo, throwing our stuff in the back and rumbling out to the Southern Highway. The agreement was that Dungo would drive us the fifty miles up to Sittee River. It was Friday, my birthday, and we would be flying home Monday, and though it had been an exhilarating few days, I felt some of that end-of-trip melancholy. The real adventurous part of the journey, getting lost and found, was over, and the rest of our time, recuperating in a cottage on the river up north, would be anticlimactic. Still, it was fun to be with Dungo again, and we had Fantas and empañadas, called pañades, in Belle Vista, a little banana worker's town full of Guatamaleans (Dungo called them "Guats"), where the outhouse smelled like marijuana. When we got back on the road, passing a man on a mountain bike almost toppling over as he tried to carry a huge bundle of plantains, Dungo was as talkative as ever at first, pointing out landmarks and people, until, after an hour or so, we all settled into a tired silence.

It was the sign to Monkey River Town that changed the day. We were already a quarter mile past it when I decided we had to go back. It was my birthday, after all. On our walk out, I'd mentioned Bruce Morgan's manuscript to Dungo and he said he remembered Morgan.

"He had wild hair and looked like that guy in the movie with Richard Pryor," he said.

"Gene Wilder?" I guessed.

"Ya, Gene Wilder. That's the guy, man."

I'd also asked him earlier if it was possible to see Artruro, but Dungo had lost touch with him. He did, however, know just where to find Artruro's old tiger-hunting partner, Santiago.

I asked Mark and Nina if I could have lunch in Monkey River Town and try to meet Santiago, and they agreed, even though it meant at least a three-hour detour. Dungo was clearly as excited as I was about not having our adventure end. We barrelled down the dirt road, and he pointed to another oropendela as it glided through the rows of orange groves, brilliant yellow against green. He also tried to find Nina her "baboons" in the palm trees, but the canopy had been wrecked by the hurricane, which had hit the area full force, with winds in excess of 200 miles per hour.

By the time we got to the end of the road, I knew we'd made the right choice. Monkey River can't be reached by car and we parked in a dirt lot and were ferried across by a guy in a whaler who knew Dungo. The town was right at the point where the river, originating up in the Maya Mountains and flowing down through Bladen, emptied into the sea, and as we took the boat across, the cool salt winds seemed to blow away the jungle's oppressiveness. We were covered in bug bites, and while we admired Jake's home in the jungle, it wasn't for us. "I know in my heart I have a beefworm," Nina had said the night before.

When we climbed off the boat into Monkey River Town, we noticed that all the streets were sand. With gulls overhead and the breakers rolling in from the Caribbean, the temperature had dropped fifteen degrees and I listened to the familiar rough mantra of waves and felt the water-thick wind against my face. Before long, I noticed an osprey hunting along the surf and I thought of Cape Cod. But this was Cape Cod with a difference: the osprey was joined by diving pelicans and great-tailed grackles and several magnificent frigatebirds hovering above the town.

Monkey River had less than a thousand residents, not a few of them gathered in the vicinity of Miss Marva's porch, where we landed and dropped our gear. "Don't worry, we don't have any crooks in this town," Miss Marva said when we glanced back at our belongings before exploring the place. I knew instantly that I wanted to spend the night in Monkey

River but when we explained our predicament to Marva she said sharply: "If you have reservations up north you should honor them." In the meantime we bought Belikins at her little bar. Marva was a large, stern-faced woman (whom I would soon learn wasn't stern at all) whose pet parrots perched in the bushes and, sometimes, on the end of her broomstick. By the time Mark and I finished our second beer, Dungo had wandered off somewhere, and Miss Marva and I had begun to tease each other. "Why don't you want us to stay here?" I asked, "You don't like the looks of us?" She laughed and said: "You stay if you want since it's your birthday." I knew I *had* to stay in Monkey River, despite her initial advice, and Nina and I wandered through town to find the one communal "town phone" so we could call someone in Sittee who would in turn radio the place where we were expected that night with our apologies. When we got back to the bar, Dungo was there with Santiago, the famous *chiclero* and bushman.

Central casting could try, but they wouldn't come close to matching Santiago for the role of tiger hunter. Deep wrinkles were scribed into his mahogany face, and his full head of gray hair curled down into beard and moustache. It was, as Dungo said, a "serious face," though there was also a near-constant hint of a smile. At sixty-two, Santiago still looked wiry and strong, and he spoke in a quiet, lilting voice that danced between Creole and English. It was often hard to make out what he was saying, but it didn't matter. I understood when he told me the route my fictional character might take up through the mountains, and showed me on my map, and I understood when he laughed and told us that a tiger had come right into town last night. Santiago had traced its prints that morning. "They like to come in once in a while and scoop up a dog," he said. I bought him another beer and he told me how he had woken up once in the morning in the jungle to find padded tiger prints circling the spot where he'd slept.

"We used to hunt them by tying sheep to a post to draw them in," he said, "But now there are too few of them."

I mentioned Jake's place and it turned out that Santiago was about to head up there to take Rose out for a five-day expedition into the mountains. "She's afraid of going alone because of snakes," he laughed, as if this was the most preposterous notion in the world.

We sat and talked and drank beer for over an hour, as fine a birthday present as I could hope for. It was an extraordinary but familiar experience: For the last year I had been talking regularly with, or rather listening to, my own elder, John Hay, back on Cape Cod, as he taught me about the place. Here was Dungo's elder, a link to an earlier time. Dungo, like me, was caught in between: He still knew the names of trees but he also had his cable TV for twenty-four dollars Belizean, and wasn't interested any longer in taking it like a Mayan. In earlier times, he would have been a *chiclero*, but now he hunted jobs, drove to the United States, watched TV, and drank. Soon the Southern Highway would be paved through Southern Belize and there would be more and more Hotel Hellos with bars where people watched *True Lies*.

When the afternoon of beer drinking was over, Dungo headed home for Independence, promising to pick us up in the morning, and we went up to our room to rest. When I woke, I walked down to the beach before dusk, passing by a mob of black vultures that hopped through an empty lot. I asked a little girl with braids what the birds were called. "John Crow," she said. She had to repeat it three times before I understood her, but she was persistent and smiling.

For all the friendliness of the people, there was a sense of melancholy about Monkey River. The hurricane had destroyed the rainforest canopy where the howlers lived, had lifted houses off their stilts and dropped them far upriver, had turned the grass streets to sand, had strangled dogs on their leashes while the people huddled in the small community center as the winds shook its aluminum sides. For these people September 11 had nothing on October 8, and everyone was quick to show photos and tell stories about that day. From one man, we heard about a howler monkey that had tried to swim for it, and had docilely climbed into his guide boat, exhausted and resigned. We also heard many stories of roofs blowing off and the beach was still littered with torn up armchairs and the black stumps of uprooted trees.

For dinner we walked over to the only restaurant in town, Miss Alice's. The sea wind blew, and a vivid orange slice of moon curled upward like a thin serving plate. Boats still sped across the channel and a small fire crackled untended in the side yard of a cinder-block house. Behind the restaurant was a patch of asphalt that served as a basketball court. There was a netless rim and a huge backboard that doubled as a billboard. "Obey your thirst," the backboard said, and then below this phrase, one word, cocked at a jaunty angle: Sprite. At the restaurant, we met the only other white people in town, a group of college kids from North Carolina who were there to rebuild the school after the hurricane. We ate a delicious meal of river fish and boilup (a mix of root vegetables), and listened to stories told by Miss Alice's son, Percy. Percy was a compact, muscular man with oodles of charm—"Correct, mon, correct," he'd say when we added something to his stories—who made his living as a howler monkey guide. But Percy was also of Dungo's generation, not Santiago's, and before we left he brought out a two-year-old copy of *Esquire*. There was Percy with his shirt off in the feature article called "King of the Howlers."

When we walked home after dinner, no lights illuminated the town except for the still-untended fire, the sliver moon, and the one bar, which was where we headed. Music throbbed from the small building, and as we walked closer, we were being watched by Santiago—as he told us the next morning—who was drinking rum on his porch. Inside, a pool table took up most of the small room, and we occasionally had to contort ourselves around the cues. The woman who served us rum had her three-year-old son at the bar and he was soon involved in an intense game of "spider" on the bartop with Nina, a newly invented game in which they would take turns running their hands along the bar while the other spider/hand tried to capture theirs.

The bad news was that the karaoke machine had been destroyed in the hurricane, but the good news was that the bar was full and everyone was drinking rum and happy. The energy level of the bar picked up with the entrance of the "baboon girls," two Canadian biology students who were living near town to study the howler monkeys, and were the subject of much speculation and wooing on the part of the young men in town. After a few drinks, we were talking with everyone and I tried to get Miss Marva's son to teach me Creole. My lame attempts met with general laughter. Mark left a little early to go lie on the dock, drink rum, and stare up at the stars.

The next morning, I sat for a while with Miss Marva and her parrots, Bigger, Ticker, and Wiley. I wondered out loud when Dungo would arrive to pick us up and Miss Marva rocked with laughter.

"Can't you hear him?" she asked. "That loud voice booming all over town?"

She pointed with the broom. "He's over at Santiago's."

I walked over and sure enough there were Dungo and Santiago, along with a couple other men, sitting on Santiago's warped porch and drinking white rum and Sprite. It was a little after nine in the morning. Santiago gave me a tour of the his ramshackle house and told me he had watched us walk to the bar. "The tiger didn't come into town last night," he said. Then, without prompting, he gave me a present. He handed me a machete scabbard that he had made himself out of two pieces of trumpet wood, wound round with tied twine. He showed me how the long machete slipped smoothly in and out. I hung it proudly over my shoulder.

A little while later, I walked through town, the untended fire still going, in search of a bottle of rum to give Santiago before we left. I finally knocked on the door of the bar, and the bartender poured from her one remaining rum bottle into a pint glass while I played a quick game of spider with her son. When I got back to Miss Marva's, Mark and Nina were packed and ready to go. I stuffed my machete scabbard into my backpack and asked whether we'd be able to rouse Dungo from his early-morning drinking session with Santiago.

"Just tell him you're ready," Miss Marva said, "Say it strong and he'll take you."

Nina pointed at me and said: "The problem is *he's* not ready."

We took our backpacks over to Santiago's and told Dungo we wanted to go, but he said it would still be a few minutes until his friend brought his boat around, so we sat with the men on the porch. Mark joined Santiago in an early morning shot of rum, and they both talked for a while about the huge deadly looking spider that had been building its web in the porch's eaves "for some years." I was quiet, knowing the boat would arrive soon and the heart of our trip would be over. Dungo was bleary-eyed from the booze, but I now had complete faith that he would get us back to Sittee, and, of course, he did. I owed this man a world of thanks, not just for saving and guiding us, but for transforming what had been a mere vacation into something larger, something like a journey. As Nina and I leaned in close to listen to Santiago tell his quiet stories, I found myself hoping the boat wouldn't show just yet. For a moment I gave into the sheer sentimentality of the traveller, mourning my imminent departure from a place I barely knew. It wasn't hard to give in to this impulse: I was three thousand miles away from my home beach in a wildly exotic landscape on an old man's porch, feeling completely out of place and perfectly at home. But then, right before the boat arrived, I stepped back from this softer emotion. I stared across town toward the basketball court where the Sprite sign served as a backboard. That sign would be the first of many of course, and Monkey River would soon enough get cable. I leaned back in my chair and tried to enjoy my last moments inside what was surely an idyllic scene: drinking rum with a *chiclero* and jungle guide in the midst of sleepy seaside town. But it occurred to me that if you looked hard enough, or cared to look hard enough, you could see a paved future beyond the sandy streets.

Soliloquy in Spartina

"What's interesting is the way that sunlight becomes an osprey."

I listened to Alan Poole, the editor of *Birds of North America*, as willets flashed across the marsh, wheezing their see-saw comedian's song, and a single tern dove into the tidal creek like a living dart. I'd just driven from my home, next to the Sesuit salt marsh on Cape Cod, to Alan's, a small cottage with a backyard that opened up on the Allen's Pond marsh of South Dartmouth, Massachusetts. As we looked out from his back porch at the marsh, he spoke of interconnections and energy flows; of marsh grasses broken down by bacteria; and of insects, fish, and crabs eating the resulting detritus.

I nodded as if I knew what detritus was, because in fact I did. I was not entirely unprepared for our meeting, having boned up on the classic, *Life and Death of a Salt Marsh* by John and Mildred Teal. I knew that the spartina grasses that cover the marsh are tough and indigestible, and that very little of the grass is eaten while alive. "When it dies," the Teals write, "the plant can no longer protect itself from attacks of bacteria which immediately begin to decompose the grass. From a bacterium's point of view, it begins to eat the dead plant. From our view, the bacteria decompose the plant and change it to detritus." The detritus, in other words, is the decomposed, enriched byproduct the bacteria leaves behind.

Alan dipped into the house and came back with his telescope, which he aimed at an osprey platform that sprouted from the marsh a couple hundred feet away. Years before, he had erected the pole and platform that the nest sat atop, and the birds had done the rest. I stared through the viewfinder as the female osprey tore apart a fish and placed it in the mouths of her two bandit-masked young.

"The thing to remember about a marsh is that it is fueled by rot," Alan said. "What ends up in those ospreys begins as sunlight, sunlight transformed by spartina. When the spartina dies, it starts the process. After the bacteria breaks down, animals feed on the detritus and predators feed on the detritus-eaters. But it all begins with decay."

As I watched, the near-final product of all this rot was now being doled out by the female osprey, fairly equitably, to the nestlings. A tiny bead of blood or fish guts bubbled on the end of her bill, and the insides of the young birds' gaping mouths shone pink.

"There were four in the nest to start," Alan said. "One was killed by rain, the other by hammering."

I understood that the hammerer had been one of the siblings, as I'd witnessed a similar murder myself. Being fish-eaters, ospreys didn't share the cannibalistic tendencies of some other raptors, so that the dead nestling had likely been tossed over and become dinner for some lucky raccoon or weasel.

Our plan for the afternoon had been to see how the other osprey young were faring, banding nestlings out on the nearby Westport marsh, but the day dictated otherwise. Tomorrow was solstice, the sun readying for its about-face, and we were in the midst of a streak of perfect weather that might be called fall-like if it weren't so much June at its best. We decided that rather than drive over to get the skiff to check nests, we'd head directly into the marsh, pushing off from Alan's backyard in his kayaks. Henry Beston had called mid-summer "the year at high tide," but this, the very end of spring, was a fuller, more pregnant time. Soon the browning and dying would begin, but for now the spartina grass radiated a vibrant, almost olive green and the marsh overspilled with bird life: willets, ospreys, gulls, swallows, terns shooting into the water all around us, and an egret, a familiar face here but unfamiliar in my neighborhood marsh less than a hundred miles north. As we paddled down the shallow tidal creeks, Alan pointed out the sparrows in the tall spartina: the bobbing tail of the seaside sparrow and the faint lisping song and orange face of a sharp-tailed.

~

In 1997, my first book was published. The book was a memoir of my father's death of lung cancer at the age of fifty-six, but since it was set on Cape Cod, and had some rocks and water in it, the publisher, and critics, dubbed it a "nature book." I had tried to write a kind of nonfiction novel, and this over-simplified labelling of the book confused me. Setting out to correct that wrong, I wrote a book about Colorado and my own recovery from cancer, focusing on the way that the American West has always served as a mythic place of regeneration and wildness. But once again, to my dismay, the finished product was dubbed a "nature book."

By that point I was truly irritated, and I decided to write a declaration of independence from the nature genre. And so I sat down to pen the essay that begins this collection, "Sick of Nature." I wrote with determination and fire: Never again would I be called a nature writer, and never again would I be asked to identify various toads, leaves, or sticks. But once again my plan backfired. The essay won a little award in a little New York magazine, and it was read by the woman who would soon become my editor. She liked the humor in the piece, but more, she liked the descriptive passages about Cape Cod. Which leads to the punchline at the end of my futile attempt at rebellion.

She called me up and asked me to do a nature book.

~

Which I did, or at least partly did. The book combined personal history and the history of our local ospreys. Ospreys, in fact, were my connection to Alan Poole. When I began to write my book about the birds, in 1999, I sought Alan out, driving down to the cottage in March, right before the ospreys began their migration back to New England. His own book, *Ospreys: An Unnatural History*, had been a guide for me while I observed the birds, and soon he'd become a guide as well, helping me dig deeper into the lives of the ospreys. In the years since, he had metamorphosed from guide to friend.

Now we glided up to the base of an osprey nest that stood on a point of land right above the creek. The two adult birds, taking their usual umbrage, swooped and circled, warning us off with their high-pitched cries. As the birds flew close, we could see their shining yellow eyes surrounded by rings of black. I asked Alan if he had ever been attacked during his field work. He said that the osprey's defense was large part bluff, at least when it came to humans, but there were exceptions and he'd once nearly lost an eye when struck while climbing a pole.

As we paddled away and the birds resettled on their nest, it occurred to me that solstice, as well as being a fecund time, was also, of necessity, a defensive time. Two osprey nestlings had already died and in all likelihood at least one of the remaining two wouldn't survive the year, perhaps returning to the marsh as food just as its dead siblings had. No wonder the birds all seemed on high alert. Fragility, as well as fecundity, defined the season.

Nearing the mouth of the tidal creek, I tried to think about the marsh as a whole. As a naturalist—a word I've only just begun to dare call myself—I have always been somewhat dim-witted. Slow to awaken to connections, when I'm finally hit by them I often take what is common scientific knowledge as something close to personal revelation. But if I'm ready to apologize for my overexcitement about interconnections, it's really only a half-apology. When we read books or watch nature shows about how all lives are tied together we nod *uh-huh* as if in response to a platitude. But it's an amazing and arresting fact, especially once you start seeing and feeling this constant intertwining in your own life. For instance, a couple of months before, in early April, I got excited the first day that I saw the insects floating lazily above the wrack line on the beach. I knew that this modest return was directly tied to the return of our local bank swallows. Of course, you might say, *of course*. But *feel* this fact and it jump-starts the mind. On dull days, on most days, we all map out our lives with an almost linear simplicity, but when things spark electric, it isn't so simple and we realize that none but the most complex maps will do. Ideas and feelings begin to interact inside as well as out, our interior insects keying interior bank swallows. Sure enough, only a day or two after I saw the insects, the swallows were back, zigging and darting close over the rocks.

~

I have been lucky enough to live on the edge of a marsh, and to walk daily across this land-in-between. Ever-changing, the marsh goes through at least four daily mood swings, never quite able to decide whether to be water or land. "Ecologists speak of an 'edge effect,'" wrote Alan in his osprey book, "the concentration of animal life that occurs where two different habitats abut." We live on just such an edge, or ecotone, a borderland between ecosystems. In fact, on a larger scale, Cape Cod itself is an ecotone, the meeting of the Gulf Stream's warm waters and the Labrador Current's cold, the northernmost and southernmost points for many species. Within that larger ecotone is our smaller one. A place in between where life is always in flux, where my every walk brings entirely different sights. Even the footing is unsure, and you can sink down into a quicksand-like muck. Woodland plants and briars grow within a few feet of seaside plants, sometimes overlapping, leading to fertility, productivity, and variety of species. In *Imagining the Earth*, John Elder explores the way that poets can inhabit a kind of ecotone of language: "The back and forth movement of an edge ... is referred to by ecologists as a 'pulse.'" On the marsh I feel that pulse daily, living with my finger on it.

For me, the marsh is a place of composition as well as decomposition. My wife Nina and I are both writers and the nearly constant uncertainty of this land has been a good thing, professionally speaking. Just as John Elder transferred ecological terms to poetry, so I've begun to employ a poetic term for our local ecology. It is as if our marsh exists in Keats's state of "negative capability," that "capability of being in uncertainties, Mysteries, doubts, without any irritable reaching after fact and reason...." The marsh, always in motion, insists on openness. Insists, in A. R. Ammons's words, on "no humbling of reality to precept." The marsh is not a neat place. It changes constantly, changes with each tide.

And so. This dead/live land gives us wordless surprise. And then, after wordless surprise, inevitably, consistently, words come. Words, ideas, sentences, whole essays looking for me when I am looking elsewhere, undermining set plans and projects. Edges are fertile places and my time here has been a fertile one. Not just the books I worked on but my own private ledger. While I foisted plots upon my various novels, my journal's plot revealed itself as a simple one: going deeper, immersing, learning the phenology of the place, becoming rooted. Not that I abandoned pre-planned projects. I still worked on my novels, even finished one, but I can't help feel that the real books were my simple records of the passing years.

My first and most basic lesson in the intertwining of lives on the marsh was an oft-repeated but still powerful one. It was the story of DDT and the way the chemical worked its way down into and then up through the salt-marsh ecosystem. The DDT, sprayed to kill mosquitoes after World War II, found its way, naturally enough, into the water and into plankton, where it concentrated in fairly miniscule amounts. The problem was that small fish ate large amounts of plankton and had no way to rid themselves of the chemicals, which lodge in their fatty tissues. Then big fish ate little fish—the big fish again unable to expel the DDT. Finally, ospreys ate the big fish and, with each fish devoured, the concentration of DDT built up in their lymphatic system. After a few hundred or so fish, the concentration in their bodies was a million times greater than it had been in the plankton. While this was still only a minuscule amount of the chemical—

a few parts per million—it nearly killed off the New England ospreys (as well as other top-level predators, including bald eagles and peregrine falcons).

Fortunately, the lesson also works in the opposite direction. Ospreys were exhibit A in the very first instance of environmental law, and the fight to stop spraying the marshes of Long Island led to the eventual banning of DDT in the United States. When human beings stopped using the chemicals, the birds came back. In fact, the Westport marsh, near Alan's home, provided perhaps the most dramatic example of the birds' comeback. After the devastation of DDT, only a handful of birds lived in the trees at the edge of the marsh, but with the banning of the chemical, and the erection of the platforms, forty to fifty pairs were living there by the end of the 1980s. The marsh now supports one of the largest, densest colonies on the East Coast, home to more than 50 percent of the Massachusetts birds. Many of the birds nest on the Westport platforms, platforms erected by Gil and Joe Fernandez in the 1970s and 1980s.

Westport was also where Alan Poole had done much of his original field work on ospreys. During that time, I imagine that he must have experienced the wonderful intensity we sometimes feel when life is reduced to one thing. His was reduced to *ospreys*, and he would often spend entire days in the field. In the spring of 2002, he had returned to the marsh to begin a survey and counted over eighty pairs.

But now things were more complicated for him. His job as editor of the Birds of North America series kept him in Philadelphia a good part of the year, and his recent survey of the marsh, though thorough by most standards, was quite casual when contrasted with his previous obsessiveness. Furthermore, his interests were varied and he'd begun to think less and less of single species, more and more of the marsh as an ecosystem.

~

Alan has taught me a lot about the marsh, but he has also given me someone to define myself against. I come to nature, to the marsh, for reasons very different than those of a scientist, but for reasons I think valid nonetheless. I don't come here for science, though certainly science, and observation, are part of what I'm after. And it isn't just personal revelations and epiphanies I want either. It has taken me a long time to understand my own relationship to the natural world, and to stop apologizing for it. One thing I have come to learn is that what most excites me is the wildness and uncertainty of places in between. "Life consists with wildness," wrote Thoreau in the essay "Walking," "The most wild is the most alive." Henry didn't stop there: "In literature it is only the wild that attracts us. Dullness is but another word for tameness."

During my hiatus from nature writing, I began to believe that that was precisely the problem with the genre: it had grown *tame*. But lately, provoked by the itch of the contrary, I've begun to read more widely in the genre, and have been surprised by the variety. What I was rebelling against, I think now, was as much a name as anything else. The fact is that the genre itself holds much: a scientist like Bernd Heinrich can dazzle us with biology or an impassioned journalist like Bill McKibben can marshal a book full of facts or an Emersonian mystic like John Hay can lift us with the sort of writing most thought long dead. What has excited me, upon returning to so-called nature writing, is just how alive it is.

A large part of my problem with nature writing is a problem of definition. It has slowly dawned on me that much of the writing clumped together under this label does have relevance—timely, pointed relevance—to the modern world. Rather than wallowing in some small side ditch, it flows very much in the main stream of American Literature. As I return to this work, I find myself using a phrase of Walter Jackson Bate's, a phrase that I once megalomaniacally applied to my own work. Bate believed that, just as romanticism had grown out of the worst exccesses of neo-classicism, so a kind of new romanticism would grow out the worst postmodern excesses. These excesses, like those of neo-classicism, were a dry emphasis on reason, on mind; a focus on games, a literature that had moved away from essentialism, from a direct connection to life. Though a scholar, not a prophet, Bate occasionally speculated that the next logical movement in the arts would be toward this kind of "new romanticism," a vital movement that would grow out of the compost of the postmodern.

Bate was never so bold as to suggest that his prophesy was already coming to pass, that this movement was already under way. This was due mostly to good sense, but also to another simple reason: He was looking in the wrong place. When Bate thought about literature, his eyes focused on England, not his own home ground. If forced to concentrate on his own country, he might consent to stick a "New" in front of "England," but he wouldn't wander too much farther afield. I remember his puzzlement over the fate of Joseph Wood Krutch: "He was a fine critic and thinker until he discovered the desert. Then all he could write about was birds and bugs."

It is in precisely this way that Krutch exemplifies the type of writing that I have grown interested in again: writing that explores the universal through the local, that focuses on an intense discovery of the whole world in one place, a literature directly connected to life, not just ideas. This is a literature that leaves behind the predominantly Northeastern, urban, and academic to explore the country's regions, while being decidedly not "regional." It is also a literature directly connected by line and lineage to the work and themes of the mid-nineteenth century, to Thoreau and Emerson, though with significant growth and change. Krutch, along with Robinson Jeffers, Rachel Carson, Aldo Leopold, Henry Beston, John Hay, and others, serve both as connection to the past and precursors to the explosion of place-related writing over the last thirty years. The word "explosion" is not overstatement. In poetry we have Gary Snyder, A. R. Ammons, Denise Levertov, Mary Oliver, Pattiann Rogers; in nonfiction the work of Wendell Berry, John Hay, Peter Matthieson, Annie Dillard, Barry Lopez, Rick Bass, Ed Abbey, Terry Tempest Williams, Robert Finch, Wallace Stegner, Scott Russell Sanders, Gary Nabhan, Ann Zwinger, Reg Saner; in fiction we have Cormac McCarthy and his many followers. This is not an inclusive list of course; I jotted it down more or less off the top of my head, but it at least suggests the quantity of writers now working in what Barry Lopez has called "the literature of place."

And what about *quality*? If these contemporary writings are part of the same tradition as the nineteenth-century romantic writers, as it seems to me they are, then the obvious question is, how does that writing stand up? The answer, of course, is "it depends." As with all writing, it varies. We could stack up prizes won, but that would be, at best, a dubious manner of judging. It is left, as always, to individual taste. It is my opinion that, at its best—Berry's essays, John Hay's miraculous flights, Ammons' poems—the work does stand up. And it is also my opinion that these are much more than regressions to earlier, old-fashioned art forms.

All these writers share an intense knowledge of place or places and, at their best, return to some of the essentials of romanticism while incorporating science and a less anthropocentric view of the natural world. I know that to call this type of writing a "new romanticism" may not be much of an improvement over the term "nature writing." Romanticism is an easily misunderstood or misinterpreted word, sounding at once vainglorious and softly gauzy. But I think it is an accurate term in this instance, at least if restricted to its strict literary definition. What these writers provide, at their best, is a grittier and more fact-based outgrowth of their romantic forefathers. A hard-headed romanticism. Seeing a pine cone not as a mirror of the human but as a pine cone. From this point of view, contemporary nature writing is as much a defining against as a growing out of the work of romantic predecessors. The modern goal seems to be not just contemplating a nightingale, but knowing its breeding and migratory habits, while at the same time trying not to be blinded by minutia. At their best, we follow these writers along on an adventure as they learn their places. They are students of phenology, the movement of phenomena, the flowering and budding and death of the year. (As in so many other cases, Thoreau pointed the way from his century to ours). There is an implicit humility here, or at least an attempt at humility. To be, in Wendell Berry's phrase, "part of" this cycle is the greatest ambition of much of this work.

There is also a deepening and continuation of the movement toward the local. Anyone who has ever written in this genre has to laugh at the way Thoreau's name is brandished about by critics. Ed Abbey mocked the way we now have the "Thoreau of Hackensack" and "the Thoreau of Pittsburgh" canvassing the country like "vacuum cleaner salesmen." But there is another side to this lazy labelling. It is, to some extent, *true*. What we have is a small army of individuals finding their individual Walden Ponds in different parts of the country, and, if we can keep from mocking, we discover that they are pointing the way to a reconnection with the local, with our home places. As Gary Snyder put it in his famous credo: "Find your place, dig in, and fight. . . ."

This then is rooted writing. Or, to return to Joseph Wood Krutch: "There is all the difference in the world between looking at something and living with it." The themes that Thoreau wrote about a hundred and fifty years ago are every bit as valid now, though we are, as Rick Bass says, fighting for the scraps. Perhaps they are *more* valid as the destruction of what we love accelerates. The American theme of the wilderness and wildness we found when we came to this country—our main theme— was never simply pastoral, it was about how we reacted to what we found and conquered, how we both celebrated the land and peoples, and simultaneously went about dominating and destroying them.

"We want concrete fact with a highlight thrown upon what is relevant to its preciousness." I underlined this quotation of Alfred North Whitehead's recently when reading through Walter Jackson Bate's books. It seems to me that this appetite for concrete fact is as deep or deeper in the contemporary writing I've mentioned than it was in the original romantic movement toward the particular. One direction of that development is a more nuts-and-bolts approach to nature. If the movement of romanticism was originally toward finding the general and ideal in the specific, then this is a movement toward the even more specific. Again, not just knowing that nightingale, but recognizing its primary feathers, its nesting habits. If that sounds reductive, it can be. In the wrong hands, this writing becomes as dry as a high school science text. But to know those specifics while also piercing the essence of the whole, leads to not just an organistic view or even to a enlightened scientism, but to a kind of deeper, grittier romanticism.

By reading more widely in the genre, I've also begun to understand the various places that various authors occupy. In doing this I've begun to see and understand where my own home ground is, and where it isn't. For instance, I've noticed that a writer like Barry Lopez seems to be attempting to move beyond himself, and beyond the anthropocentric, trying as best a human being can to empathize with other species. When Lopez writes about birds and animals he tries to see the thing itself, to eliminate the taint of the personal. I have also begun to experiment with getting beyond myself, trying to understand the lives of our local birds, but I find that what interests me more is the personal in nature, that is, the story of the human beings who are doing the trying. Lopez is involved in a fascinating experiment, but it is not *my* experiment. It is the human story in nature that interests me. The *human* story of a person getting obsessed with birds, for instance, or the *human* story of going into the woods.

In fact, after six years of living on ecotones, I've begun to finally see that the place I occupy, and would like to defend, is exactly the edge between the personal and the wild, where Thoreau bumps into Montaigne. The places I love—both physical and metaphoric—are edges, and I have learned that I need the stimulation that an edge provides. It is from these rich, overlapping areas that I would like to write, an unstable, uncategoriazable place that isn't one thing or another. Mine has been a search for identity as much as anything else. And now, having finished my little experiments in the personal essay, it is precisely to that ecotone, that edge, that I am eager to return. There is a risk in going back to nature, of course, but so be it. If I'm called a nature writer, I can live with that. It's funny to me how much time I've spent thrashing against my fate. Now, rather than rebel, I find myself happy to return to a modest role in a great and various genre.

~

Right before the tidal creek emptied into ocean, Alan and I beached the kayaks in the lee of a line of dunes. He pointed down a sand spit at the tern colony that was thriving less than a few hundred yards from his cottage.

"Three years ago there were thirty pairs," Alan said. "Last year maybe a hundred, and this year over three hundred."

Despite this recent success, what struck me was the utter precariousness of the terns' enterprise. As we walked along the edge of the colony, the birds rose and dropped as a group, then flew directly at us before suddenly veering away. Recently, while checking on the osprey nests, Alan had found his interest drawn to the competing attraction of the tern colony, and with the help of Mass Audubon interns, he'd marked the nests with tongue depressors placed near the nests (but not so near as to be "EAT HERE" signs to the neighborhood predators.) The nests themselves were no more than slight indentations in the sand, and the small blue and brown splotched eggs lay out in the open just like the rocks and sand they were camouflaged to look like. Fox prints wound their way through the nests and a dead loon, a remnant of winter storms, rotted in the middle of the colony. When we came across a newly born chick, it huddled next to two unopen eggs and, as Alan pointed out, looked like "a slightly fluffier egg." The colony was open not only to predators, but to the weather, the whole of it being nothing more than a raised hump of sand. If terns are a famously defensive bird, it seemed to me they have every reason to be.

"A moontide northeaster would wipe out the whole colony," said Alan. "Their strategy is to re-nest quickly, and their failure rate is incredibly high."

The terns settled again as we walked back to the kayaks. They would soon face another night with the marauding fox, and for all their fierceness, they were not comfortable in the dark. Only luck or fate would determine which birds would lose their young.

We climbed into the kayaks and paddled back up the creek. Ahead of us, fish broke the surface and terns dove. Then, in the day's final display of aggressive defensiveness, a tern swooped directly into the back of an osprey that had flown too close to its territory, chasing the bigger bird through the air. After watching that spectacle, we paddled a little farther and beached the boats on a small sandy spot amid the spartina. We stripped and swam in the shallow, warm water.

"If you're going to study the marsh, you might as well get *into* it," said Alan.

We emerged from the water and used our shirts to dry off while I asked Alan more questions about the marsh.

"Just keep reminding yourself of the role of detritus and bacteria," he said. "Focus on how energy flows through the ecosystem."

In March, Alan and I had taken a trip together down to a marine lab on an island in Belize, and now I mentioned the crabs that fed below the outhouses. The crabs had adapted quite well to this human innovation, even having the good sense to back up when people sat down.

"Exactly. Mangrove ecosystems are also detritus-based. They are the marshes of the Caribbean."

We climbed into the kayaks and pushed off. I let Alan go ahead and floated for a while, watching sunlight pulse in lines down the banks of muck below the grass. I understood that my previous maps of the marsh were too simple and, following Alan's lead, I tried to imagine the marsh as a complex whole. For instance, any notion of a "food chain," with a direct and upward flow of energy, was far too reductive. To chart the real flow of energy, you would have to consider not just the simple fact that the ospreys eat fish but that a raccoon—or possibly insects—had just feasted on a dead osprey nestling. And then you would have to factor in the great sweeping motion of the tides, keeping the marsh in constant flux, sweeping in and dragging out nutrients, pulling in larval invertebrates and fish, nurturing them, finally ushering out many of them in late summer and fall.

Anyone with eyes could see that this was a time of great fertility and risk on the marsh. But what was harder to see was the festival of rot that had led to all this vibrant life. Sunlight becoming grass becoming food for bacteria becoming detritus becoming food for crabs and snails becoming food for birds and shrews becoming food for other birds and predators becoming food for insects and bacteria. No simple chain but a wild interweaving. In *Moby-Dick*, Melville wrote of the great maw of the sea, fish devouring fish, but here was a devouring at a dense and microscopic level he never imagined, all that he described but within a few square feet. I didn't pretend to understand it all yet, but to even consider the flow of energy meant making the first tentative beginnings toward a more complex map.

While I floated in the channel, Alan reached the shore and pulled his kayak up on the lawn below his cottage. The sun was lowering itself into the creek, laying down layers of violet in both water and sky, and a three-quarter moon was brightening. Tomorrow would be the longest day of the year. I paddled below the osprey nest again, and the female swooped down until she was only ten feet above me, looking huge and eagle-like with her nearly six-foot wingspan. The brown and white patterns of her underwings glowed in the early evening light. The bird made a couple of passes above me but there seemed something obligatory about her defense, and soon I was gliding back toward the cottage and she was flying back to the nest. Before paddling to shore, I took one last look back at the bird. There she sat on nest's edge, proud and upright, her yellow eyes gleaming, the glorious end of a process that had begun as sunlight.

The Punctured Pastoral

A second before the plane hit the first tower, pigeons lifted off the side-walks and fluttered toward the sky. Not long after, as if in reciprocation, stationery and paperwork fluttered back down with the rain of ash.

The day before the attack, I had been taking notes on *Columba livias*—I called them rock doves, but they were still pigeons—watching as they lifted and flapped upward with a noise like light applause, the sound echoing off the walls of Eldorado Canyon in Colorado. The next day, the day of the attack, my wife Nina and I, along with the writer Reg Saner, hiked several Trade Towers–high up to Lake Dorothy at the base of South Arapahoe Peak. We would have spent the day in ignorant bliss, not know-ing a thing about the disaster, had not Nina run down to town before we left to get last-second supplies. The day grew quickly surreal: We clambered onto the country's rooftop—snow-streaked peaks everywhere, the clarity of quiet, falling water—while wondering if the world below was ending.

Nina and I wouldn't see the televised images of the planes and crum-bling buildings until almost a week later. We were staying in a small cabin above the town of Boulder with no TV, no radio, for a while not even a clock. Our time there had been an idyl, a break from worry. The world slanted upward from our backyard. Each morning during the trip I had gotten up early, pulled on a flannel shirt, and set to writing outside while the moon floated over the roseate foothills. I would take breaks from my writing to listen to magpies mobbing in the trees overhead or to watch flycatchers flit through the grasses, immersed as much in the romantic setting as in my work. Early fall in the foothills is a time of reddening sumac, Chinook winds, and occasional bracing afternoon thunderstorms. "Our little pastoral time is almost over," I wrote in my journal the day before the attack.

We were due back home two days after our hike to the top of the world with Reg, on a United flight back into Logan, which was, of course, cancelled. The harried woman behind the desk at the United office told us that tickets might be available in a few days, but like a lot of people we decided we didn't want to fly that week. Being in a metal contraption up in the sky, an idea that had somehow sounded reasonable just a few days before, no longer seemed wise. So we commandeered our rental car (the company initially responded to the tragedy by tripling their daily rates, but relented after being buried in furious faxes and letters, including my own) and set out across the country. I felt a twinge of regret as the white peaks receded in the rear view mirror, and Nina recalled that Boulder had been the place where the righteous survivors had gathered after the holocaust of biological warfare in Stephen King's *The Stand*. We were leaving behind what seemed like a safe haven. Soon enough, we found ourselves driving through flatlands of tarweed and sage, relieved by an occasional cottonwood, the smell of slaughterhouses pervading the car even before Nebraska.

The great American road trip is East to West, a movement from restriction and crowds to freedom and space. Nina and I drove in the opposite direction, drowning ourselves in NPR, unsure of what we were heading back into. We stopped at our friend Burns's house in Columbus, Nebraska, where he showed us slides of his summer trip to the Arctic Wilderness Refuge and bemoaned the fact that war would spell doom for efforts to save that beautiful land. The next night we had a wonderful, drunken meal with friends in Wisconsin; the next morning we hiked the Ice Age trail through blue stem and goldenrod that alternately turned the hills purple and yellow. But for all the beauty of the trip, we never really got away from "it." It travelled with us, Nina bursting into tears from time to time during the drive. I felt things shifting around inside me. Three days later, we drove up the Jersey Turnpike to Nina's parents' house and had our first look at the gap-toothed New York skyline.

As far as we could discern we knew no one who had been killed in the attacks. Our New York friends all had horror stories, but they were alive. My sister had watched the towers fall from the top of her building at work, but my mother reported that she was okay. I couldn't get through to her by phone, so the next morning we woke up before dawn and headed over the George Washington Bridge. The first pink streaks hadn't yet lit the dark, dusty sky as we sped down the West Side Highway, and it felt as if we were driving onto the set of *Blade Runner*. It was Tuesday, exactly a week after the attack. Nina said that it was wrong to be going into the city and though I argued at first, I relented when an eerie convoy of dump trucks full of rubble rumbled by in the other direction, escorted by police motorcycles complete with sirens and lights. Another convoy, heading back into the city, soon appeared in our rear view mirror, lights flashing in the dark. We were in the way, mere voyeurs, gawkers. This was not our place. I pulled a U-turn, drove out of the city, right back to our home on Cape Cod.

~

By September 19, I was on the beach watching plovers peck along the shore and a sharp-shinned hawk skim the wind over the harbor. I watched the crazy abundance of bird life, listening to the inhalation and exhalation of waves, staring out toward Provincetown and the Atlantic beyond. The year was turning toward October, the tourists leaving, but the beach no longer seemed the retreat it once had. Not just the fact that the nuclear power plant by the bridge would make a tempting terrorist target, or that there was talk of anthrax being sprayed by cropdusters, or that armed guards had been posted at the Quabbin Reservoir to protect Boston's drinking water. *A Place Apart* is the name of an anthology of Cape Cod writing, and a place apart the Cape had always been. But suddenly the ocean—which had until then seemed a moat—no longer offered protection. Perhaps, after the horror of the deed, that was the immediate message we took away from September 11. *Welcome to the world.* There is no place apart.

While many have commented on the symbolic genius of the terrorists' assault on capitalism, we, as a people, were also hit on a deeper mythological level. Wasn't the American pastoral myth, the myth of a separate place, a *new* place, central to our national consciousness? Home of the noble savage and the not-so-noble savages, home of utopian schemes, home of Transcendentalism, later home of the Wild West. All of these myths dependent on our *apartness*. Dependent on the fact that the rest of the world was *over there*. And suddenly what seemed fact was proven illusion. Even the lightweight president, who just a few short weeks before seemed hell-bent on creating a New Isolationism, was thrown into the global scrum.

One impulse in the face of crisis is to head for the hills. And one of the standard tenets of American romanticism is that there are always hills to head for—whether Thoreau's Walden or Wendell Berry's farm or Robinson Jeffer's Tor House on the California coast. It was a tenet that I, settling in for another winter on the Cape while the world readied for war, began to question. Particularly, I questioned my own personal isolationism, my private instinct for retreat.

I understand that the literary repercussions of the event were hardly the most noteworthy, but they were an example of how the terror of that day pervaded each of our lives, how Bin Laden, for all the gruesome death involved, succeeded spectacularly if his goal was to unsettle and overturn each small corner of our private worlds. "Everything has changed" was the sentence you heard over and over. After the initial shock, people began to wonder how their little worlds were affected. The fallout on the arts, for instance, preoccupied many. Blowhard pundits quickly predicted the death of irony (while more level-headed journalists suggested that it was just taking some well-deserved time off). I also heard it prophesied that we would see the death of many other things, including memoir, spy novels, stupid sit-coms, and action films, though the prophets quieted down after a little while.

It wasn't the fate of the action movie that most concerned me; rather it was my own little domain of nature writing. The pastoral is not generally considered rough and tumble, and I wondered: How would such a quiet and countrified genre stand up in the face of this withering assault? It's a standard part of the myth of the nature-writing tradition that Thoreau *retreated* from the world, and it was suddenly hard not to hear the military implications of that word. Who hadn't felt the impulse to run away in the face of what was happening? Nina and I had felt safer tucked in the mountains two thousand miles from the East Coast, still wrapping ourselves in the illusion of a safe place. But was heading for the hills, even the metaphorical hills, a cowardly retreat in the face of this new world? How could I spend another year observing and writing about ospreys or snails? I suspected very few nature writers were working in Israel, for instance. What use was it now to write of titmice or the migratory pattern of the semipalmated plover? Wasn't this a time to think only of war and politics?

~

By October, we were all being urged to return to "normalcy." I wasn't exactly sure what that meant, but I supposed that for me living in rural retreat *was* normal. By then, people had begun to get their bearings. For instance, I knew that I wasn't going to be flying off to be a war correspondent any time soon, no matter how inspired that idea had seemed at first, and I knew that it was on Cape Cod that I would have to regroup and rebuild.

During that time of chaos, I felt the need to seek out elders. During our hike on September 11, Reg Saner had talked about Korea and what it felt like to lead young infantrymen into battle as a captain. The day's events seemed to bring back his own experience in that war. "I wonder if I'm not one of the few poets to have handled heavy explosives," he said.

Soon after we returned, Reg sent me a letter complaining of the country's "unremitting jingoism." "I've been embarrassed by such blather all my life," he wrote, "and have repeatedly heard the media turn it on like tap water. Perhaps the day will come when our politicians grow tired of their adolescent baloney and talk like adults." Reg, having fought on the front line of a vicious war and watched men under his command die in combat, had more than earned both his opinion and his own brand of skeptical patriotism.

While homesteading in Alaska, John Haines wrote of "someplace called Korea" that so concerned his countrymen. Some might take offense at this, but not Reg Saner, who, having had a direct experience of the horror of war, also seemed to have a larger perspective on the events of September 11 than anyone else I'd encountered since the attack. "I know it will sound pompous," he said during our hike. "But the relationship that concerns me is that between myself and the universe." Thoreau had written much the same, expressing a faith in the planet and a skepticism toward most things human. I was glad that there was a tradition of both, glad to have ancestors to turn to.

I also began to pay more frequent visits to John Hay over in Brewster. John often wrote of our human need for the "fixity of the past" and "permanence and stability." There was precious little of that going around these days, but nature could at least give some distance and perspective. John, almost ninety, had a longer perspective, having witnessed the events of the world for the better part of a century, the inevitable flux and reflux of the national mood. But he had little immediate wisdom to offer, seeming just as undone as everyone else. It occurred to me that it must be even harder to handle the shock of what was happening as an old man.

Settling was one of the primary lessons of John's work, and this event, more than any other I'd lived through, was *unsettling*. Other threats—nuclear, chemical, biological—that we'd cordoned off in remote sections of our brain, were now set free to mingle with everyday thoughts. The nightly news, which for so long had seemed like just another TV show, was finally hitting home. It was a time of uprooting for almost everyone, a time when "I don't know" seemed the best and most sensible answer, and only the shallow rushed back to their prejudices.

John had written of his encounters with Native Americans:

The difference between uncertain, anxious, and impatient people like ourselves and the Navajo seemed to lie in a calmness, a dignity of inheritance. As I heard it described, Americans facing danger, real or imaginary, say, "Don't just stand there, do something." The Navajo says, "Sit tight, and in that way you may escape evil and harmful results."

But even those ready to "do something" were uncertain what to do. For most of us, preconceptions were lost along with lives in the rubble. It was hard to remain obsessed with the old obsessions. We returned cautiously to what was once firm ground.

Personally, I tried to resist the urge to simply re-trench, to merely repeat a litany of the beliefs I held before September 11. It seemed to me that the event was, among so many other things, a demonstration of how the weakest, most dogmatic minds were the quickest to run back to their preconceptions, barely taking time off to be uncertain. Witness Jerry Falwell's response or Billy Graham Jr.'s talk of the need for "a vengeful God" and the unleashing of "our most hellish weapons of destruction."

Chastened by this kind of reaction, I made my own conclusions only tentatively, picking through my personal rubble to see what I could rebuild with. It's hard to respond to crisis with creativity, but I found I was a little better at it when walking out by the bluff. One of the things living by the bluff had taught me was that "I don't know" is often the best answer, at least initially, to the questions the world poses. I needed to rebuild on the foundation of this uncertainty.

And I needed to approach the task with humility, as that is one of the lessons my observations of the natural world had taught me again and again. This humility is born, at least partly, from understanding just how varied life is and just how urgent each type of life is to those living it. Two years before, I had spent six hours a day watching ospreys, fish hawks that get their food solely by diving from the sky for fish, and I could state confidently that those hawks cared about catching fish as passionately as any human ever cared about making money or war.

There are more ways to be in the world than the human way, and while that may be little consolation when faced with the loss of loved ones, for some of us it helps to think of the world as a home to more than just us. The bird migrations coming through Cape Cod didn't make me forget the Air Force Jets from Otis Air Force Base that they shared the sky with, but they did lend some perspective. In fact, my own first moment of that much-coveted "normalcy" was a moment of immersion: the sky filling with staging tree swallows, five hundred of them spinning as if riding a giant carousel before shooting off, shimmering black wings to white bellies, jabbing and darting in every direction like hallucinogenic flecks.

To find an older world I headed out to greet beach and birds. In the face of crisis I gradually began to try again to learn from the natural world, while no longer believing in the fantasy that it was "a place apart." By mid-month I had another small success with this when, armed with my bird books and binoculars, I became absorbed in the intense concerns of golden plovers, ruddy turnstones, and sandpipers for over an hour. Then I snapped out of it as if out of a dream. This was an example of the newest symptom of September 11, a symptom that other friends described: the strange discomfort of succeeding at what we were being urged to do, "getting back to normal."

But my hour of bird-watching was hardly "normal" anyway. Looking at cormorants trying to take off in their desperate way, slapping the water before gaining altitude, I suddenly saw exactly what had startled them: a black helicopter from Otis Air Force Base breaking from the clouds. Jutting out into the sea, farther east than the mainland, Cape Cod was, after all, a kind of front line, ahead of the rest of America. I watched the helicopter patrol up and down the Cape's shore for the next half hour, my thoughts leaving nature and returning to the "real world." It's hard to wax poetic about Walden Pond when Walden is patrolled by a copter. "Everything has changed." And everyone was suddenly affected by the daily news. For instance, one night after teaching my class, I slept over at a friend's in Boston. Nina called the next morning to insist I leave early, having heard the Secretary of Defense announce that Boston might be a terrorist target over the next few days.

We were all similarly affected, and in a strange way unified. In this lack of a safe place, we joined not just the citizens of the rest of the world, but the other species that populate this planet. Vulnerability is a reality of life on earth, a fact we have tried so desperately to bury under layers of control. I thought back to the migrating monarch butterflies we saw while undergoing our own abrupt migration back from Colorado. They were engaged in their great and preposterous enterprise, their generational migration down to the hills of central Mexico, flickering and floating in a pattern of flight that at times looked no more purposeful than that of a falling oak leaf. Our rental car alone probably killed a half-dozen of them, but that wasn't about to deter the rest. It seemed, in my troubled state of mind, to be a perfect symbol of the fragility of earthly efforts.

~

In November, Cape Cod becomes another country. Long-billed northern gannets dive into the surf and the cold shadows of gulls ripple over beach rocks. The water, so inviting only weeks before, takes on a darker, bracing shade of blue and the clouds bulk up purple and muscular. As the northeast winds bluster across the bay, it isn't hard to see why Cape inhabitants, from the native Wampanoags to the captains of clipper ships, have always chosen, quite sensibly, to winter away from the ocean.

Our own choice for the coming winter was a less sensible one: We had decided to rent a house right on the beach again. As November stretched into December, and the cold deepened, I began to spend more time walking the beach and searching for stranded turtles. The winter before, sea turtles had stranded in record numbers on our Cape Cod beaches. In the late fall of that year, hundreds of turtles, mostly young loggerheads and Ridley's Kemps, had become hopelessly confused due to the weather. They had spent the previous summer gently paddling in and around the warm waters of Cape Cod Bay, and in a normal year would have begun their epic migration by turning sensibly south after the first shock of cold weather. But last year hadn't been a normal year. Like the turtles, humans carried on with summer activities long into October, even November. Since the cold never came, the turtles never left. Scientists couldn't say with certainty that the reason migration didn't begin on time was because of the prolonged unseasonably warm weather, but the layman, not quite so burdened with responsibility toward conclusive evidence, could easily make the jump. Whatever the reason, far too many turtles were lingering in Cape Cod Bay when the cold finally hit in December. After the first storm, our beaches became littered with dead or near-dying turtles.

The turtle news from the year before had not been entirely depressing. On December 15, Nina and I were returning from a run at twilight, walking back to our house along the beach. Nina later heaped much credit on me for "discovering" the turtle, but the truth is I almost tripped over it. I was walking on the flat, hard sand of low tide and thinking about nothing when I stumbled upon a rock where there had never been a rock.

In the gloaming, the shape loomed dark, vague, large, and it took a moment of staring and eye adjustment for me to understand what I was seeing. It was a sea turtle, a 48-pound loggerhead it later turned out, with a shell twice the diameter of a garbage-can lid and no real business swimming around in our northern waters at that time of year. The turtle looked near death and pushing him back in the water would have killed him. If it had been mid-day, we would have marked the spot, wrapped him in seaweed, and headed home to call the Mass Audubon Society's Welfleet Bay Wildlife Sanctuary, as our friends up at Audubon had instructed us. But since it was almost night, I decided we should try to get it back home ourselves.

The plan was for Nina to run ahead and call the Sanctuary while I wrestled the turtle down the beach. It didn't move at all when I hefted it up against my chest, carrying it with hands below and leaning it into my chest the way a schoolgirl might carry a tall pile of books. It was cold and covered with seaweed and one thing I learned quickly about turtles is that they reek. (I never did get the reptilian odor out of my coat.) I looked down at the shell leaning against my stomach, studying the turtle as best I could, as I walked. Its head was much bigger than you'd expect and pointed like a bird toward a beak of a mouth; its eyes remained closed and squinty, and its enormous flippers hung down by the sides of its shell. The color, in the fading light, glowed burnished orange; the skin was hard, wrinkled, and leathery like my father's high school baseball mit.

The first sign of life was sudden and startling. The turtle lifted one flipper, then another. The orange of the flippers was divided up like puzzle pieces, as if it were made of a hundred different sections of rock. I moved down the beach in choppy, awkward steps, putting down the turtle every twenty yards or so. The third time I picked it up, it came truly awake, straining its head back toward my neck, and lifting both flippers up over its head and then down and up again as if doing slow-motion jumping jacks. I stumbled home with my now-live turtle.

We kept the turtle on our patio while we waited for Bob Prescott of the Audubon Sanctuary. When he arrived, Bob explained to us that the turtle was likely suffering from hypothermia and that it would have to be warmed very gradually, only a few degrees at first and then five degrees a day. It would be tended by the staff at the Sanctuary and, if it was lucky, then would be driven up to the New England Aquarium in Boston for further nursing. If and when it was ready, it would be flown down to be released in southern waters off North Carolina or Florida.

The next day, Bob called to tell us that it looked like our turtle would make it. He asked me to name the turtle, and after some thought I decided on Kronos, the mythic Titan who rode atop a turtle's back. Bob told me that loggerheads were classified as "threatened" while the Ridley's Kemps were endangered, with only about 2,500 nesting females. In other words, every turtle mattered. In a time when the daily environmental news was overwhelming—the usual litany of crushing population, habitat loss, global warming—it was heartening for me to take things down to an individual level: one person saving one turtle, feeling for a moment that my actions could have some influence.

Now, in the wake of September 11, my turtle walks took on more purpose. Looking for the turtles was an activity I came to value, a ritual that required looking outward, not inward, as I walked the beaches. It also made me feel as if I were a part of something. Part of a larger network of people certainly, a group of volunteers hoping to help a species not their own. But also part of a larger connection, a web that threaded my life both to the turtles and to my place, this rocky point of coastline, as well as to other places around the world, such as the turtle's nesting grounds off Northern Mexico or the warm waters of the Gulf. The invisible strands of this web were the mysterious migrations themselves, the underwater journeys that were absurd in their ambitions, journeys that barely would be believed by human beings if the evidence didn't occasionally wash up on our beaches.

As the winter wore on, I was reminded that the beach, in many ways, was the opposite of retreat. In mid-winter, I almost tripped over an immature snowy owl while I was walking along the shore. It flew off over the bay with a unearthly screech, soon chased by several terns, always protective of their turf. The fact was that here, on this isolated spit of land, I was bearing witness to a great cosmopolitan battle between one bird who had dropped in from the Arctic and several others who had just circumnavigated the globe. The tern and owl confirmed the lesson of the turtles. They helped me understand that my return to my childhood beach, to Cape Cod, was not just a withdrawing, and that by becoming intensely local I had become inadvertently cosmopolitan. Knowing this one small stretch of beach, I was beginning to know wider connections. If I looked closely and well enough, I could see the entire world from East Dennis.

~

I am not saying that the turtles allowed me to make sense of the senseless murder of September 11. There is no sense to make. These notes are no more than the stray thoughts I have gathered from my personal rubble. They are all very tentative and admittedly threadbare. Even when I write confidently I feel the world's uncertainty inside me. I also feel my philosophy constantly slipping; I picture not shorebirds but the thousands of sheets of paper flying everywhere, paper that once seemed so desperately important, paper covered with type like the coda of the interior lives lost, paper like the one I type on now. Maybe, in the face of all this uncertainty, we can do without grand conclusions. Maybe those of us who like to declaim the death of this or that genre should keep our mouths shut out of respect for those who actually died.

I can say only one thing with confidence. Of all the deaths I will mourn in the face of September 11, the one I will no longer mourn is that of our myth of isolation. The expiration date on that particular myth had come and gone. It has always been too simple, too illusionary. Even Thoreau, our most famous literary retreater, was not in fact retreating but plunging into the world. It's hard to be both a good naturalist and a xenophobe. Nature teaches again and again the interconnectedness of all life, of different types, different species; it teaches, for instance, how the bank swallows key on the return of the insects each spring, and how the ospreys key on the return of alewives. Human beings, just like every other animal, are forever intertwined. The old myth of our separateness is dead. It's a brand new world and there are no hills to head for.

IV.

Howling with the Trickster:
A Wild Memoir

Firm ground is not available ground.
—A. R. AMMONS

trickster in the city

Here is how it begins:

I am driving from Cambridge to Cape Cod to get my last load of belongings, my final trip before our move to the city. I am resolved to make this move, despite some apprehension. The sun is out and the snow melting when I start the drive, but by the time I reach the bridge at the canal the clouds have bulked up, and fifteen minutes later I am in the midst of something just short of a blizzard. Right after exit 8, the car in front of me slows and I slow to see why. There, by the side of the road, stands a beautiful black and gray coyote in its full winter coat. The coat gives it the illusion of great heft, so that an inexperienced observer might think it a wolf. Snow swirls around the animal as it waits patiently at the very edge of the highway, waiting for a gap in the traffic to cross. I glance to my left, the north, toward the woods that are its destination. Then, before I pass, I get one last look at the coyote's eyes. They shine orange. They are intelligent, watchful, intent.

It is that glimpse of the eyes that scrambles something inside me. Before then I had resolve, plans, deadlines. But the eyes introduce uncertainty. Somehow they change everything.

~

Until recently, my wife Nina and I lived on the beach with coyotes as our neighbors. We grew used to seeing them skulking across the backyard to the beach, hunting in the field next door, staring back curiously from the brush by the sides of the roads, hopping down the street like kangaroos in our headlights. Though they favor night, coyotes are neither truly nocturnal or diurnal, and they seem to appear any time and anywhere. These sights became increasingly common, but I never found myself quite getting used to them. They were a happy reminder that, for all the development on Cape Cod, there was still some wildness left. But more than that, they were the thing itself: each sighting brought an electric jolt of wildness.

During two of those winters on the Cape, Nina and I had the good fortune to rent a house right on the edge of earth and sea. While living in the edge house, I walked the beach obsessively, up and down so often that it almost took on the regularity of vocation. The stretch of Bayside beach below the bluff near our house contained a point of shoreline among the rockiest on Cape Cod. Those large rocks, as well as being a congregating point for eiders, cormorants, and seals, were a great catch-all for whatever the tides dragged in, and in winter what they most often dragged in was death. "A vast morgue," was how Thoreau once described a Cape Cod beach, and ours was certainly that. All winter long I hiked the beach and all winter long the ocean kicked up cadavers. Thoreau called himself "the inspector of snowstorms"; during those cold months my title might have been "the examiner of corpses." Morbid surprises greeted me almost every day. There were the usual gulls, cormorants, fish, crabs, and dozens of horseshoe crabs; and there was the dead seal that lay where it had been thrown up against the rocks, the seal's bones and its resilient all-weather pelt a landmark for my walks. And then there were the more unusual finds: the plump, little dovekie, like a miniature penguin, that washed up practically on our lawn, and the thresher shark that beached at Linnel Landing in December. The shark was thirteen feet long, half of that length taken up by its blade-like tail, a tail that it had once swung scythe-like to herd and stun small fish. It bled from its teeth.

My prize find during those winters was a coyote that washed up below the bluff. A young coyote, it had probably weighed about thirty pounds while living, but the sea had soaked it through. When I first found it, I dragged it above the tideline and called the Natural History Museum, but their coolers were full and so it was left for me to study alone. I pulled it up behind some rocks, above the tide, where I hoped no one else would disturb it. The thick winter fur, surprisingly white, had bunched up on its side and swept down through the bushy fox-like tail. Its legs, long and rangy, stretched out straight from the torso as if it had been killed in mid-yawn; its teeth, stained pink with blood, were set in a grimace; its eye whites red. The people I talked to at the museum suggested it might have drowned.

Over the next two years, I watched the gradual process of decay, and soon I was studying the coyote's bones. By the second February the bleached ribs were delicate and thin, the vertebrae almost weightless as if hollow, like a bird's bones. Reddish hair still clumped atop one of the leg bones, black toenails studding the end of the bone—small little bones like knuckles. Next to it sat several more small bones, bones in a row side by side like one of the multiple-chambered flutes played by satyrs. The skull itself had been washed and weathered almost free of meat. It stared out with enormous eye sockets, like a gull's skull, but with teeth and fangs like no gull ever had. The jaw bones still held to the upper skull, seemingly glued by the last adhesive scraps of muscle and cartilage.

~

It wasn't just *dead* coyotes we saw on the beach. The family that rented the house to us also owned the house next door, and one of the ways we lived cheaply—in what was by no means a cheap neighborhood—was to dogsit for them when they were away. Their dog was a black standard poodle named Beau, a moody animal, stubborn as a camel, though loved by its owners more than most children. Despite occasional spasms of puppyish energy, Beau was generally placid, even slightly mournful with his owners gone. But one day around sunrise he started acting strangely, running in circles, and yelping and whining to be let out. When Nina got up to open the door, Beau went flying across the yard and disappeared over the bank down to the beach. A second later, Nina heard a burst of loud barking and yelping. Then, right at the spot where Beau had disappeared over the bank, a large coyote came trotting back up. Ruling out the possibility that Beau had been magically transformed into a coyote, Nina came to another conclusion, one she yelled up to me where I still lay in the bed: "A coyote killed Beau!"

Coyotes don't kill dogs Beau's size, at least not often, but that fact didn't reassure us as we pulled on our clothes and scrambled around the yard and beach, searching for the missing poodle. Ten minutes later when we found him, he was unhurt, except psychologically. The formerly placid dog seemed to have suffered a temporary psychotic break and it was with great effort that we herded him back into the house. While we did this the coyote just stood there, watching the whole thing from the edge of the garden. When I came back outside it only backed up slightly, studying me as I studied it in the rising morning light. It had a thick, whitish winter coat, like the dead youngster I'd found, but it was much bigger, maybe forty pounds. The coyote took its time looking me over before showing me its tail and turning away. Then it casually trotted off toward the cranberry bog.

Though often described in books as "elusive," the coyotes I've encountered can just as often be brazen. Certainly Beau's coyote was. Maybe, in this case, it was simply a question of asserting its domain. It was Beau's yard during the day, but part of the coyote's core territory during the night. At sunrise, that wild edge between light and dark, the two animals met, and a decision of ownership, of property rights, had to be resolved. I'd heard many stories about domestic dogs scaring off coyotes but not in this case. Maybe Beau, with his well-groomed curls and fancy hairstyle, was an affront to the wild dog who roamed along our beach, and maybe the coyote needed to at least briefly assert his supremacy. No poodle was going to stand in his way.

~

During those winters in the edge house I learned that I need to live near water. A place where land stops and something different (and wet) begins. We are both creatures of edges, Nina and I. Never having bought a house of our own, moving almost every year since college, we have lived more like jellyfish than barnacles. Uncertainty and rootlessness have been our themes, and when we left the edge house we began again, jamming our lives into boxes. As we packed, I had the sneaking suspicion that I was leaving the best place I had ever lived and the best place I would ever live. We lost something when we left, something less obvious than a nice view. "How to live?" has always been a question that obsessed me, maybe to an adolescent degree. But living on the edge, the question became slightly modified, sharpened and polished. It became more limited, but at the same time began to imply its own answer.

Here was my new question: *How to live wild?*

~

And now our time of captivity has begun. As captivities go it isn't a bad one, but we feel the domestic closing in. Our city house has gates around it and the gates are locked at night. Just before six each morning we wake to the sound of enormous dump trucks, letting out their hydraulic sighs and rumbling down the narrow streets like dinosaurs.

For years we have drifted so that we could write and live in beautiful places. But now we are moving to Cambridge to start the first leg of a new sort of life. I am finally going to give in and teach, and we are going to have nice, civilized things like paychecks and health insurance. Everyone agrees it's about time. I'm over forty years old, for God's sake, and we have a baby due in three months. It's time, as everyone says, to *get serious*.

But when I get back to Cambridge I start to read about coyote. I begin slowly at first, fending off what may be a newly rising obsession. After a week the coyote books have piled up in our apartment, and I put the skull from the beach on my desk. A few of the teeth have fallen out but the skull still looks savage, a bird-like point to the nose, some dried scraps of carrion still hanging off, undigested by bacteria. I bring it to my first class and place it in front of me on the podium like Yorrick, hoping to scare off freshmen. If I have to live away from Cape Cod, then at least I can bring a little of the Cape with me.

The fact is that while our digs may not be as spectacular here as a seaside cottage, they still have some of the sheen of the romantic. The visitor's suite we are renting, in Adams House at Harvard, is usually rented out to the Nobel Prize–winning Irish poet, Seamus Heaney. As we move in, we discover Heaney's notes to himself around the apartment, scanning them for literary content but only finding exhortations to get milk or Kleenex. I make a note of my own to get hold of Heaney's translation of *Beowulf*. Living here brings us more than just the usual name-dropper's thrill. Having left our wild beach behind and begun our time of domestication, we are reassured to find ourselves in the lair of Seamus.

After I teach my first class, I head over to the library to take out some of Heaney's books of poems, and then migrate over to the Ernst Mayer Zoological Library to continue my fledgling coyote studies. Much of what I learn I know already, from my years living out West, but some of this is new. "Dog cortex has been mapped for neural function, but coyote has not," I read. Yes, that is precisely it: the unmapped. Beau's behavior was always more or less predictable, except on days like the coyote day when the wild was introduced into the doggy equation. But coyote itself is unknown to us. In Native American myth, coyote is the bringer of change, of chaos, the Trickster. Coyote won't stay still, won't settle, and this fact excites me. He is a wanderer who could serve as totem for my coming time of wandering.

The pastoral was not just my mode of living during the years on Cape Cod, but my mode of reading as well. While staying on the beach, I devoured the work of contemporary nature writers. Though I loved most of what I read, I occasionally found it to be pious and dull. The overriding metaphor that I discovered, the metaphor that I tried to live out myself, was that of marriage to a place. The work, as a whole, preaches that we must find the place we love, commit to it, fight for it, and never leave it. For me, the best thing about this idea is its radicalness, given the transience of much of American life. But the worst thing about it is its dogmatism. I couldn't marry Cape Cod for many reasons, cost of living among them. My relationship with the Cape could better be described as a stormy love affair: All my life I've been coming back to this peninsula and then leaving again, trying to settle down but never quite managing. At the same time, over the years, I've fallen in love with other places: the slickrock of Utah, the mountains of Colorado, the white city of San Francisco, the concrete canyons of New York, the brick world of Cambridge. I am a fickle sort of nature lover.

What I like about the coyote stories I now read is their tendency to thumb their nose at the pious and predictable. Coyote comes to town and farts and fornicates; coyote laughs and drinks and cheats. Coyote has no use for false humility, but he is often humbled in the end through the usual roads of arrogance and self-deception, and he knows—or at least momentarily learns—the futility of imagining he can predict or plan how the world will proceed. Perhaps, it occurs to me, coyote is not the greatest role model as I begin my first real grown-up job and await the birth of my first child. On the other hand, I like the effect the stories have on my insides. They tweak the orthodoxies of place. They loosen me up, breaking things apart, leaving me feeling wonderfully free.

I drop the books at the apartment and walk down to the water. Our own bit of wildness is now reduced to this narrow patch of nature along the Charles River, but I am happy to go there daily. Yesterday I heard a kingfisher rattle along above the shore and saw a red-breasted merganser floating in a small puddle of open water, one of the few places where the river hasn't iced over. Later, two red-tailed hawks let out a war cry on my way to class and I looked up to see them circling Memorial Hall. Last fall on Cape Cod, I watched a pod of humpback whales break through the waves, simultaneously breaking through some barrier in my consciousness. I suspect I won't see whales breaching in the Charles, but I may find more than I bargained for.

~

In fact, I am in on a wild secret that makes my time here more exciting. My secret is this:

Coyote has come back to the city with me.

It's true. When most people picture *Canis latrans*, they place them in the dry tumbleweed deserts of the West, but by now coyotes have spread throughout the entire continental United States. Their migration was a characteristically contrary one from West to East, gradually moving eastward as cultivated fields opened up meals of mice and voles. The other factor allowing the early stages of this movement was the human slaughter of wolves. Wolves not only compete for the same foods with coyote, they kill them. With the wolves gone, the coyotes crossed the Mississippi and then, both curious and pressed by each generation's need for new territory, they pushed on, reaching northern New England by the 1930s. By the early 1970s, they had spread through eastern Massachusetts, and by the late 1970s and early 1980s, they were being occasionally spotted by surprised observers on Cape Cod.

How did they get onto a peninsula—an artificial island really thanks to the canal—only accessible to us by bridge or boat? At first, most people hypothesized that they swam across the canal. But coyotes, like humans, are famous "path followers," and, as the Cape Cod coyote expert Peter Trull argues, they could easily have slipped over the bridges in the dead of night. Like the coyote I saw by the side of the highway, they simply waited for traffic to die down, as it always does after midnight. "Coyotes apparently have little concern for the comings and goings of humans, as demonstrated by the continual reports of coyotes trotting through yards and along streets," Trull writes. "The most credible hypothesis, then, is that coyotes did walk (or run) over the canal bridges."

If it was surprising to see coyotes along the beach, imagine what it must be like to spot one while driving on Boston's southeast expressway. Supremely adaptable and canny about the human ways of things—as any animal must be to thrive in this compromised modern world—they have lately made inroads into the city itself. This past summer a young biologist named Jon Way captured and collared a coyote in the town of Revere, following it by radio surveillance as it trotted through the wild patches of the city. The coyote, named Maple by Way, jogged down abandoned railroad tracks at night and shot through alleys. Her den was behind Weylu's, the Chinese food restaurant that sits like an anchored junk on a hill above Route 1, and she regularly prowled behind the Burger Kings and used-car lots along that same trashy strip. When moving through suburban neighborhoods, Maple would travel surreptitiously, like a cartoon spy, pulling over and hiding behind lightpoles as cars drove by. Coyotes are wide-ranging and Maple would often range as much as fifteen miles a night, all within the city boundaries of Route 128. Jon Way believes that these nightly peregrinations are only partly motivated by the search for food. Just as often they are driven by curiosity. By the dog equivalent of *wanderlust*.

~

During our six years on Cape Cod, I became friends with the great nature writer, John Hay. John's life was an admirable attempt to live close to wildness. He had come to Cape Cod in 1946, after World War II, back when the place still had a rustic feel. He came in part to be close to his mentor, Conrad Aiken, but he also came for another reason. "I suppose I came here following some vague urge for 'space,'" he said to me. By space, as I finally figured out, he meant freedom. There were only 800 people in town in those days and he bought twenty acres on a hilltop for practically nothing, a house where he still lives today. He liked the sense of sprawl, of having plenty of room for both his art and his family, and he liked to get away from people so he could think.

The Cape Cod I have left behind is running out of the space John came for, if it hasn't run out already. As with many places, a sense of suburbia has encroached on the old rustic feel.

Fortunately, the ocean helps mitigate this encroachment, as do the returning coyotes.

"I'm glad the coyotes are back," John said to me when I visited him recently. "It's nice to have truly wild neighbors again."

~

Wildness is defined, in part, by wide ranges. That is why we are kidding ourselves if we believe we can confine the wild to parks. Mountain lions require the largest range of any animal on the continent, about 200,000 acres to a black bear's 15,000. Canids are great roamers, too, wolves most famously, capable of ranging from 100 to 200 square miles. Typically coyotes only manage to cover a tenth of that, between 10 to 20 miles, which still makes for a lot of wandering. When Maple was found dead, hit by a car, she was up in Peabody, on the other side of Route 128, over eight miles from her den.

Since we moved to the city a few weeks ago I have confined my previously wide range to three-mile walks along the river. Yesterday, February 7, I walked during a morning snowstorm. The snow added a layer of wildness to the place, piling up on streets and sidewalks, as well as covering the river ice. As the snowfall intensified the whiteness began to illuminate other whitnesses. The birches along the water gleamed and a gull with black-tipped wings was transformed into a stranger, more exotic bird: a white dove of some sort. I walked to the open water near the grate where I knew I would find the great blue heron, and sure enough he was there, hulking, long neck pulled in, solitary. I worry for the bird: How will it survive? What is it eating? As I moved forward it leaned forward too, poised for flight. It has become habituated to the walkers and joggers and cars but this new unusual creature with his curious movement forward, and his pauses and uncertainties, must have seemed uncategorizable and therefore predatory. Finally the bird pushed off into the snowstorm, gray legs straight behind it as if in a steep dive. It disappeared in the white for a moment before reappearing by the other open grate. It dipped into the sewer tunnel as if into a cave.

Snow makes for good tracking and when I got home I put in a call to Dave Eatnough, a science teacher at Revere High School. Eatnough and his students have been working with Jon Way to try to track the coyotes within the Boston area. For over a year now, they have been setting box traps in hopes of capturing and collaring the coyotes, but other than Maple they haven't had much luck. They have seen prints and scat and other signs of activity but the coyotes seem to be on to them. The box traps are like giant Have-a-Hart traps, with spring doors that close once the animal enters, but recently Eatnough has been trying a new method, luring the coyotes in with meat before firing a net launcher over the dogs. Two nights ago, I was supposed to join Jon and Dave for an all-night stakeout in hopes of catching a coyote. But, tired from a trip and teaching, I called to beg out. I fell into my usual routine: dinner, a couple beers, some dumb TV, and early to bed by 9 o'clock. That night, while they were readying the new net launcher, a coyote wandered into one of the box traps. If I had been there, preparing for the stake out, I would have seen the coyote, and the next morning I chastised myself for not following my first wild impulse.

Today, the snow having transformed Boston into a wilds, I head out with Dave Eatnough to track the new coyote that they have named Bart. Bart, Eatnough tells me, has a terrible case of mange, with very little hair, though he weighs a surprising thirty-two pounds (as contrasted with the relatively healthy Maple's thirty). After Bart was sedated and collared, he was given medicine for the mange before being released. Now we are driving along Route 1, my arm frozen from holding an antenna out the window, listening to little electronic beeps on our receiver that will tell us where Bart is moving. We drive behind Stop N' Shop and Petco, following our electronic trail. When we pull into neighborhoods we immediately explain ourselves to people so they don't think we're with the CIA. A man gives us permission to tramp across his backyard, and his three-year-old son asks him what we are doing.

"They're trying to find the coyote so he doesn't eat you up," he says.

~

We track for a while, getting close a few times, but without much luck; Bart is likely hunkered down for the day. The point isn't to get too close anyway, as that would disturb him, but just to get a reading on where he is, which we have done. After a couple of hours I thank Dave and head home.

But then double back to a spot he brought me to earlier. Before we began tracking, Dave took me over to a cemetery where another of the box cages was set up. Coyote tracks ran all through the snow, and Dave showed me a den where the local pair lived. He told me that he had seen two coyotes there the week before.

I am glad to be alone. Dave is a fine companion, with a passion for coyotes and the energy to allow him to teach all day and check cages at night. But I'm not sure how I feel about the sedating and radio collaring of a large wild predator, especially one that has had the wiles and wherewithal to survive within the borders of metropolitan Boston. There are all sorts of scientific rationalizations for the trapping, the best being that knowledge about the coyotes can be used to protect them from human beings through education, but we are still talking about *using* the coyotes for something. Confinement and control are the opposite of the wildness I purport to be after, and confinement and control are a large part of any radio collaring experiment. It's true that my own curiosity isn't exactly pure; I am not without my own *uses* for things. Still, as I follow the coyote prints into the junk-heaped woods behind the cemetery, I begin to think that I prefer this kind of tracking to the kind that involves electronics.

This is a bruised landscape—refuse piles, car dumps, iron bars jutting out of rock mounds—but the snow smooths and heals. The coyote trails weave beside a half-frozen tidal canal, encased in a concrete trough. The trails cut like a wake, dark blue shadows through the snow, or, as Dave said earlier, like contrails. Coyote tracks, at least adult coyote tracks, have little of the wayward wanderings and random playfulness of dogs. Coyotes place their feet in the prints they've already made—this is called "perfect stepping"—so that the lines cutting through the snow are surprisingly narrow. Like humans, coyotes make it easy on themselves. They follow paths: frozen rivers, old railroads, even sidewalks. As I quickly learn, they particularly like to hug fences.

I follow the coyotes wanderings all through the woods, sometimes winding like ski trails and sometimes very straight and direct, meaning business, on the way somewhere. For a while I trace a single violet trail as it jogs down the side of a hill to a creek, crossing a little footbridge. There are signs of a pounce, a meal of a mouse along the way, and then a brief stop to urinate. I get down on all fours to follow the track below a low canopy of prickers and briar. Snow falls from the branches on the bare skin below my shirt and coat, and melts instantly. When I emerge, I see a small group of sparrow-like birds, possibly longspurs, fat with chestnut heads, picking berries off what looks like a dead branch. From there I follow the tracks to a small den under the rocks, the den carved into a sort of mulchy pile below the roots in a hillside, the hillside itself located below a car dump. It's too small for a coyote den but just right for a badger or possum. The coyote probably stopped here in hopes of a snack, though it also might have been partly house hunting, since coyote dens are usually just excavations of the dens of smaller animals like these. I am not yet a good enough reader to tell the whole story of this coyote's afternoon. Nearby are wild weavings of some smaller animal: crazy scribbles through the blue-violet shadows. But how would even mice or voles stay on top of such light snow? Then the little fork marks give a hint, and I remember something Dave told me this morning. The prints are the steps of birds, and the marks next to them snow angels created by their fluttering wings.

I follow the tidal canal, which seems to marry the urban to the wild. Where the ice has melted a Big Gulp cup floats next to two dozen nervous mallards, and weed-strewn shopping carts jut up from the dark water like half-sunken ships. Each squirrel nest in the area seems topped off with the insulation of a plastic bag, as if this were a local status symbol. This is a place neither urban nor wild, though, in moments, it is both. Mythic coyote occupies borderlands, places in between, always wandering between different spheres of being. "In short, trickster is a boundary crosser," writes Lewis Hyde in *Trickster Makes the World*. I cut through a hole in the chain-link fence, with barbed wire on top in prison-camp fashion, and follow the tracks up a refuse pile, remembering that coyotes like ridges, often climbing them for no other reason than to get a good look around. Below me the outline of an abandoned tire pushes up through a foot of snow, looking like a sugar donut or a lifebuoy thrown overboard. I descend from the hill and trot through the snow for a while like the coyotes I've seen on the Cape.

I get a sense of the animal's range just from the wild perambulations of the one I've been following, all these paths created since yesterday's big snow. I also get a sense of the kind of "wilds" a city coyote must occupy, the way they must patch together a necessary wilderness where no obvious wilderness exists. Coyotes can survive where wolves cannot in part because of their "human" qualities and human-style adaptability. Here you can see how they move behind the back of the human world. They patch their territory together out of parklands, cemeteries, backyards, car dumps, schoolyards, train tracks. And of course they occupy that other wild territory: night. At night the deeds of human property transfer into their names. When the path I'm following ends at a road, it isn't hard to imagine the coyote trotting right over into the backyard across the street, after which, hopefully, it will reach another larger patch of wild.

Hiking mindlessly through the snow, I'm more convinced than ever that this is a better way to track the coyotes than with the radio collar. Despite the usual scientific rationalizations and despite the fact that they are getting high school students involved in something other than Gameboy, I feel less enthused about the coyote project. Clamping radio collars on the few wild animals strong and wily enough to survive in the Boston area seems the opposite of the wildness I am after. It seems—as usual—about control.

By the time I head back to the car I've walked for three hours and the shadows on the snow have turned from blue to violet. I haven't spent an afternoon like this since I moved to the city, and haven't spent an afternoon tracking in this manner perhaps in my whole life. A whole day of coyote. It's been a long while since I felt this full.

With my body content plowing through the snow, my mind begins to work better, too, and I feel new questions taking hold. Why does this thing called "the wild" really matter? We repeat the notion that we need the wild—it has become environmental dogma—but what do we really mean by it? In an increasingly controlled and pre-packaged environment why do we need the wild? Does it have an evolutionary purpose? Or is purpose beside the point? And this: If the wild is so important, how can most people live without it? Thoreau had a blunt answer to this last question: They can't. Or at least, they can't live well. Better than the famous "quiet desperation" line is this quote from "Walking": "When sometimes I am reminded that the mechanics and shopkeepers stay in their shops not only all the forenoon, but all the afternoon too, sitting with crossed legs, so many of them,—as if the legs were made to sit upon, and not to stand or walk upon,—I think that they deserve some credit for not having all committed suicide long ago." His prescription was to get out and walk four hours a day, a prescription that most of us would have a hard time fitting into our schedules. I already understand that my daily tramps by the Charles River are not enough to keep me sane, which may be why I am suddenly attaching myself to coyote, or at least the idea of the coyote, with such ferocity. I want to believe that I can find wildness here, in this crowded, controlled city on the country's eastern edge. Wildness, as many others including Thoreau have said, is not necessarily synonymous with wilderness. Mine is a potentially hopeful obsession: If I can find the wild here, in this time and place, then I can find it anywhere.

Of course I don't expect to actually see the coyote I've spent the day tracking, and I don't. But I see plenty. This afternoon of following wild dogs has also been filled with wild birds. Four red-tailed hawks, two adults and two immatures, with white winter bellies, keep flying off in front of me, and two gregarious snow buntings, with their delicate butterscotch cheeks and caps, come within a few feet of me. As the light slants lower a yellow-shafted flicker swoops across my path, a white flash of tail and red patch on the back of its head. For a split second I see its undersides, pure gold in the afternoon light. A minute later that same color is echoed by a willow tree, its yellow buds the first to bloom each year. The tree glows an eerie gold, flicker-colored, and seeing it defines and elevates the afternoon.

I return to my car and from there I walk back over to the box trap, following a path along the fence by Mr. Epstein's grave, then through a stand of shrivelled sumac. You can tell by the way the prints angle through the cemetery that the coyotes are on intimate terms with this landscape: They know where the open gates are and they go right for them. I find eighteen crows mobbing by the box trap. Dave told me that the crows go in and pull the hocks of meat out of the trap, as do the red-tails. This seems behavior undignified for a hawk, but the two that were captured in the cage last week confirm it. At another trap they keep capturing the neighborhood pit bull, but so far the owner has been a good sport about it. In many ways this has become a community project, and local butchers are also helping out. "Ya, you can use this meat," one of them said to Dave. "Just get us a coyote we can hang on the wall."

Now the cage door is open, poised, and the hocks of meat, big hunks of something that look like cows' feet, still half-frozen from the night before, have begun to melt and turn rank. The coyotes understood what's going on, know it's a trap, otherwise they'd be on that meat in a second. From my reading, I know that both mythic and actual coyotes have been known to urinate on traps, leading some to conclude that the animal must have a sense of humor. It's no surprise that the coyote they caught the other day was mangy, since no self-respecting coyote would fall for something this obvious. The disease must have made the animal more desperate, causing it to brave the cage in hopes of a meal.

Before I leave I decide to take one last look at the den that Dave showed me this morning. Right in the middle of the cemetery, its entrance is a circular opening in the base of the tree stump, with roots hanging down over the hole like Rasta-man dredlocks. I get on my belly in the snow and peek inside where smooth sand slants downward. The entrance to the den is so small—a womb-like entrance—that the coyotes must squeeze in each time they enter or exit. How long does the tunnel slant back? Dave and Jon Way excavated an abandoned den, digging it up to twenty-five feet before they stopped. The den delights me in a way that

I can't quite articulate, reminding me of childhood forts in the woods. "All children want to crouch in their secret nests," writes Seamus Heaney. Dave told me not to spend too much time by the den, fearing I might scare the coyotes off, but I run back and get my sketchbook so I can draw and remember it.

~

I climb back into the car and drive home before sunset. But first a detour to the Middlesex Fells, the rocky parkland that sits perched like an eagle aerie above the city. I hunt for coyote prints, wondering if this space connects by some pathway to the cemetery. Though I find no tracks, I am sure that this is one of the wild patches the coyotes use to move through this crowded, human world. I return to the city from above it, slanting down on Route 93. I'm new here, but I'm happy that I've started to get to know my neighbors, particularly the hairy, four-legged ones. Change and chaos are the twin trickster gods of my existence; I have left Cape Cod behind "for good," have moved to the city, and will soon move again to a place a thousand miles south. But for the moment, I don't mind. Driving back down from the Fells, I have a fine view of the downtown skyscrapers in the violet crepuscular light. It is still a city, true, that hasn't changed. But I feel it becoming a wilder place.

walled-in

This is the winter that never ends. This is the aberrant winter that puts the lie to all those milquetoast global-warming winters that we've had since returning east. This is the childhood winter, where snow comes to stay, piling up in drifts that rival memory. I like all the snow, but winter itself has started to seem trying. Sometimes I feel trapped in the season, just as I feel trapped in the city.

I continue to worry about the great blue heron. The Charles remains frozen, except for the tub-sized spots by the sewer grates where the street run-off comes bubbling up. How can an animal that survives by fishing survive now? Winter is a time of retreat—turtles sinking themselves deep in the muck below the ice, small rodents scrambling in dark tunnels below the snow—and with the chance to fly south long since past, where does the heron retreat to? I watch it stand proud and upright above its dingy ice-chocked fishing hole, but its posture seems to lack the poised excitement characteristic of the species, as if it were just going through the motions. Patience is the heron's great motto and lesson, but what if you wait and wait, and nothing comes? Another day I take my class out walking in a blizzard and we see the heron again, flying desperately from grate to grate. One student decides to keep dibs on the bird as part of his winter project.

My own project continues apace, as does Nina's. She is now beginning her third trimester, while I, less ambitiously, try to learn about coyotes. On the days I don't teach I drive out to the Stone Zoo in Stoneham to watch five coyote siblings roam the wilds of their cage. The landscape within the chain-link fence is meant to replicate the Sierra Nevada but lately resembles the Arctic. I sit on the snowy bench in front of the cage and take notes on coyote behavior. Today—a cold beautiful day in early February—the big news is the flock of starlings that tease the coyotes by roosting on the top of their fence. The coyotes bark up at them with barks that sound surprisingly doggish. They occasionally take time out from chasing the birds to play their usual games of dominance and sub-mission. Cane, the largest female, stands over Caon, the second largest, while Late, the runt, cowers far off behind some trees in the corner of the cage. Lupe, the dominant male, pauses to sit on the rock that juts prominently in the middle of the cage. (I will later learn two significant facts about this rock and its appeal: One, it is where Jon Way, the coyotes' surrogate mother, comes to pet and play with the pups, and two, it is artificially heated from below.) When the starlings fly to the other end of the cage all the coyotes except Late follow. The coyotes cast blue shadows as they mince across the new snow. Then the birds, apparently done with their taunting, fly off all at once into the blue cold sky with a sharp explosive noise like applause.

Watching the coyotes, particularly Lupe, I understand how I mistook a pack of coyotes for wolves when I first moved to Colorado. Winter may not add bulk, but it adds fur: Lupe's coat is full and he looks both tall and husky at once, white underneath and foxish red throughout his tail. The same beautiful red fur curls behind his ears where it ruffles in the snowy wind. When the wind blows, Lupe squints into it; when it stops the squinting stops too and he reveals orange eyes like those of the coyote I saw at the side of the highway. I have never seen a coyote's eyes from this close or for this long before and they remind me of the intense burning orange of young osprey eyes, a predator's eyes, the opposite of a goat's dull unfocused pupils. When the wind picks up again Lupe returns to squinting and hunching, then decides to plop down and curl around himself right there in the snow, forsaking his throne-like rock.

If you watch coyotes long enough it isn't hard to see how they earned their mythic nicknames and reputations. The eye-squinting, a way of jogging that looks guilty like a skulk (sometimes exaggerated even more in an arced run called "active submission"), the alternate cowering and posturing, and a mouth that often seems turned up in a slight smile. Combine this with behavior that is scavenging, adaptable, and sometimes something less than what we would call noble. And of course smart. Jon Way tells the story of following a coyote around a golf course on Cape Cod. The coyote usually let golfers pass "within 15 or 20 meters of him," but, while ignoring the golfers, he started barking at Jon from 300 meters away. The coyote recognized the scent: It was that guy who kept putting those traps out and putting collars on his friends and family. Mimicry is another of the trickster's talents and that too is on display here at the zoo. The female Caon has begun to emit a strange, low growl that Jon calls "cougar-like," a handy simile since the neighboring cage is occupied by two mountain lions kidnapped from the American West.

Always quick to look for symbols that reflect on my personal mythology, I make note of the fact that these coyotes were taken from Cape Cod and now live fenced-in in the Boston area. Of course, it is preposterous to compare my semester within the gates of Harvard, which I could quit at any time, to the lifetime incarceration of these five canids in a cage not much bigger than a full-length basketball court. I'll resist the urge to go on an anti-zoo tear, but to say that the animals themselves are changed by the fence around them is not just metaphoric hooey. To bring up just one obvious example, there is the fact that Lupe is sleeping peacefully in the snow only twenty yards from a mountain lion that with a couple of leaps could break his neck in the wild. The same goes for human beings. "The mind is a powerful thing," Nina says when I bring her out to the zoo the next week. She means the way that we can stand a few feet away from cougars and leopards without fear, but also the way we respond relatively blandly to animals that would send a magnificent jolt through us in another, wilder context. As it is, the bars and fences strip these creatures of danger and therefore strip us of both fear and wonder. I even walk by the cage with the snow leopard without a jolt. It's as if a mute button has been pushed in our centers of delight. Walking out of the zoo, I pause in front of the cougars and feel only pity and low-level curiosity. It makes me wonder: Is the wild just a construct of the human mind? And why confine it to "human": Not only are the coyotes blasé about the cougars but the cougars pay no mind to the hawks who seem uninterested in the nearby snakes. Perhaps it is as simple as this: Too much fear muscles out wonder, but eliminate fear and uncertainty altogether and you also eliminate the possibility of awe. We think we can have our cake and eat it too, but we can't. By living over-safe and pre-planned lives, we eliminate what is most unsettling about being human—terror and panic—but also what is best. When we withdraw from the edges, the ecotones spilling over with life and danger, we settle for life in the middle.

But I have grown suspicious of vaguely Emersonian sentences like the last one. I claim that I am searching for wildness; I claim that it is that quality I am after. "In wildness is the preservation of the world," Thoreau said. Sure, but what the hell does that mean? *Why* is the world preserved by wildness? Love of the wild has become an environmental cliché, but can't it be more than that? It's not wildness as an abstract quality that I'm interested in, but wildness as a possible way of living. If we had the gumption, we could all head off to the woods like Doug Peacock and live with the grizzlies. But how many of us are unrestrained and confident enough to do that? And if we did, the woods would be crowded with poets. Is it possible to live wild without living in the wilderness? That's what I need to know.

~

Today the United States declared a high risk of terrorism. While I don't quite have my color-coding down, I think we are now at the second-highest, orange, maybe, or red. In other news a pair of red-tailed hawks have been perching on the weathervanes atop Memorial Hall and yesterday a flock of cedar waxwings filled the crab-apple trees down by the river, beautiful black-masked marauders on a winter-long quest for fruit. Meanwhile snow continues to coat the city. My student reports that he hasn't spotted the great blue heron for several days now.

Today I see two signs as I walk around the snowed-in city. This one in front of a church with eaves piled high with white:

God is in the midst of the city. Psalm 46.

And then later, on the way home, this homemade sign, black marker on posterboard, in a student's dorm window:

Let's Kick Saddam's Ass and Take His Gas.

~

At night I read more coyote stories before drifting off. After a while they all start mixing together: coyote steals fire from the hags on the hill,

Coyote eats his own intestines or excrement, Coyote sleeps with his wife by accident, Badger screws Coyote's wife, Coyote steals fire and makes the world. It occurs to me, as I start to doze, that if it is "wildness" I am really after, then I may have the wrong man. This vain, self-conscious, ridiculous figure is far from the pure noble-savage visions of wildness we nature writers usually worship. Thoreau, for instance, would be unlikely to admire an animal that stalks the streets of L.A. stealing garbage. "They're just big raccoons," a friend says. And if the actual animal has proved perfectly adaptable to modern life, so has the myth. It strikes me, as it has struck many before me, just how contemporary a creature this mythic coyote is. If he is wild, it is the wild of randomness, capriciousness, and humor, not of wild nature and the uncultivated. This, too, seems right for my present purposes.

In *A Coyote Reader*, William Bright summarizes the myth: "But Old Man Coyote, even when he brings fire for the benefit of humankind, is far from being a Promethean hero: he is an insatiable glutton, a gross lecher, an inveterate thief, liar, and outlaw, a prankster whose schemes regularly backfire." (Bright also suggests that, if we want a modern cartoon equivalent, think Bugs Bunny, not Wile E.) Appetite, and an inability to contain that appetite, define Coyote. Though he knows they are trouble, Coyote can't stop himself from eating the grasshoppers that are roasting in a big brushfire. When they don't seem to be filling him up he plugs his ass with tar pitch. And then, of course, the pitch catches fire from the remnants of the brushfire and Coyote's ass catches fire, too. The story ends with him vowing never again to eat roasted grasshoppers, a vow we know he won't keep.

It is a commonplace to say that Coyote stories dance back and forth between the sacred and profane, but you can read a whole lot of Coyote without finding much sacred. I challenge anyone to discover the divine in the story of Coyote covering himself up with rocks to suck himself off. If not for their sanctification as native myth, some of these stories would be on par with Farrelly brothers movies. In fact, in his Id-driven behavior, Coyote seems almost a caricature of modern Americans. In *Trickster Makes the World*, Lewis Hyde writes:

If by "America" we mean the land of rootless wanderers and the free market, the land not of natives but of immigrants, the shameless land where anyone can say anything at any time, the land of opportunity and therefore opportunists, the land where individuals are allowed and even encouraged to act without regard to community, then trickster has not disappeared. "America" is his apotheosis; he's pandemic.

Coyote works as myth because he is a boundary crosser, but to be a boundary crosser you need boundaries to cross. As any class clown knows, the easiest place to get a laugh is in the schoolroom (or in church), where it isn't permitted. That is why we get the most pleasure when Coyote dances through our most sacred groves. I take some small comfort in the fact that my current attempt to interweave the coyote myth with my own life is something of a minor boundary crossing. Not just that I am "usurping" Native American myths (as if all cultural myths shouldn't be fair game for human beings) but that I am intruding on the turf of contemporary Western writers, both native and non-, from Gary Synder to Peter Coyote, who have claimed Coyote as their own. Of course Coyote himself wouldn't care who or what used him. My own uses are selfish, not academic. Since *Canis latrans* has returned East, I reason, his myth might as well come along, too.

~

Jon Way begins his work days with a howl. He comes into the zoo the back way through the working entrance, rounds the snake pits and the leopard cage, and then, still out of sight of the pups, does a fair impression of a coyote in the wild. It only takes a second or two for the pups to respond. They let go with a wild cacophonous chorus that sounds like fifty coyotes, not five. "Howl" isn't really the right word or, at least, it doesn't quite contain all the sounds: The cries are ridiculously high-pitched, punctuated by even higher individual yelps like the noise a dog makes when hit. There is yowling and yodelling and whining and there are all sorts of sounds in between. Jon enters the cage and the group, man and coyotes, continues to howl around the warm rock. "Ghostly" is a lame adjective, but the howling would make a fine soundtrack to the scene where the spirits all rise up in *The Christmas Carol*.

On days when I come to the Stone Zoo alone, the coyotes sometimes mistake me for Jon for a second. But only for a second. They come running toward me, up to the edge of their cage, as if to greet an old friend, but then register disappointment and slink away. Jon *is* an old friend but only as much a friend as someone can be who captures you and takes you away from your mother. On the other hand, not long after they were taken from their den behind an old shed in Falmouth, Jon became, in effect, surrogate mother to the pups. On April 12, 2002, when the pups were three and a half weeks old, Jon took five pups out of a litter of nine, including two runts and three of the seven more normal-sized pups, and brought them back to his basement apartment in his parents' home on Cape Cod. Jon admits that he was nervous at first about bonding with the coyotes. Late, the runt, was sucking on anything he could get his mouth on, including Jon's fingers. On his Web site Jon wrote:

It took 2 1/2 stressful days to get the middle three pups to eat. They had lost weight up to that point and I was getting nervous that they wouldn't eat (we offered them Esbilac, which is puppy milk, and puppy weaning formula). By the end of the third day, I gave them a package of raw chicken. It was like a light switched on in them because after that they were all completely bonded to me. They all devoured the chicken and thereafter have approached me during all subsequent feedings. They mostly liked to eat meat (we gave them partially cooked meat scraps that I got from a butcher) but did eat dog food and Esbilac milk.

For a month Jon slept next to the cardboard den box and let the pups chew up his apartment. Then, after another month spent in quarantine, the coyotes were transported to the Stone Zoo outside of Boston. Jon visits almost every day, continuing to bond with the now almost full-grown pups and following them around to study their behaviors. He knows the hierarchical relationships of the coyotes from the inside, being in effect part of that hierarchy, and often it is the dominant male of the group, Lupe, who gets to sit on his lap during the group howl.

Jon is tall and affable, still in his twenties, with a shaved head in the style of his generation. I got his name through a friend on Cape Cod and first met him when he came to speak to my environmental writing class in the fall of 2002. His talk and slide show were informative and there was something happily guileless about him as he described a coyote's need for a large home range (average of 11.5 miles on Cape Cod) and then, with the next slide, revealed the smallish cage in which "his" five pups would spend the rest of their lives. I had fed the class Jack Turner's subversive *Abstract Wild*, in which he makes a persuasive case against radio collaring, and I could sense a communal bristling as Jon obliviously described the twin goals of his Boston coyote research: to study his captive pups and to radio collar as many urban "ki-yots" as possible. His own ambitions showed on his Web site and in person, where he had no qualms about saying he wanted to be "a famous naturalist," and a kind of boyish enthusiasm mixed unselfconsciously with a strict devotion to the language of scientific research. On the Web site, he wrote of how his team had collected as much scientifically sound coyote data as they could to "gain reputability." Aside from the usual scientific justifications, and the fact that kids at Revere High School were aiding in the studies, there is one undeniably positive result of the research: More is being learned about what happens when coyotes and human beings live near each other.

For instance, as Jon points out one cold morning at the zoo, the bold daylight behavior of some coyotes that frightens suburbanites can usually be attributed to a single (and understandable) behavior.

"What they are seeing is a perfectly natural coyote behavior, usually by females during pup-raising seasons," he said. "It's natural for them to act bold to protect their home. But there's big difference between acting bold and being a threat to humans."

Since it isn't that commonly known that coyotes have moved inside Route 128, there hasn't been too big an outcry from Boston pet owners yet, but it will come, along with cries to "move" (i.e., exterminate) the coyotes. In fact, pet owners in the East have become a small-scale version of Western ranchers. Since Cape Cod is a decade ahead, the coyotes having arrived there earlier than in Boston, the controversy has already been brewing for a while. Pet owners talk and write of the "coyote menace" and, in truth, it can't be denied that coyotes occasionally snack on cats.

Down on Cape Cod everyone has a story about coyotes and pets. Last spring on the Cape I talked with a guy from Sears who was delivering a new washing machine to our house. He told me a story of riding a bike with a friend through the Punkhorn, a section of preserved woods in Brewster. They turned the corner and suddenly there were ten coyotes howling. He was big guy, but he and his friend just turned around and tore out of there. Then he told me about a coyote den only fifty feet behind his house in Falmouth.

"We went down to dig it up and get them out," he said. "And we found fifteen cat collars in there."

~

Depending on whether you are a pessimist or an optimist, the great blue heron is (a) dead, or has (b) flown off to find open water. Either way, the bird is nowhere to be seen on this stretch of the Charles.

It's funny how even the name of the river here sounds pompous, begging to be pronounced in a Thurston Howell accent. You wouldn't say that about the Rio Grande or the Missouri or the Klamath, but *the Charles* just sounds different. Nina, whom I have dragged back East and now to the city, mockingly calls it my "beloved Charles." Of course, the river doesn't care about our names for it, and, whether we think so or not, those of us who live in this part of Cambridge live within the river's watershed. I have become particularly aware of this while walking at night, and during the recent snows. For instance, you feel how the winter winds use the river as a pathway, and how those winds fly up off the water through the man-made canyons between the school's old brick buildings. With the river frozen and blanketed with a layer of snow it's easy to study the prints now covering it. For the more bold animals, the river is a natural pathway, devoid of human obstacles. It doesn't take much imagination to picture a curious coyote on his nightly peregrinations using the frozen river as a highway wending right into the heart of downtown Boston.

Living up here in the city I can't help but begin the process of looking back on and romanticizing my six years of "retreat" on Cape Cod. It's just the way the mind works, at least my mind. There is a tradition of writing about nature while in the midst of it, but there is also another less-known tradition. I'm reminded of the fact that Ed Abbey wrote good chunks of *Desert Solitaire*, a radiant book stuffed full of the outdoors, while in his cramped apartment in Hoboken. And that my friend Brad Watson recently created the vivid fictional world of Mercury, Mississippi, while laboring in the academic mines of Cambridge. If living right in a place can set the mind on fire, then sometimes exile serves the same purpose. As if the mind, ever adaptable, can feed on both immediacy and remove.

It might seem strange to teach a nature writing course in the city, but even before we moved here I was counting on the river as an ally. What I hadn't counted on was all this snow. The city is usually a place to get away from, the cliché is that the city's business intrudes on us; we feel people around all the time. But the snow mitigates this feeling. The assignment I gave my class last week was to watch spring come in, studying the budding progress, and by now the willows usually would have begun to hint at yellow. But this year spring won't budge. We remain locked in winter.

If it's strange to teach nature writing here, then Harvard must seem like an even stranger place for me to write about nature. It shouldn't. How many of our cultural wildmen are dead white guys from Harvard? It's nature writing's dirty secret. Thoreau and Emerson for starters, of course, though it could be argued that in both cases Harvard represented what they were rebelling against, what they were fleeing from. Flip through the old *Norton Nature Anthology*, before they got the PC religion, and it looks like a Harvard alumni bulletin. Take my home turf, Cape

Cod, for instance. Pretty much the whole canon went to school here: Thoreau, Henry Beston, Henry Kittredge, John Hay, Robert Finch . . .

I'm not sure what, if anything, to make of this. The postmodern take is that one should feel embarrassed to be associated with Harvard: with its pomposity and with being among those Reagan derisively called "pencil pushers and intellectuals." But why? Of course there are snobs here in abundance. One member of the Classics faculty, whom I met recently at a party, can't speak, let alone write, without sounding like he's using a thesaurus. This intimidated me, and when I apologized to him "for not being more articulate," I managed to mispronounce the last word, rhyming the final syllable with "hate." I kicked myself the rest of the day, and told Nina that everyone here had poles up their asses. And it's partly true. If I want to extend my coyote metaphor and see the gates around Harvard Yard as a boxtrap, then there's little doubt that prestige and status are the bait.

But there's a lot more than just snobbery here. For instance, I love the class I'm teaching (though, since it's called "Environmental Writing," it is a culmination of my long misunderstanding with the world.) The kids in my class are the Harvard equivalent of hippies, relative nonconformists coming from all disciplines: biology, environmental studies, classics, and, of course, English and literature. Passionate and funny, they are eager to write and also fairly earnest environmentalists. They give me some hope that not everyone is grubbing after money.

They also seem much more mature than I was at their age, perhaps because they drink a whole lot less. Harvard, I've noted, looks a lot different when you're not drunk all the time. You notice the architecture, and the way nature hides in the city niches, like the pigeon building its nest where the cinder block fell out below the Eliot Bridge. The river has become my daily haunt, just as it was twenty years ago when it provided a refuge from school and city, and I sneak out onto it at dawn, tracing the tracks of voles and raccoons. On my morning hikes down the Charles I follow my own assignment, hunting for signs that spring might finally break through.

~

Twenty years ago I lived a different, more Bacchanalian kind of wildness in this city. Being back in this place old stories keep coming to mind. I have tried to resist telling most of them, fearing I will come off as a middle-aged bore, but the story of my fractured skull may now be worth telling in full. It seems emblematic of my first stint here, and also, maybe, emblematic of the wildness of my twenties, which spilled over into my thirties. During that time, whenever people told me that they felt like they had a split down their middle, I could only nod in agreement.

The moment I remember today is one that long colored—and almost ended—my life. It was late in my sophomore year and I was out carousing with my friends Bill and Griff, trying to pick up women at Boston College. Around two in the morning I began serenading an uninterested brunette with Looking Glass's *Brandy*, the song I always sang when drunk back then. I followed her down the hallway crooning, "There's a port on a Western bay . . ." Minutes later we found ourselves sitting out on a small balcony off of the second floor of the Hillside dorm. I wrongly believed I was beginning to impress her, when Griff appeared below.

"Come on," he yelled. "It's late. We gotta go."

I ignored him but he kept on yelling—like a cat yowling to come in—making a game of it. This went on for some time while I ignored him and tried to talk with the girl.

"Come on," he yelled finally. *"Jump."*

This last word sparked a romantic notion in my soggy brain. I looked out at the tree branch five feet in front of me and envisioned a glorious end to the night. In leaving I would dazzle my would-be date, would leap out and catch the branch and swing, Errol Flyn–like, letting go and alighting ten feet below on the concrete. A swashbuckling finale to the evening.

And here, looking back, is the strangest thing: I didn't just think it; I actually did it. I bid farewell, leapt, caught the branch, and swung just as planned. But then, as I was swinging forward, about to let go of the branch and make my glorious landing, it broke off with a loud SNAP. Now I was almost parallel to the ground. And falling.

A moment of quiet as I dropped through the night air and then impact; a slow-motion second before neck and skull cracked into pavement.

There were screams, doors opening, a crowd gathering. I didn't pass out, but pushed myself to my feet, staggering around like a wobbly prize fighter until the ambulance arrived. The last thing I remembered, before being driven away, was looking out through the ambulance window at Bill and Griff. They were dancing around and making funny faces.

At the hospital in Newton, I was awakened on and off through the night. Though I still felt nauseated, the doctor released me the next morning without an X-Ray. Back at Harvard I reported directly to the student health center. Again I was somehow released without an X-ray. I was told to "use my own judgement."

This was not a good thing to tell me at that age. That weekend I played in a Frisbee tournament and then, Monday afternoon, I quarterbacked our intramural football team. We had our worst game of the year and our offensive line was particularly leaky. I was sacked six times. That night I couldn't sleep, nagged by persistent nausea and headaches.

I returned to the hospital the next day. Finally I was sent down to be X-rayed. Alone in the elevator on my way back up to the doctor, I snuck a look at the pictures. There was my whitish skull. And there was the crack. You couldn't miss it. A blue lightning bolt running jagged right down the middle of my brain.

When the doctor saw the picture he told me I couldn't leave the hospital. In fact, he told me I couldn't move. A nurse wheeled me to a room and deposited me in a bed for the next week. Griff brought me my clothes and books but my head hurt too much to read. I was kept under constant observation. My skull was severely fractured.

"Sometimes the skull just heals itself," the doctor told me before I left the hospital a week later, "Sometimes problems don't crop up until years later."

Looking back, it occurs to me that there was already a pattern at work that would continue over the next decade or more: I had failed and almost died because I had had—and then followed through on—a grandiose drunken vision. In a flash I'd seen it all: the branch, the brilliant dive, the perfect landing—all of it—and, intoxicated by the picture my brain created, nearly broke that brain in half.

As I recall it now, it reminds me of a Coyote story. Coyote is always coming back from the dead, usually having been killed by his own idiocy and appetite. Come to think of it, most of my youthful stories, most of all our youthful stories, are stories of misadventures driven by appetite. Appetite as in lust, gluttony, ambition. I think again of Thomas Wolfe roaming the stacks of Widener Library, devouring all he saw, wrought up in a swirl of reading and visions of glory. This was one of my early misdefinitions of wildness, confusing it somehow with ambition and glory. If I am going to continue to idealize the word, and not discard it completely, then I obviously need a more mature definition. The other day, the house secretary told me that a boy, a junior, had almost died in Adams House, where we live, by drunkenly jumping out the window. I winced and recoiled, as I still do whenever I climb a ladder or walk over a high foot bridge.

~

Coyotes' howling is, among other things, a "territorial advertisement." It is also, more simply, a greeting.

At the zoo each morning the battle really begins when Jon walks into the cage. The two males jump in his lap first while everyone else runs around jockeying for the seat. "If the others come too close, you'll see Trans react," Jon tells me. The hierarchy of this coyote family seems the opposite of what we romanticize as "wild." At times the cage is like some kind of nightmarish junior high school lunchroom that the coyotes can never graduate from. Though Jon still calls them pups, and though they *are* pups, since coyotes, like humans, are very slow to become independent, they look full grown. Lupe, a huge coyote at almost fifty pounds, rules. Second in command is Trans, who, though also the second lightest, is a male, dominating the females. This can be comical, and points to the psychological element of the hierarchy, when you watch Trans pin down Cane, who is nine pounds heavier than he is and could easily reverse things. At the low end of the pecking order is the runt Late, who won't even approach the group despite the appeal of seeing Jon.

"Late doesn't even come over because she knows she'll get beat up."

While Lupe luxuriates in Jon's lap, the rest of the coyotes chase each other around, nipping at each other's haunches, running in circles of active submission or lying down in a passive form of the same. There is a lot of high, squeaky whining, like the sound of basketball sneakers scuffing on a gym floor, and what Jon calls "preliminary whines—not getting hurt, just anticipating."

Gradually Lupe allows others to edge into Jon's lap, and then the rest of the coyotes, all except Late, gather close. Sometimes Jon will then lead a second howl right there on the rock, the whole group, including him, stretching their muzzles up to the sky. All the while, Jon, wearing his fingerless wool gloves, pets and roughs up their coats.

I like Jon, and admire him despite a vague Tony Robbins-ish quality. He is still a kid and wears his ambition on his sleeve, but it is only the rare person who doesn't start out with some excesses. For all I know, he may very well develop into a thinker as well as a scientist, into a kind of George Scaheller of coyotes. But for the moment, our two projects are to some extent running at cross-purposes.

Of course, I am using him and studying him, in my writerly way, as surely as he is using the coyotes that he is also so genuinely fond of. But it's more than that. It's not so much the zoo project that bothers me as the radio-collar project that he is running concurrently. In the weeks since I went tracking with Dave Eatnough, the box traps still haven't captured any coyotes, but they have inadvertently trapped six crows, two more fishers, and two red-tailed hawks, who flailed about inside the traps. The hawks were injured and had to be killed, and it was about then that I signed off on the project for good. I am still going to the zoo on a regular basis, but I am convinced that if it is really wildness I'm looking for then I should want no part of this other project. It's not that I think myself morally above it, it's just that I am after a different quarry.

The coyotes themselves have avoided the traps, though that isn't putting it exactly right. Their footprints are all around the cage, and during this frozen winter they are certainly well aware of the meat that sits inside the bars, tempting them with its rank smell. But coyotes are famously savvy when it comes to human traps. Gary Synder points out that coyotes, unlike wolves, would never take the poison meat that the pioneers laid out to exterminate them. The fact that coyotes actually urinate on man's traps is a case in which the behavior of the biological coyote and the mythic one are perfect reflections of the other.

The one Boston-area coyote who was stupid enough to take the bait was the bald, mangy, starving creature who Jon Way and Dave Eatnough named Bart. Half-dead to begin with, with his hairless cord-like tail, Bart looked more rat than canid. Being a coyote, he likely knew that the meat in the trap was trouble, but being desperate, he decided to risk it. "The coyote is a living breathing allegory of Want," Mark Twain wrote, and Bart fits the bill. (Though despite a severe case of mange, he weighed in at 32 pounds, almost twenty pounds less than Lupe, but not bad for winter.) After Bart was caught, he was drugged, collared, and finally released. He now roams the Breakhart Reservation in Saugus (the same reservation that, in a semi-acronym, gives him his name). Bart kept very still in the days after his release, leading Jon to worry that he was dead, but on February 11 he was seen trotting along with two other coyotes through what Jon described as "a potential summer-time rendezvous for his social group." Still, hopes aren't very high for Bart as the snows continue, and I can't imagine a half-pound collar helps his cause. I picture families neighboring the reservation pointing out their windows and exclaiming over the bald, collared oversized chihuahua jogging through their back yard.

~

I have said that the challenge is to keep the wild within us as we live increasingly domestic lives. I have no interest in the wildness of my youth—the wildness of jumping out of buildings—any more than I want my moods to swing wildly. Like my brother, who, having been homeless, mocks the hip Kerouacian version of homelessness, I am tired of clichéd wild ways. Part of my current process has been peeling off and discarding the husks of old definitions of the wild. "Lacking discipline, restraint or control, unruly." I don't care for that, my youngest definition. "Full of ungovernable intense emotion." That isn't my wild any longer either. "Reckless, risky?" Possibly, but . . . "Random or spontaneous." That might be getting there. Or the last definition, that of card games: "having a random equivalency value to be determined by the dealer's needs or choice: *playing poker with deuces wild*." This, it seems to me, is closer to the Trickster's wild: the unexpected, the fortuitous, the random. The fact that, for all the claims of reason and science, life remains a stubborn intractable creature, essentially out of our control. And it would make a neat Zen package to wrap this all up by saying that we need only accept this uncertainty, except that our constant frustrated battle for some foundation, something certain, is part of what makes the whole human situation so messy. And telling us to accept what we can't accept doesn't help much either.

Like the rest of us, I am a creature of chaos, and after forty-two years it may just be time to admit it. I am finally figuring out that ambition is just a grid you place over the green thing, often a wildly implausible and inaccurate grid. "Firm ground is not available ground," said A. R. Ammons, but that doesn't stop human beings from spending the better part of their lives looking for something firm. Trickster hates firm ground. He chops up the ground below our feet, keeps us moving, leads us into that place that Lewis Hyde calls "betwixt-and-between." If the world has a sense of humor then so should its gods, and the trickster gods—from Hermes to Loki to Eshu to Coyote—are undoubtedly gods with senses of humor. Life, real life, seems almost to resent an earnest mindset, and instantly turns to making a mockery of it. Any philosophy that excludes laughter cheapens life. To paraphrase a now oft-quoted saying: "When the last human being is gone coyote will lift his leg on the grave."

~

After a few days of melting—during which brown creeks of filth and snowmelt ran down from Mass Ave. to Mt. Auburn, and the grackles and sparrows stirred—the cold has returned. Last Saturday Nina and I went to the Baby Fair at the Expo Center. Hundreds of people jammed aisles filled with hundreds of carseats and strollers and cribs, inducing a few moments of deep panic and tightening in our chests. But we fought through it and even ended up with a great find: something called a Graco Metro Lite Travel System, a combination car seat and stroller. Then, last night, Hadley started pressing with a new ferocity, kicking against Nina's belly and my back for the better part of the night. Clearly, she wants out.

Meanwhile there have been rumblings from my brother. When I drove by his house to pick him up for dinner, he had that hollow look that I have come to fear. He was scribbling on his hands with a ballpoint, glaring up at me when I hadn't said anything, wearing a slight, frightening smile. There was a lot of dead air, and some nodding to voices I couldn't hear. When I brought up the subject of taking his medication, he snapped. "Leave it to me and the doctors, okay?" "Are you doing okay?" I asked. "Great, I'm doing great. Just fine." A moment passed and then he added, "I'm doing fine, okay?"

A disturbing visit but not as disturbing as the news I receive when I get home. His roommates call to tell me he has been staring at them when they watch TV, that he is smoking obsessively and walking around naked laughing to himself, that one day he began wildly jumping up and down shouting obscenities. "He's been a whirlwind of shit and destruction," one roommate says. Sounds like the brother I know, though I am not so sure the roommate telling me this tale is much of a reliable narrator. Reliable or not, they now want to kick him out of the apartment and they want me to help.

We have had two good years, two "tractable" years with me as his guardian, two years at the same job and in the same apartment. But with this illness, you learn never to think in the long term. Spring is the season of danger. It usually happens the same way: In late winter he stops taking the medication for a while and then feels his mind spark alive. Who can blame him for stopping? The medicine, which allows him to be effective in life, which allows him to be in control and less of a bother to us, also deadens his once-lively brain. And when he first begins to come alive in late winter, it *does* seem such an innocent and positive thing. He is funnier; he laughs more freely; he reads. A hint of this aliveness is all it takes for him to want to stop the medicine entirely. And so he does, he does stop. But then, soon after, all the rest starts coming alive too: the voices, the spiels, the paranoia. Coming with spring as surely as snowmelt. What is first a thaw quickly becomes a flood.

Meanwhile, the world's news is no less chaotic. After I get off the phone with Peter's roommates, Nina and I head down to a candlelight vigil on the river. We walk up onto the high point of the foot bridge, holding our candles like supplicants. Some folks send their candles floating out onto the Charles attached to small chunks of ice, the waving lights reflecting back up from the black water.

~

Last night, the police went to Peter's apartment in Brighton. He yelled at them about how his rights were being violated by his doctor and that skinhheads were after his sister in New York. The cops took him to the emergency room at Beth Israel and there the psychiatrist on duty took over. He had to be restrained—not because he was violent but because he kept trying to get up to walk out. They gave him some Haldol and will try to get him into a private room today.

Meanwhile war has begun. The news people cover the war like it was sports, calling the death and destruction "shock and awe." This afternoon I cancel my class due to the "walk out," joining hundreds of other students and teachers in a march to Government Center. We pound drums and give peace signs in a manner that prompts one onlooker to say into his cell phone, "I just walked out of my office into 1973." There is a comic military aspect to the long-haired leaders of the march, who order us around with bullhorns. There's something very military about these organizers, and they clearly think this is their moment in the sun. One of them gets into a shouting match with a burly construction worker.

"You're a bunch of jackasses," the construction worker yells. Then, after the leader/bullhorn guy yells back, the construction worker walks up to the man, jabs a finger near his chest, and shouts in his face: "You fucking virgin hippie. Fuck you!"

But that is as bad as the confrontations get. For the most part, people in the streets are remarkably supportive, hanging out of their office windows and flashing back peace signs as we walk through the high-rise canyons of downtown.

Later, on the nightly news, the networks demonstrate their usual distorted definition of "balance." After they show the thousands of us marching, they give equal time to twenty people waving American flags on a street corner in Acton.

When I bring a pizza by for Peter at the hospital, we barely mention the war. The strong medicine has begun to kick in already, the doctors practicing their own brand of "shock and awe." Peter is no longer the frightening large man he was a few days ago, but a big, dully smiling, tractable boy. He nods vaguely when I tell him about the peace march. He was once the most political member of our family, and the dark family joke of all this was that George W. Bush was the very first person Peter was paranoid about, during Peter's brief stay in Austin. He was convinced that Bush was out to get him and to destroy the world. Now, medicated again, he could care less what George Bush does.

It is an ugly choice that life and biology have dealt Peter. Numb safety or wild paranoia. For the family, there is no choice. We want safety, control, quiet. Bring on the drugs, we say. But the patient remembers a life before medication. The patient remembers the freedom of spontaneous thought, of ideas crackling, of laughter. For all the touting of new "miracle" drugs, that remains the crux of the problem. They will need to find a way to allow for the *good wild* without the bad. They will need to do the impossible.

~

Jon Way tells me that a coyote was shot in Malden. It was one of the coyotes they were hoping to catch for their study. He doesn't have many details but the first indications are that it was shot by a Malden police officer sometime after midnight.

Coyotes are considered troublemakers, but trouble for who? We resent them because they have adapted almost as well as we have to lives of cars and trash. Our cat, Tabernash, formerly a stray who made his living hunting, has not taken to the city. He yowls all night, keeping us up, mourning his former wild life. We keep him inside for "his own good." But it isn't safety he's interested in.

By the way, we were just told that Harvard made the list of top terrorist targets. This makes us feel important.

~

Is it any wonder that I should embrace a philosophy of uncertainty? The real wonder is that anyone wouldn't. Perhaps that is what is so irksome about those currently in power. Their *certainty*.

We all have the impulse to say once and finally: "This is the way it is." Even now, I feel that urge bubbling up again. As I sit here, awaiting spring and war's end and the birth of my daughter, I try to make sense of the world. And that, Coyote tells me, is my big mistake.

But still . . . what to *make* of all this? Carl Jung suggests that modern students can return to long-gone Trickster myths "like an old river-bed in which water still flows." I like the image, though I am careful to point out that I'm not trying to re-invent my own Trickster religion. What I'm after is something closer to a personal chaos theory, an uncertainty principle of the self.

What life serves up most consistently is the inconsistent, the chaotic, the unexpected. Again, what to *do* with this? "Be in uncertainties" as Keats said? Well, yes, for starters. At the very least, be suspicious of whole-cloth philosophies. Moments of wonder in the natural world, for instance, don't necessarily have to translate into a philosophy of wonder. One of the functions of Coyote is to overturn, disrupt, unsettle. Being in uncertainties may not be very comfortable, but at least it has the value of being truthful, being honest, about the world. Why pretend the world is neat, ordered, within our control? Coyote will not let us have air-tight theories, just as *Canis latrans* itself is always demonstrating intelligent aberrant behavior that contradicts the accepted behavior of the species.

If the Trickster does allow moments of contentment, they are only moments, not lasting long enough for any kind of self-satisfaction. As I get older, the phrase "It's always something" has begun to seem more philosophic than cliché. I can't make a philosophy out of secondhand biology and pilfered Native American myths, but I can study the Trickster. And if I listen closely, I can hear what Coyote is trying to say:

Don't be afraid of getting your hands dirty. Splash around like a child playing with finger paints. Cross borders. Cross boundaries. Laugh at the whole thing but at the same time take it seriously, "play for mortal stakes." Value your brain but also your anus: They both have their roles. Be suspicious of traps. Of walls and gates, and aphorisms. Fight duplicity with urine.

Not an airtight philosophy, true. But it will have to do for now.

~

We continue to bomb the cradle of civilization. Yesterday we attacked what was once Babylon. Since the war started, we have dropped 8,000 pounds of smart bombs between the Tigris and Euphrates.

Peter headed home today. I talked his roommates into giving him two more weeks while he looks for a new place. He is, as they say, a new man. As we walked out the front door of the hospital, I realized for the first time that you can see the windows of the floor where Nina will soon give birth.

~

The news is that Bart is dead, the most recent victim of this brutal winter. He was found curled up like a fetal rat near the wood pile where he made his den. Back on February 16, Jon had hiked in and discovered Bart asleep on a pile of steamy mulch, giving him a clue as to how an almost hairless canid could survive the winter. According to Jon's Web report, the mulch was "probably about 70 degrees despite the air temperature barely reaching 10 degrees today." The mulch belonged to a small pig farm and the farm's caretaker told Jon that he had seen the coyotes coming around searching for garbage. He had noticed Bart before, collar and all, and declared him "one of the ugliest things I've ever seen." Jon continued his report: "Apparently, the caretaker sees these coyotes on a daily basis and also sees flocks of wild turkey, groups of deer, and occasional fishers and bobcats. This is all within the urban metro-Boston Route 95/128 belt. We were surprised to learn the potential of bobcat being in our urban study area."

Three days later, on February 19, the day I saw the heron with my class and the day after the record snow, Jon, Dave Eatnough, and a friend hiked in. Using radio tracking, they found Bart curled up deep inside a wood pile that he seemed to be using as a den. Jon writes:

> . . . after a brief search (with a flashlight) we found him under an approximate 10 × 5 foot piece of plywood (from an old deck). It was like a normal coyote whelping den with a narrow entrance. He was safely lying in the back of the den in an apparent catatonic state. Clearly he must have been very frightened from the noise we were making outside the plywood den. . . . After taking a few minutes of video, we left the area. . . .
>
> This is one of the first instances that I am aware of a non-pup or whelping female using a den-like structure. Contrary to common belief, coyotes do not seem to use dens beyond a couple months of age (except when females give birth.) Bart clearly seemed to be in there because of the blizzard last night. I wish he needed a new collar because we easily had him trapped!

We are taught not to anthropomorphize, but it's hard not to imagine Bart's thoughts upon seeing Jon and his pals shining their flashlight and pointing their video camera. *Not these guys again*, the poor coyote must have thought. *Why can't I shake these guys? What do they want from me? Why won't they stop hounding me?*

Less than a month later, the next time the gang saw Bart, he was dead. He had starved, the fate of many animals this winter, and was down to 24 pounds. This was half the weight of Lupe, eating his dogfood and butcher's meat at the zoo.

~

Coyote, it should be clear by now, is not all fun and games. It's easy to talk vaguely about wildness without consequences, but it is important to remember that it was Trickster who brought death into the world. He had his reasons, worries about overpopulation being one, but he was the first to pay the price: His daughter was the very first creature to die. He ached with regret and tried to take back what he'd done but, as usual, could not. Coyote also brought us fire, and ushered in a time of tools and technology. Coyote is both creator and destroyer, bringer and taker.

~

This semester I force-fed my Harvard students Turner's *The Abstract Wild*. Like the Trickster, Turner is a Westerner, and he tends to make Easterners uncomfortable. Here, for instance, are his thoughts on the radio surveillance of animals:

Biological controls are now ubiquitous. Biologists control grizzlies, they trap and collar cranes, they have cute little radio backpacks for frogs, they bolt brightly colored plastic buttons to the beaks of harlequin ducks, they even put radio transmitters on minnows. And always for the same reason: more information for a better, healthier ecosystem. Information and control are indivisible. . . . It (control) is the main point, perhaps the only point, of surveillance.

The great need now, is to begin to imagine an alternative. Perhaps we don't need more information; maybe the emphasis on biological inventories, species recovery, surveillance, and monitoring is a further step in the wrong direction.

The biologists in the class were irritated, and a little unnerved, by this, as well they should be. Recently, I sent Turner a note that said, "You'll be happy to know you frighten the scientists a little." He wrote back: "It does make me happy. No one—scientists least—likes confronting their shadow. The 'wild' elk here in Jackson Hole are now fenced, inoculated, fed elk kibble, and shot with hormones for birth control. That's wildlife biology for you. . . ."

I take Turner's phrase, "imagine an alternative," as a challenge. We need to find a way to imagine the lives of animals, of all nature, not in either a purely romantic or purely scientific way, but in ways where they intermingle with our own wild lives. With Bart's death, I am officially quitting Jon Way's coyote project. I do not want to make Jon into a villain, because he isn't one. But nature for him has very specific uses, and wildness isn't even a part of the equation. Here are the on-line lessons he has taken from Bart's death:

We are now down to [zero] coyotes radio-collared in the north Boston area. We are still actively box-trapping and a coyote (on video) regularly goes halfway into the traps but never to the back of it to get captured. Very frustrating indeed. We are now exploring the option of buying bigger box/cage traps. We strongly feel that a bigger opening will entice coyotes to enter the trap a little easier.

The lesson then is to get a bigger trap! In this looking-glass world, Jon is Wile E. Coyote and *Canis latrans* is the Road Runner. It seems appropriate that Jon's coyote project, that my coyote project, that any "coyote project" should end in frustration and failure. Though I wish Jon no ill will, I can't help but find myself rooting against him and his traps. Or, to put it more positively, I find myself rooting for the Trickster.

howl

In the city, sparrows fly out of the mouths of lions.

It's true. It happens every spring, right above our apartment, where a row of leonine gargoyles line the eaves of Claverly Hall. Starting in late March, straw and sticks drool from the lions' mouths as house sparrows gather bunting for their spring nests. Their chatter wakes me up earlier every morning, even before the rumbling of the dinosaur garbage trucks.

With spring I have begun to try to imagine the city as it once was. When it was first settled by Europeans, in 1636, it was called Newtowne. Below Watertown, the Charles is a man-made river, and when the settlers first arrived the basin was a salt marsh like the one by my home on Sesuit Neck, tidal creeks flowing down toward the harbor. Night-herons still roost by the hundreds along the river, and a simple kayak trip upriver will let you travel back in time, allowing you to imagine the water as a highway for much more than powerboats and crew shells. Just as it did twenty years ago, the river provides me a refuge from school and city. Hiking through the Charles basin, I begin to notice that spring is finally showing signs of breaking through. The crew coaches are out in their motorboats, poling their way through the ice flows, breaking them up and hurrying along ice-out, while several gulls, amused, watch their labor as they float by on harbor-bound icebergs. The willows are finally giving their yellow hints of spring and mockingbirds are everywhere, trying to sing in the season. It comes slowly, grudgingly. April showers bring May showers. On one particularly rainy day, I stop on my way to a student-faculty dinner at the Co-op. A red-tailed hawk is hunting a squirrel in Harvard Yard, right near Johnson Gate, the Yard's front entrance. The hawk swoops from tree to tree, ignoring both the drizzle and the crowds of people walking below, focused on the squirrel, which cowers below a yellow-poplar. It is strong drama: the hawk's intense patience, the squirrel's panic and eagerness to run (just what the hawk wants)! Finally the squirrel makes a dash and the hawk swoops, almost nailing the rodent before it scrambles into a hole in the brick wall of the gate. Though there is little chance the squirrel is coming out any time soon, the hawk stays and watches from a branch of the poplar, never taking its eyes off the hole.

It's funny, but I don't think I've ever seen a hawk from closer up. I was only about fifteen feet below it when it was staring down the squirrel and I can't get over how burly it looked (though I knew that—due to its hollow bones—it didn't weigh as much as our housecats). Only one other walker stopped to watch the show, but there is constant foot traffic and it occurs to me that one of the red-tail's adaptations to life in Harvard Yard is habituating to the crowds of humans. I am soaked through by the time I leave, and I run up to the Co-op to make up time, appearing at my student's dinner dripping both sweat and water but still filled with a wild buzz from hawk-watching.

~

When I got back home a few nights ago something strange had happened to Nina. She was dusting—actually dusting!—an activity previously unknown to our homes. We had read about how expectant parents begin to experience the "nesting impulse" and here it was. Over the last few days both of us have turned into neat freaks and everything is clean and in place. Today I put together the co-sleeper and the net we bought to cover it (to keep the cats out), installed the car seat, and then assembled the crib and changing table. We are getting ready . . . but for what? For the world to change, of course.

If I ever needed more proof that we are driven by simple biology, the nesting instinct provides it. Meanwhile, my brother gives me even more evidence that the brain is just another organ. He is back at work, getting along with his roommates, calling us to inquire politely about the arrival of our firstborn. And I imagine that I will have little problem letting this man, who just weeks ago had to be restrained in the hopsital, hold our newborn. Why not? You wouldn't recognize him if you saw him first a month ago and then now. He is transformed, though his transformation has none of the pleasures of traditional narrative. His isn't an inspiring story of persistence, insight, and bravery. Oh, there is plenty of bravery, and effort, but most of the change is due to the pills he swallows once a day.

We will take our miracles where we can find them, however. The fact is, we wouldn't have time to help Peter if he were to break down again. With anticipation of the big event preoccupying us, everything else has fallen by the wayside. Suddenly everything is *baby*. There is little time for coyote tracking, for instance. Originally, I'd hoped to become as obsessed with *Canis latrans* as I once was with ospreys, but that will not be happening. I have had some coyote successes but they have been small. By sheer good luck, I was at the zoo on the day that Jon first saw the coyotes exhibiting sexual activity, with Lupe trying to mount Cane. Jon seemed almost as excited as Lupe, and told me that, despite the fact the animals were siblings, it was possible for them to form "a copulatory tie if they mate . . . just like dogs get stuck together so will they."

That is about the extent of my zoo discoveries, and though I have made it out to the den at the cemetery a couple of times, for the most part I now take my nature where I find it. The other day I pedalled with my friend Hones to the tiny city park where he had seen a sharp-shinned hawk take out a sparrow in mid-flight, but the hawk was not around. Last night Nina and I went to a movie (our last?) at Kendall Square, and while walking to the theater, Nina saw something dart across the road and pointed. I didn't see it but she swore it was a wild turkey, so I ran up around the corner and tried to catch a glimpse. This was dead in the middle of the city, buildings everywhere, with the train tracks running through providing the only possible "wilderness." I saw some twelve-year-old boys with a basketball chasing something, and so I followed them. "That's one big fucking chicken," they said, and laughed. I asked where it was and they pointed down the street to a vacant lot. I tried to sneak up on it, keeping downwind, but it ran off when I got within forty yards. I couldn't be 100 percent sure, but it looked like a wild turkey.

~

"It's amazing how many Harvard students dress like prostitutes," Nina says.

On the warm days, the clothes come off in the Square. Young girls everywhere.

Nina's comment may sound prudish, but it's true. Whoever inspired this style of low-cut pants—Britney? Christine Aguiellera?—didn't do most of these kids any favors. It is only on the rare person that the inch or so below the belly button looks attractive.

Along with the low-slung trousers, out come the cell phones and other electronic devices. They all walk around chattering to themselves like schizophrenics. Half of the people seem to have those little earphones jammed in their ears and they happily converse right out loud, seemingly with no one. It brings out the moralist in me and I can't help but think that, as well as looking crazy, these people are losing the capacity to dwell in their own minds. Yesterday I went to a reading and there were so many little electronic burbles and twits that you might have thought it was taking place inside a great computer. Watch alarms and Walkmen and beeps and squibs and rings. Then, to top it all off, the *author's* cell phone rang right before she was about to speak.

Like the collared coyotes, these people never shake their electronic devices. They are constantly hooked up and never *out of touch*. The first thing my students do, after walking from the library to their next class, or from one class to another, is check their e-mail on the hallway computer, lest they *miss something*. Again, like the collared coyotes, they are made both easy to track and tractable by all this.

I know all this muttering makes me sound like the middle-aged curmudgeon I am. And I know I'm a hypocrite: I own a cell phone and rarely go a day without checking my e-mail. But hypocrisy won't stop me from moralizing. In fact, being aggressively (and hypocritically) judgmental is one of the true pleasures of living in the city, with so many people around to judge. I've noticed that this aggressive hypocrisy is most pointed when it comes to traffic. Put me in a car and I hate arrogant pedestrians; set me out on foot and I mutter about obnoxious fucking cars; give me a bike and I hate both cars and walkers. It seems to me that there is a freedom in this low-level venting of spleen, spleen that might turn ingrown in a more rural, isolated setting.

~

Trickster reared his head again last night.

First, Jon Way e-mailed to tell me that Harvard, despite its billion dollar endowment, hasn't paid him the hundred dollars it owes him for speaking to my class last fall. He also forwarded the latest updates from his coyote Web page. The coyote study continues to be, in Jon's words, "very frustrating." More and more coyotes are sniffing around the cages but not going in, or if they go in, they will back out before they spring the trap. "Adult females should be giving birth soon (or already)," Jon reported on April 14, so "hopefully, a few hungry females will enter traps in the next month of so." In the meantime, the traps have snared yet another fisher and a turkey vulture.

Before I dozed off last night, I picked up my coyote books and skimmed through randomly. I read these words in an essay by Karl Kerenyi:

> Trickster is already present, exhibiting his true nature as—so we might sum up, under a single active principle, the component elements "phallic," "voracious," "sly," "stupid"—*the spirit of disorder, the enemy of boundaries.*
>
> . . . Disorder belongs to the totality of life, and the spirit of disorder is the trickster. His function in an archaic society, or rather the function of his mythology, of the tales told about him, is to add disorder to order and so make a whole, to render possible, within the fixed bounds of what is permitted, an experience of what is not permitted.

~

Pear tress like rooted clouds bloom along Dunster Street, white blossoms drifting everywhere. It is May now and the early glory of the magnolias is over. That southern tree bloomed from the top down and reigned over the courtyard outside our window until it was overthrown recently by the pink and white crabapples. The long-restrained spring is finally and truly breaking free. Tonight Nina's contractions are coming almost five minutes apart, but it isn't like a TV show. We don't throw our bags in the car and rush to the hospital, but are told by the doctor that we must wait until Nina's body convulses in a more precise and orderly manner.

I am not the first person to have a child, I understand that, but it sure feels that way.

~

Birth catches me unawares.

Wait a second—that isn't right, it sounds too literary and old-fashioned. And it is putting it too mildly. The experience doesn't merely "surprise" me either. It shocks me. How can something you have been preparing for for nine months, something you have heard about your whole life, something that is the basis for all life . . . how can that have the power to shock? I don't know.

It is a long and grueling labor. Nina gets to experience all flavors of childbirth. First, some thirty or so hours of building labor at home. Then a period of pain in the hospital where she can barely move. The rooms have showers and once Nina gets in she can't get out. She is down on all fours, the steaming water hitting her lower back full on, easing what is uneasable. She has it in her mind that she will do this without drugs, in part because they have told her that if she gets an epidural she won't be able to "move around." But as it is she can't move anyway. Then the nurse says that if she does get the epidural "the pain will go away." It is that magic phrase that resonates in her mind. *The pain will go away.*

And it does for a while. Neither of us slept during the erratic labor of the night before but after the drugs kick in we both rest, on and off, for a few hours. Until the middle of the night when we hear the word "complication." The baby's heartrate is decelerating during contractions, not a big worry, we are told, but worrisome enough because Nina has not dilated as much as they would like. The worry continues into the morning when the doctor lays out our options for us. It is clear that she thinks— and soon we agree to think—that a C-section is necessary. Once we say yes to the operation, someone pushes a fast-forward button. Less than half an hour later, Nina is lying on the operating table and I am in scrubs looking from my wife's face, bravely smiling, to, on the other side of the sheet, her bloody middle. It is exactly the same set-up as my own operation, twelve years before, down to the separating sheet and epidural, though that doesn't occur to me until later. In the moment, nothing much *does* occur to me, and I am not expecting anything, when the doctors reach into my wife, up to their elbows, and then a bloody head emerges, straight up, in the style of Kurtz emerging from the water in *Apocalypse Now*. That was when the perpetual state of shock—the state I remain in—began. Next comes the full bloody emergence and a wild squall of life as Hadley's little arms raise over her head in victory. The cord is cut, the placenta comes splashing out into a pail (Nina is a small woman—how can all this come out of her like bloody clowns piling out of a circus car?), and the baby is whisked off into the corner to be cleaned, and immediately, *tested*. I am whisked along with her and she passes her tests, and is wrapped in a blanket and, before I know it, handed to me. For the nurses and doctors, this is an everyday experience but they are sensitive enough to at least mimic awe. I don't have to pretend. I have been relatively calm to this point, but my one fear was that I would not know how to hold the baby, and that, worse, I would drop her. But it turns out I do know how to hold her, naturally, and I will not drop her. I know that with the utmost confidence as I cradle her in my arms.

It isn't fair that I am the first to hold her after all the work that Nina has done. From behind her curtain she is calling, "Where is she? What does she look like?" I carry Hadley over and dip her down to show Nina her pink perfect body. And it is somewhere around that moment that I feel a great rush come surging up. Sure it is physiological—goosebumps and tingling scalp and a hundred other physical symptoms—but it is also more than that, a wild gushing love of the sort I've never felt before. The only experience that even compares to it is the obverse: holding my father's hand as his breathing slowed and ended. But even that pales. Before I know it my chest is throbbing and I am holding Hadley tighter and I am feeling things coming up from someplace too deep for words.

~

"Isn't it the wildest thing?" a friend will ask me much later. And maybe that is what surprises me, what shocks me, about birth. Why didn't somebody tell me it was like *this*? They don't pitch the idea of children the right way when they talk about car seats and sleeplessness and play dates. They forget to mention the wild, drug-like rush.

I am not a big crier, or maybe I should say I *was* not a big crier until now. The next day I am at it again, sobbing as I dance around the room with Hadley in my arms in the twilight as Nina sleeps, recovering from birth and major surgery. I am a father—an idea I can't quite get my head around—and this helpless pink animal is my daughter. I suspect I will soon be offending all my childless friends by becoming a proselytizer of procreation, just the way people used to bug the shit out of me by only talking about their kids. But I know myself well enough to know I won't be able to help it. Meanwhile I dance to James Taylor—James Taylor! Already I am becoming a soft-rock parental caricature—while Hadley reaches out with her long fingernails and wraps her perfect old-man hand around my forefinger. Whatever the quality of the music, the experience itself is primal, only comparable with falling in love or certain LSD trips and even those obviously paling, both in terms of intensity and duration. By the third day these evening dances will have taken on the feel of ritual, but it will take a while longer until they are crusted over by repetition. For now the moments remain alive.

The reason we have a CD player in the room, the same reason we have the painting of a Cape Cod beach and that I took a massage class, is that we were prepared for a long natural labor with lots of coaching and caressing. We had none of that, Nina screaming at me every time I tried to touch her. Out of all the classes and books and manuals, I gleaned only one bit of information that, in retrospect, was worthwhile. It was a piece of advice that Trickster could have given: Be prepared to abandon your plans. Those who swear they won't take drugs end up getting epidurals while those determined to get an epidural right away find that they are caught up in labor and now it is too late, and those vowing to have a natural birth end up with a C-section. In short, birth can't be pre-planned. As I dance around the room with Hadley I wonder how much time and energy we waste trying to maintain the illusion that we create our own fate. We play imaginary games, make charts and graphs, and sing ourselves reassuring songs. But it doesn't help in the end. The future is chartless.

~

"Everything happens for a reason," the true believers say.
"Yes," Old Man Coyote says. "And that reason is accident. That reason is chance."

~

Back home we stagger sleepless through the finally blooming city. Hadley howls deep into the night, her furious and seemingly constant proclamation of existence. I push her around and around in the stroller, rumbling over the Adams House courtyard bricks until midnight, under the crabapple and Hawthorn trees, pausing to breathe in the hemlock on the corner. Classes are over and the Harvard students let loose after a year of restraint, yipping and roaring until six in the morning. After a dozen laps I notice that one kid is taking a leak by the courtyard gate. I sneak a peek to see if Hadley is sleeping. A little disgruntled Buddha stares back up at me.

Throughout the spring, the birds fly in and out of the lions' mouths. The other day a kestrel found itself trapped in one of the dorm rooms three floors above us. Kestrels are feathery missiles, small, fierce falcons that hunt other birds, and my thought is that it must have been going after one of the songbirds that nest below the student windows. In usual Harvard fashion, experts were called in to trap and release the bird. Once released, the kestrel bolted into the air but then circled back and alighted on the tower to assess where it had been, the mistakes it had made. It would not be trapped again.

One day, on my way down to river, I notice that the tree swallows are back, carving up the air. Life bursts out of the concrete world. Look up at any of these lightposts and you see nests: Near the old gym I watch chickadees fly out from under one of the stanchions and catbirds emerge from behind a pompous old Veritas crest on Quincy House. Meanwhile, in front of Lowell House, a mockingbird is doing a perfect imitation of an oriole, and then a little while later, by the water, I see the oriole itself. It shines fierce orange and black, flitting boldly from branch to branch and letting out its liquid cry in purer form than its imitator. The river is cluttered with scullers, galley slaves involved in some ancient form of discipline the rest of us don't understand. "We have an advantage over other boats," a driven young coach yells through his bullhorn across the water. "We have the athleticism and discipline to make the slight adjustments they can't." He will make them believe.

While the crew shells dominate the river, geese cover the riverbank. I watch four Canada geese with dozens of goslings, down-covered, pecking at the grass. There is a yellow-greenish, almost urine-stained, color to the goslings, a yellow-greenish shine to their heads. When humans get too close they hurry back to make sure they are in the phalanx behind the adults. At this point in the goslings' development, their necks not long yet, their bills are the thing they have most in common with parents. During the course of the day several different mothers tend them in a kind of communal goose daycare.

The birds I am most excited about are the night-herons. They lead a strange nocturnal life, and during the day they try to rest. But they've picked a bad place for roosting, here in this center of human community, and they are constantly disturbed, flying back and forth, complaining with loud "sproak"s, trying to seek out some privacy. On the days that I kayak I can get close enough to see their burning eyes. One day I watch dozens of them roosting around the small camp of the homeless man behind a concrete barrier. I keep perfectly still, drifting in the slow current, and they don't fly off, their eyes reflecting the red-orange of the blooming maple they sit in. They have large feet, silky white underfeathers, gray backs, black black bills, and a distinctive hunch. They hop nervously from branch to branch. Then, before they fly off, they dip down a little, as if they need to push off.

~

My brother visits and we talk about the war for a while. The war is over, we are told, though more soldiers die every day. My brother speaks in a calm, quiet voice. He looks good. Before he leaves, he holds the baby, just as I imagined, gently rocking her in his arms.

~

"Spring has its sappy wisdom," writes Richard Rodriguez. It is sap that interests me now. Blood, juice, life. And youth. This spring, rather than be an apprentice, I have become a mentor to many young students. They see their friends heading off to internships on Wall Street, and they want to know what kind of internships they should get. "How to be a writer," is the hidden question below all the other questions. I tell them funny stories of my own struggles and give pep talks about persistence but what can I really say? "Go out and get a series of crappy jobs while you struggle"? "It will take ten years or so to get started"? I understand this isn't very glamorous advice. So I take them out for beers at Daedelus, our neighborhood bar, and I encourage them, knowing that rewards—and glamor—have to be exaggerated at the start. Once we are a little drunk, I help out when I can with practical advice no one gave me, (the same way I wish someone had given me a practical talk about sex when I became a teenager), how to write a cover letter, say, or which grad schools are worth considering. I don't find myself rolling my eyes at their idealism or naiveté, at least not very often. I write notes to myself about trying to be "relentlessly generous" as a teacher, but I have my selfish motives, too. I like their energy. I like being around them. I like the juice they give me.

And, I can say finally, I like being in the city. I never had Paris or Rome, or New York for that matter, and, to paraphrase Wallace Stegner, Cambridge is the closest I've gotten. Now, back here after twenty years, it somehow seems the right place (as these random happenings so often seem "right" once forced upon us.) Throughout this wet spring I've been dipping into city books: so far I've read through *Patterson, Tropic of Cancer*, and *A Moveable Feast*. I've found that Hemingway's book fits into my new role as a mentor, a helper to young writers. If it is filled with viscious caricatures of his fellow writers, notably Fitzgerald, and with plenty of middle-age romanticizing of youth, there is also something sweet and domestic that is missing from his other work. To his claims about being poor and happy, it's natural to reply, "Well, that's easy for you to say . . . poverty didn't last too long for you, did it?" But that said, I'll admit I've used selections from the book for pep talks in my classes, especially his famous anecdote about losing the suitcase filled with his apprentice work. This spring, worried that I wouldn't be able to write once the baby came, I also used the book as a way to give myself pep talks. Here is the excerpt I taped up on the mantle over the fireplace:

So the next morning I woke early, boiled the bottles, made the formula, finished the bottling, gave Mr. Bumby a bottle and worked on the dining room table before anyone but he, F. Puss the cat, and I were awake. The two of them were quiet and good company and I worked better than I had ever done. In those days you did not really need anything, not even the rabbit's foot, but it was good to feel it in your pocket.

Our Hadley, I should point out, is no Mr. Bumby, and grows impatient if anyone pays much attention to anyone other than her. But despite this, writing has not been a problem for me; it just comes in smaller chunks. I have been getting to work on a city book of my own, a kind of anti-*Walden*. One of the things I need to get across in the book is that the domestic does not necessarily have to be the domesticated. That is what has most startled me about Hadley's birth. "Cuteness" has nothing to do with it. When people told me about children they forgot to mention the sheer animal energy of the experience. The euphoria. The throbbing tears. Of course it makes sense—that procreation would be tied to pleasure on the other end too. "Joy is a symptom by which right conduct is measured," said Joseph Wood Krutch of Thoreau's ecstatic periods. It isn't so strange that, given the biological rightness, the act would be accompanied by overwhleming joy. The other day I ran into the writer Jamacia Kinkaid on the street and she put both hands up to my face. "You've been transformed," she said. And then, less joyfully, "You'll never be this happy again."

The city has been the perfect perch to look back on the failed Walden of my last six years. I would have loved to stay on Cape Cod for much longer, maybe my whole life, but I have begun to see how the ability to root is tied to privilege. (Thoreau, for instance, doesn't get to squat at Walden without his Emersonian connections.) Privilege got me to Cape Cod in the first place, but then, like most of us, I eventually had to go where my work took me. I think the life that John Hay lived on Cape Cod, rooting down there for over half a century, is a fine life. It just isn't *my* life. Despite my own intentions, it turns out that I am a traveller, a mover. Though these constant uprootings tire me out, I take some small consolation in the fact that Coyote never settled. In fact, many of the stories, stressing movement, begin the same way: *Coyote was going there* ... This phrase is Coyote for "Once upon a time."

As well as the importance of movement, here is another thing Coyote teaches through his actions: *There was no golden age. There was no garden.* When Hemingway's suitcase was lost, I imagine, he wasn't quite as calm in real life as he was in his pages. Jung writes that one of the functions of the Trickster myths is to remind us that there were no "good old days," no halcyon time when the native people lived their simple lives in perfect harmony with nature. There were always accidents, adultery, and rectums. It never was any better than this. Even Walden wasn't *Walden*.

~

Part of the pleasure of a city is leaving it.

Today we fly back down to Cape Cod in our Honda Civic, babyseat and all. Hadley is too young for a road trip but here we go. We feel like we are playing hooky and when we cross the bridge there is a sense that we are heading over into a life other than our ordinary one. I talk a lot of nonsense these days and I find myself yelling out "Wheeeee" or something like that as we bomb down the other side of the canal.

This time there is no coyote by the side of Route 6 but that's okay. It was the pure accident of that event that led to my interest in Jon Way's project, but it is choice that has led me to turn away from it. I no longer have any interest in getting to know animals by collaring them like slaves. It's not that I am turning my nose up at information, but I do not merely want information, and I certainly don't want "control." I want more than facts; I want something that mingles with my life. I want, as Jack Turner put it, "to imagine an alternative" and on Cape Cod, where we are heading, I know of two men who have done just that, getting to know coyotes as more than mere subjects.

One of those men is Peter Trull. Trull was the first to record his scientific observations of the Cape Cod coyotes and continues to write extensively about the wild canids. I had hoped to spend some time in the field with him, but he has proven even more elusive than the coyotes, never returning phone calls, and breaking appointments when I finally pin him down for meetings. During the times I did encounter him, before I started trying to meet him, he seemed a charismatic and energetic—if somewhat unreliable—character. Some might have described his study of coyotes in a similar way, full of exciting anecdotal evidence though lacking the "objective" electronic surveillance of Jon Way, but that isn't fair. For instance, his DNA studies of Cape coyotes are helping determine the possible wolfish origins of Eastern Coyotes. More fascinating to me is the way he has *immersed* himself in his study. Here is a description of one of his coyote encounters from his recent book, *Coyotes in the Neighborhood*:

On a gray November day I was investigating an area in Eastham, Massachusetts where several coyotes had been seen and heard by residents. I was dressed in full camouflage—head to foot, gloves and all. My binoculars were around my neck. I had no camera. As I ducked into a dense cedar grove behind an empty summer residence an amazing thing happened. I was alarmed yet mesmerized as eight or ten long-eared owls swooped silently, like great moths, out of the dense cedars and vanished silently into the adjacent pine and oak woods . . . I decided

I would try to entice them back making the sound of a small mammal. By using my thumb and index finger pressed together and "kissing" them hard I can make a loud squeaking or chipping noise. To a predator like an owl, this squeaking sounds like a small mammal in distress and will often attract them. The owls didn't respond . . . but a coyote did. I knew I had awakened a coyote from a late afternoon snooze the second I heard the steps in the dry leaves a hundred feet or so away. . . . The footsteps were getting nearer and louder. I visually probed the thickets ahead of me through tiny slits in my camouflaged hood. I saw nothing yet sensed I was being watched. I squeaked again with just a kissing sound. The coyote came towards me at a brisk walk, stopping 15 feet away, searching the ground, looking at the sky, perplexed, and then piercing my gut with a real hard look directly in my eyes. I squeaked again, but then immediately wondered why I'd done it. The hair on my arms and neck stood straight up as the yellow eyes of the coyote came to within six feet of my face, staring directly into my eyes. . . .

This—much more than following the electronic beep of a radio—is the sort of coyote encounter that interests me.

~

If Peter Trull is Cape Cod's Coyote Man, than Eric Levy is our resident Bicycle Poet. I met Eric when he was writer-in-resident at the Cape Museum of Natural History, but he lost that position as part of a bloody coup among the nature lovers. Now he works as a park ranger, spending his afternoons and evenings bicycling through Nickerson State Park and along the Rail Trail, a bike path that runs down the Cape's morainal spine. Eric has been sending me Cape nature updates throughout my captivity in Cambridge, poems and other effusions about flora and fauna. Almost a week before we returned to the Cape, Eric was biking through Nickerson at sunset when four coyote pups came bumbling toward the bike path. He pulled over and the pups ignored him, too busy bumping into and biting each other, round balls of fur that behaved, according to Eric, almost exactly like domestic dog puppies. They spent a while nosing each other and mock fighting and not-so-mock fighting. When their mother caught up with them she shepherded them away from the nosy human being, but until then Eric had an up-close view of the siblings at play.

One of the first things I do upon arriving on the Cape is to go for a bike ride through Nickerson with Eric. We head out at dusk, though we both know it is unlikely we will re-create the coyote pup experience.

"I like my job," Eric tells me as we pedal. "I get to know the wildlife as neighbors, not as part of a study."

I note that he isn't being particularly quiet, lecturing me on nature as we pedal along the trails, but I decide not to mention it. Instead, I keep my eyes on the dark fringe of the woods, hoping for another happy accident of our paths crossing coyotes.

"Don't get me wrong, I want to get all my biology right," Eric says. "But then I want to go beyond biology."

Okay, I think, that sounds good. Now let me watch the shadows.

~

It feels so right to be back on Cape Cod. The year is turning toward solstice. Across the harbor the young osprey nestlings stretch their spindly necks up toward their mother's fish-filled bill. Orange-bellied tree swallows chase insects down at the marsh. When Hadley sleeps we constantly check to make sure she is breathing, nervous in the face of this new and massive responsibility. Rain drenches the trees and plants and the whole house smells like honeysuckle.

I no longer have the city courtyard to walk Hadley in, and at first I wonder how I will placate her when her yowling starts since the streets here are too dark and dangerous. But on the second night, out of necessity, I come upon my solution. I push her down to the harbor in her Graco Metro Lite Stroller, and then wheel her back and forth on the wooden dock where they haul up tuna. The rumbling over the wooden slats soothes her as does, I like to think, the steady breathing of the ocean. We see almost no one except for Dave Howe, washing off his charter boat, *The Albatross*, and an older Russian couple in Hell's Angels jackets who come here every night to fish with hand lines. As I push the stroller up and down, the fish jump and light pulses under the dock, our shadows cutting across the sterns of the charter boats. After twenty or so laps of the dock, Hadley sleeps soundly. One night when the moon is almost full I push her across the parking lot to the edge of the marsh. We did not pick Hadley's name for purely literary reasons; it means "field of heather," which is what this marsh becomes in the fall, filled with beach heather. She is sleeping but I let out a loud howl to see if I can get the marsh coyotes started. No luck. Another night I think I hear them but it is only a dog across the harbor. The clouds keep the moon obscured and I hear nothing. I had secretly hoped that spring would end with a great coyote chorus.

I will admit that it's hard to approach wildlife stealthily while pushing a stroller. But if my new burden handicaps me as a naturalist, then I soon find that the Graco Metro Lite is more maneuverable than you would think. One afternoon I am pushing Hadley around the cranberry bog when I see something that looks like a log from a distance. But then the log moves. It *minces* actually. I was hoping for a coyote but the movement is fox-like. And it is, or must be, a fox, with black tail, black leggings, black back, and orange head. It retreats to the woods but not entirely out of sight. It watches us from the shadows as we stroll by.

Then, the night before we head back to the city, something happens. After walking Hadley to sleep on the tuna dock, I decide to push her down the road to the beach. I carry the whole contraption up a sandy path to an overlook above a revetment wall. And just when we get to the end of the path I see something: dark shapes in a cluster. A second later the something I see sees me and they are off, small rounded shadows bounding for the safety of the rocks. These are distinctly dog-like shadows, but they are not domestic dogs, and I am pretty sure I have seen the neighborhood coyote pups. I carry the stroller to the beach and search through the openings in the rocks, but the animals are long gone, likely having climbed the bank and headed into the woods. Later, after we put Hadley to sleep, I return with a flashlight and find hundreds of canine prints, many of them cluttered around a half-eaten fish head.

~

The next day, before I leave, I return the coyote skull to the spot where it formerly rested. Then I walk past where the seal decomposed, and reach the rockiest point below the bluff. I turn out to face the water, where a flotilla of eiders rise and fall on the waves. I try to listen to the ocean's crash and seethe without letting the static of my thoughts interfere. I stay relatively still for half an hour, and do a fair job, by my standards at least, of keeping personal plans and worries from spilling over into my mind. Then, as I return along that familiar stretch of beach, the plans rush back in but in a cleaner way than usual. I feel a strange certainty about my future; I know I will keep returning here, in whatever way I can. This place, for all its over-development, is not quite used up. John Hay has written about the Cape his whole life, but there are still a thousand stories here. It remains, it seems to me, an inexhaustible source, and though it might take some time, I will eventually find a way to return here. A time of movement and unsettling is coming, a time of being away. But the thought of circling return is something I will cling to while in exile. Before I leave the beach I take one long look back, trying to imprint the sights of the seals and eiders and cormorants.

~

Back in the city. All winter long the guy at the corner has been asking for change for "some coffee." At first I was the easy rube, giving him all the change I had and even some bills. But after a while I hardened, until he knew not to even waste his breath on me. As I pass I notice that he has a new pitch for the new season.

"Spare a little change for an ice coffee?" he asks passersby.

Is it only me or does this seem like a little too fancy a line? Like saying "spare a little change for a soy decaf latte?" I walk by without making eye contact.

If I have become hardhearted toward this man, I find I now have the opposite problem with others. Since Hadley's birth my powers of empathy seem to have become uncorked, often spilling out in wild directions. I pass a mother and child sitting on a stoop. The daughter is blind and the mother is stroking her hair. I think "Hadley could have been blind," then "Hadley could become blind" and before I know it I feel my heart open up to the child and the mother, and the world, and all of a sudden these new things—these tears—are starting to form in my eyes. What the hell is happening to me? It is crazy. There are too many people in the city to start caring about all of them. It would make living here impractical.

I'm sure that the way I am feeling now will slowly harden over. But for the last few weeks I can say, without exaggeration, that I have felt a closeness to the source of life. To something not calcified by habit and crusted over by routine. And if I already sense this time ending, becoming something else, I still get small glimpses of the miraculous. On a rainy day walking by the river I stare at the rainwater, like sweat, beading on rhododendron leaves. Across the water a dozen cormorants sit lined up in orderly fashion on one of the boathouse docks, leaning into the rain. Somehow, without my noticing, green has filled up this gray world. Maybe God *is* in the midst of the city. Grass and weeds break up through cracks in the concrete.

This state, as I say, is temporary. We are leaving anyway and in two weeks this will be just another place we once lived, just as these glimpses will be memories. *Coyote was going there . . .* To tie up loose ends before we leave I check in with Jon Way to see how the coyotes are faring. All is well with the group out at Stone Zoo, but his box-trap project is looking like a failure. They're still onto him, sniffing around the traps but not going in. Jon recently posted a picture of Wile E. Coyote and one of his ACME traps on the Boston coyote Web site. Next to it, Jon wrote: "When will Coyote get stupid?"

"The Coyote is not a villain," said Chuck Jones, the creator of the

Road Runner series, "He just *wants* something." If you need to think of Native American myth in terms of a Warner Brothers cartoon, then don't think of Coyote as Wile E. Coyote. Better to think of Coyote as both Wile E. and Road Runner, both the trapper and the one who won't be trapped.

~

Old Man Coyote offers us no conclusions. As Gary Snyder wrote famously: "He's always travelling, he's really stupid, he's kind of bad—in fact, he's really awful, he's outrageous." Coyote continues to spread throughout the country. William Bright writes, "Like humanity, he is an omnivorous, ubiquitous inhabitant of the North American biosphere . . ." In the end Coyote is not "about" anything. Coyote is survival. Coyote is life.

But that is not enough for me, a planner, a thinker. I need an ending, and the time for that ending is now. I am packing up my coyote books along with the rest of our belongings. Heading off to a new place, a place without coyote (for now—he *will* come).

Jon Way will publish his coyote findings in a few years. In the meantime, though no scientific journal will take them, I feel the need to publish my own findings:

1. Coyote has broken the boundaries of suburbia and is now taking on our cities.

2. Coyotes move through our neighborhoods on rivers of smells.

3. "In wildness is the preservation of the world." Okay, sure, maybe.

4. If we are going to try to get close to life—life's source, life's energy, life's wildness—then we need to let in life's uncertainty. We can't have it both ways: We need to be open to what is given.

5. The thing about coyote is this: Both animal and myth are as adaptable as we are. Just when we think we've extinguished them they're back. Therefore:

6. No matter how much we may want to, we can't get rid of coyote.

~

And, finally, Coyote is messy.

Having published my findings and closed my books, I now need to add a couple of footnotes.

The first concerns the wild turkey we saw in Kendall Square. It turns out it has become something of a celebrity. There was a big article about it in the *Globe* the other day that said that crowds now gather and that people snap pictures. A wildlife biologist suggested that the bird had followed "electrical wires, rivers, and parks" into the city. It mostly eats acorns but will also occasionally take handouts from people. Fame seems to have domesticated the bird and some local security guards have made it a kind of mascot of Kendall Square. They even gave it a name. They call it "Mr. Gobbles."

The second footnote concerns the coyote pups I saw with Hadley. I was thrilled to have seen the pups; it seemed such a fitting end to my year. Chance and accident had once again delivered just what I needed. (And had delivered a neat end to this essay.) I scribbled down the conclusion to this chapter, feeling quite self-satisfied, but it only slowly dawned on me that I was the butt of another of shape-shifter Trickster's jokes.

At first I only glimpsed the foxes. When I returned to Cape Cod right before solstice I saw an adult running across the road with a squirrel in its mouth, and then I saw the kits at night in my headlights on the road. But soon I began to see more and more signs of fox, and a friend told me that they had watched one run across the road with a four-foot-long hog snake in its mouth. Then one day, around noon, the four fox kits came bumbling right onto our front lawn. They played, dawdled, and stretched for twenty minutes or so, letting me get close enough to take pictures without running off. As I watched them, something about the way they moved rung a bell. And then, over the next few days, as they continued to explore the neighborhood, it became more and more obvious why they looked so familiar. These were the "coyote pups" I saw on the beach. Oops.

I was looking for coyote and so I saw coyote, but the world decided to give me foxes. Nina tells me I should write an essay called "Sly Fox in the City," but I think not. Anyway, I still believe it might have been shape-shifter Coyote at work. I, like Jon Way, have been duped. Coyote has the last laugh.

~

But I didn't plan this, we say. *I didn't expect this.*
Get used to it, Coyote says back to us. *Welcome to the wild world.*